Container Gardening For Dummies®

W9-BSM-342

Container Gardening Tools

Most of the following items are available at garden centers or through mail-order suppliers.

✔ **Hose-end bubbler:** Screw this attachment to the end of the hose and use it to soften the flow of water — so that you don't wash out soil. A metal hose-end extension allows you to water overhead baskets and containers that are normally beyond arm's reach.

✔ **Scrub brush:** Use a brush to nudge soil, moss, and salt deposits off your containers.

✔ **Hand truck:** You need one of these if you want to move heavy containers indoors, or if you do a lot of outdoor redecorating.

✔ **Watering can:** With a watering can, you can also apply liquid fertilizer as you water.

✔ **Soil scoop (trowel):** This tool comes in handy when filling containers with potting soil or when mixing small quantities of potting soil (for larger quantities, use a shovel).

✔ **Mister:** Indoor plants often need extra humidity. Apply moisture with a small hand sprayer.

Hardiness Zone Table

Throughout the book, we often mention what zones various plants are "hardy to." The following table shows you the average winter minimum temperature (according to the United States Department of Agriculture) for all of the zone numbers you will encounter in this book.

Zone	Minimum Temperature	
	Fahrenheit	**Celsius**
Zone 1	Below −50°F	Below −46°C
Zone 2	−50°F to −40°F	−46°C to −40°C
Zone 3	−40°F to −30°F	−40°C to −34°C
Zone 4	−30°F to −20°F	−34°C to −29°C
Zone 5	−20°F to −10°F	−29°C to −23°C
Zone 6	−10°F to 0°F	−23°C to −18°C
Zone 7	0°F to 10°F	−18°C to −12°C
Zone 8	10°F to 20°F	−12°C to −7°C
Zone 9	20°F to 30°F	−7°C to −1°C
Zone 10	30°F to 40°F	−1°C to 4°C
Zone 11	40°F and up	4°C and up

Insects That Are Good for Your Plants

The following are some beneficial insects that you can buy to help control pests that can trouble your outdoor container plants.

✔ **Lady beetles:** Both the adult and the lizard-like larvae are especially good at feeding on small insects like aphids and thrips. Release a few thousand of them in spring as soon as you notice the first aphid.

✔ **Green lacewings:** Their voracious larvae feed on aphids, mites, thrips, and various insect eggs. Release them in your garden in late spring, after the danger of frost has passed.

✔ **Predatory mites:** This type of mite feeds on spider mites and thrips. Add them to your garden in spring as soon as frost danger has passed.

✔ **Trichogramma wasps:** Harmless to humans, these tiny wasps attack moth eggs and butterfly larvae (that is, caterpillars). Release trichogramma when temperatures are above 72°F (22°C).

For Dummies: Bestselling Book Series for Beginners

Fertilizer Lingo

Before you buy fertilizer, be sure you understand what's out there.

- **Complete fertilizers** contain all three macronutrients — nitrogen (N), phosphorus (P), and potassium (K).

- **Incomplete fertilizers** are missing one or more of the major nutrients, usually the P or the K.

- **Chelated micronutrients** are in a form that allows them to be absorbed into a plant quicker than the more commonly available sulfated forms. If your plants just won't green up (they stay mottled yellow and green, or just plain yellow), no matter how much nitrogen you apply, you probably have a micronutrient deficiency of iron, zinc, or manganese.

- **Foliar fertilizers** are applied to the leaves of plants rather than to the roots. Most liquid fertilizers can be used as foliar fertilizers, but make sure the label instructs you accordingly.

- **Organic fertilizers** derive their nutrients from something that was once alive. Examples are blood meal, fish emulsion, and manure.

- **Slow-release fertilizers** provide nutrients to plants at specific rates under particular conditions. Some slow-release fertilizers can deliver the benefits of their nutrients for as long as eight months.

Design Ideas for Mixed Plantings

Here are some tips for creating some eye-catching color combinations when planning a mixed planting:

- For bold, vibrant looks, choose contrasting colors (on opposite sides of the color wheel), such as yellow and violet.

- For pleasing, compatible combinations, choose harmonious blends of related colors like blue, violet, and purple.

- Create a soothing style with variations or shades of the same color — from pale pink to rose.

- Add plenty of pizzazz with energizing warm color combinations using red, orange, or yellow.

- Or cool things down with refreshing blues, greens, and violets.

- Don't forget white. It adds welcome dimension, lightens dark areas, and works with all other colors.

- Consider foliage too. There's much more than green. You can find stunning results with silver and gray foliage, and variegated (two-toned) leaves are sure to add interest.

Praise for This Book

If you're tired of the same old pot of red geraniums, be sure to check out *Container Gardening For Dummies*. This book is packed with planting and design ideas that will transform even the humblest of pots into a flower festival. Bill Marken's clear, concise, step-by-step instructions are worth the price of admission.
—Doug Jimerson, Editor-in-Chief, *Garden Escape*

Who better to turn to for everything you need to know about container culture than a guy who has "been there, done that" for a careerful of years? You meet that person in Bill Marken. And Bill enjoys a remarkable ease of communication, which makes absorbing detailed information on his subject as easy and pleasant as chatting with a neighbor.
—Joseph F. Williamson, Former Garden Editor and Managing Editor of *Sunset* magazine

Praise for the NGA

As an all-organic gardener, I've always dreamed of having a rose expert/enthusiast come to my gardens for tea and spend the afternoon sharing and teaching me all about roses. *Roses For Dummies* is written as a friend, answering all my puzzling questions and providing easy solutions that are budget-friendly.
—Jan Weverka, Editor of *The Rose Garden*, a monthly organic newsletter

. . . an outstanding reference for beginners and first-time homeowners . . . clearly explains how to retrieve garden information online.
—Carol Stocker, *Boston Globe*, Boston, MA, on *Gardening For Dummies*

. . . a thorough, readable beginners' guide. . . . Readers will enjoy the straightforward, yet light-hearted tone.
—Cheryl Dorschner, *Burlington Free Press*, Burlington, VT, on *Gardening For Dummies*

This book has much to recommend it . . . a simple, well-laid-out introduction to basic gardening.
—*Library Journal* on *Gardening For Dummies*

. . . easy-to-read and fun to thumb through . . . a wealth of information on all aspects of gardening. . . . A good choice for beginning gardeners, *Gardening For Dummies* would also be a good gift for longtime growers.
—Beth Dolan, *The Tampa Tribune*, Tampa, FL

. . . you'll find you're in the company of the real geniuses — the folks who can help you dig through the mounds of gardening information available and get growing soon.
—Amy Green, *The Journal-Constitution*, Atlanta, GA

The beauty of *Gardening For Dummies* . . . is its clear, jargon-free text. This should be a great relief for you if you're truly interested in learning about the subject, but afraid to spend big bucks on a serious gardening book that will only amaze and confuse you.
—*Country Decorator* magazine

Humorous, down-to-earth information anyone can understand. Covers every detail of creating a flower garden from beginning to end. I'm impressed — a book filled with valuable lessons covering each phase of building a garden, keeping one from making timely mistakes. It could help any beginner have a successful, flourishing flower garden.
—Judy Wigand, owner of Judy's Perennials, San Marcos, CA, on *Perennials For Dummies*

Whether you live in the sun-bleached subtropics or the misty snow belt, you will be able to determine just what perennials grow best for you, how to combine them for the optimal effect through the season, and perhaps most importantly, you will have some real design concepts instilled in you. . . . I know no other book that presents these ideas more intelligently.
—Panayoti Kelaidis, Plant Evaluation Coordinator, Denver Botanic Gardens, on *Perennials For Dummies*

CONTAINER GARDENING FOR DUMMIES®

by Bill Marken and The Editors of The National Gardening Association

WILEY

Wiley Publishing, Inc.

Container Gardening For Dummies®

Published by
Wiley Publishing, Inc.
111 River Street
Hoboken, NJ 07030
www.wiley.com

Copyright © 1998 by Wiley Publishing, Inc., Indianapolis, Indiana

Published by Wiley Publishing, Inc., Indianapolis, Indiana

Published simultaneously in Canada

For general information on our other products and services or to obtain technical support, please contact our Customer Care Department within the U.S. at 800-762-2974, outside the U.S. at 317-572-3993, or fax 317-572-4002.

Wiley also publishes its books in a variety of electronic formats. Some content that appears in print may not be available in electronic books.

Library of Congress Cataloging-in-Publication Data:

Library of Congress Control Number: 97-81237
ISBN: 0-7645-5057-8

Manufactured in the United States of America
10 9 8 7 6 5 4 3
1O/TR/QR/QV/IN

About the Authors

Bill Marken is an editor and writer who lives in the San Francisco Bay Area. He served as editor in chief of *Sunset, the Magazine of Western Living,* from 1981 to 1996. While at *Sunset,* earlier in his career, he worked as a writer for the magazine's garden section, pitched in on several editions of the best-selling *Western Garden Book,* and generally nurtured his interests in subjects related to gardening, landscaping, travel, and other aspects of the good life in the western U.S. He claims to have developed an early interest in gardening by working at nurseries while going to school; he may have been the only English major at the University of California at Berkeley who knew what U.C. soil mix was.

Bill's interest in the natural world includes a strong dose of environmentalism. He has served three terms as president of the League to Save Lake Tahoe, the major watchdog of the threatened lake. A vacation garden at 6,200-feet elevation gives him insight into cold-winter climates with 100-day growing seasons; he knows what it feels like to see Father's Day snow wipe out containers that were just planted.

Bill currently is serving as an editorial consultant to Hearst Magazines Enterprises, developing a new magazine based on the television show *Rebecca's Garden.* He is also California editor for *Garden Escape,* an Internet publisher and catalog. He is a past winner of the American Horticultural Society's Horticultural Communication award.

The National Gardening Association is the largest member-based, nonprofit organization of home gardeners in the U.S. Founded in 1972 (as "Gardens for All") to spearhead the community garden movement, today's National Gardening Association is best known for its bimonthly publication, *National Gardening* magazine ($18 per year). Reporting on all aspects of home gardening, each issue is read by some half-million gardeners worldwide. These publishing activities are supplemented by online efforts, such as on the World Wide Web (www.garden.org) and on America Online (at keyword HouseNet). Other NGA activities include:

- **Growing Science Inquiry and GrowLab** (funded in part by the National Science Foundation) provides kindergarten through grade 8, science-based curricula.
- Since 1972, the ***National Gardening Survey*** (conducted by the Gallup Company) is the most detailed research about gardeners and gardening in North America).
- **Youth Garden Grants.** Every year NGA awards grants of gardening tools and seeds worth more than $500 each to schools, youth groups, and community organizations.

For more information about the National Gardening, write to 180 Flynn Ave., Burlington, Vermont, 05401 U.S.A.

Dedication

To Mike MacCaskey of the National Gardening Association, who told me enough about the plans for this book to get me excited but not enough to persuade me to do something more sensible. Thanks, too, for pitching in all along the way.

Acknowledgments

Special thanks go to Lance Walheim, who wrote several chapters and supplied expertise throughout the book, all the while writing a book of his own (*Lawn Care For Dummies,* which I highly recommend; read it).

I relied on Peggy Henry for the chapters that involved design and step-by-step advice (what's left for me to do, you say?), including chapters on mixed plantings, hanging baskets, and miscellaneous containers.

Martha Polk Wingate deserves a lot of credit for her work on the chapters about vegetables, cactus/succulents, and indoor plants. Nan Sterman was responsible for the chapter on perennials. Thanks also to Emily Stetson for tackling one of the toughest chapters, soil mixes. Catherine Boyle compiled the frost charts.

NGA thanks Sarah Kennedy at Wiley for her vision and enthusiasm about both gardening and these books. Also at Wiley, thanks to Ann Miller who is always ready to lend her able hand. Much thanks to Project Editor Tim Gallan and Copy Editor Linda Stark. Thanks to key participants at NGA: David Els, President; Michael MacCaskey, Editor-in-Chief; Bill Marken, ...*For Dummies* Series Editor; Larry Sommers, Associate Publisher; and Charlie Nardozzi, Senior Horticulturist. Special thanks to Suzanne DeJohn and Kathy Bond-Bori, NGA Staff Horticulturists, for their help.

Publisher's Acknowledgments

We're proud of this book; please register your comments through our online registration form located at www.dummies.com/register.

Some of the people who helped bring this book to market include the following:

Acquisitions, Development, and Editorial

Project Editor: Tim Gallan

Acquisitions Editor: Sarah Kennedy, Executive Editor

Acquisitions Coordinator: Ann Miller

Copy Editor: Linda Stark

Technical Editor: Denny Schrock

Editorial Manager: Leah P. Cameron

Editorial Assistants: Donna Love, Jill Alexander

Composition

Project Coordinator: Regina Snyder

Layout and Graphics: Lou Boudreau, J. Tyler Connor, Angela F. Hunckler, Todd Klemme, Jane E. Martin, Drew R. Moore, Brent Savage, Janet Seib, Deirdre Smith, Michael A. Sullivan

Proofreaders: Nancy L. Reinhardt, Christine Berman, Kelli Botta, Michelle Croninger, Nancy Price, Rebecca Senninger, Janet M. Withers

Indexer: Anne Leach

Photographers: David Cavagnaro, Crandall & Crandall Photography, R. Todd Davis Photography, Inc., Allan Mandell, Jerry Pavia, Michael S. Thompson

Illustrator: Mark Zahnd

Publishing and Editorial for Consumer Dummies

    Diane Graves Steele, Vice President and Publisher, Consumer Dummies

    Joyce Pepple, Acquisitions Director, Consumer Dummies

    Kristin A. Cocks, Product Development Director, Consumer Dummies

    Michael Spring, Vice President and Publisher, Travel

    Brice Gosnell, Associate Publisher, Travel

    Suzanne Jannetta, Editorial Director, Travel

Publishing for Technology Dummies

    Richard Swadley, Vice President and Executive Group Publisher

    Andy Cummings, Vice President and Publisher

Composition Services

    Gerry Fahey, Vice President of Production Services

    Debbie Stailey, Director of Composition Services

Contents at a Glance

Introduction 1

Part I: Container Plants: To Know Them Is to Grow Them 5

Chapter 1: Neat Things to Do with Container Plants 7
Chapter 2: Cultivating Your Little Corner of the World 17
Chapter 3: Containing Your Excitement 25

Part II: How to Plant 35

Chapter 4: Soil Mixes 37
Chapter 5: When Plant Meets Container 53

Part III: The Plants 65

Chapter 6: Annuals 67
Chapter 7: Perennial Pleasures 79
Chapter 8: Lighting Up Containers with Bulbs 93
Chapter 9: Big Shots of the Garden: Shrubs and Trees 103
Chapter 10: Vegetables and Herbs 129
Chapter 11: Fruits and Berries 141
Chapter 12: Cactus and Succulents 153
Chapter 13: Indoor Container Gardening 163

Part IV: Designing and Decorating 171

Chapter 14: Matchmaking, Container-Style 173
Chapter 15: 12 Tested Recipes forMixed Plantings 181

Part V: Special Effects 197

Chapter 16: Hanging Baskets 199
Chapter 17: Containers with Extra Character 219

Part VI: Maintenance 233

Chapter 18: Thirst Quenching 235
Chapter 19: Feeding 247
Chapter 20: All the Other Chores 255
Chapter 21: When Bad Things Happen: Pests and Diseases 265

Part VII: The Part of Tens 281

Chapter 22: More Than Ten Container Plants for Special Situations 283
Chapter 23: Ten Container Plants for Spring, Summer, Fall, and Winter 287
Chapter 24: Ten Handy Tools for Container Gardening 291
Chapter 25: Almost Ten Words about Bonsai 293

Appendix: Additional Resources *297*

Index *315*

Cartoons at a Glance

By Rich Tennant

page 65

page 35

page 171

page 233

page 281

page 197

page 5

Cartoon Information:
Fax: 978-546-7747
E-Mail: richtennant@the5thwave.com
World Wide Web: www.the5thwave.com

Table of Contents

Introduction 1

How to Use This Book 1
What We Assume about You 2
How This Book Is Organized 2
    Part I: Container Plants: To Know Them Is to Grow Them 2
    Part II: How to Plant 3
    Part III: The Plants 3
    Part IV: Designing and Decorating 3
    Part V: Special Effects 3
    Part VI: Maintenance 4
    Part VII: The Part of Tens 4
Icons Used in This Book 4
What and Where Next? 4

Part I: Container Plants: To Know Them Is to Grow Them 5

Chapter 1: Neat Things to Do with Container Plants 7

Taking the Container Plunge? 8
    1. You can grow plants in impossible places 8
    2. You can make plants look good 8
    3. You can grow plants that you think you can't grow 10
    4. You can do stupid container tricks 10
Enjoying an Out-of-Garden Experience 10
    Advantages of plants in pots 11
    Advantages of plants in the ground 11
Designing with Container Plants 12
    Thinking about style 12
    Growing that one special plant 13
    Combining plants in containers 13
    Making arrangements: How to combine containers 14
Putting It All Together 15
Down-to-Earth Advice 15
One Last Thing: Plant Names 16

Chapter 2: Cultivating Your Little Corner of the World 17

A Climate to Call Your Own 18
    Bottom line 19
    Bottom bottom line 19

Climates and Container Plantings 19
    Seasonal performers 19
    Permanent plants: A few words about winter 20
Your Garden's Microclimate 22
    Sun or shade? 22
    Wind 23
    Slope 24
    Reflected heat 24
Flexibility for Flourish 24

Chapter 3: Containing Your Excitement **25**
Types of Materials 25
    Terra-cotta or unglazed clay 26
    Glazed clay 26
    Wood 27
    Plastic 28
    Other materials 28
    Improvised containers 29
    Raised beds 29
    Containers of your own making 29
Container Sizes and Shapes 29
    Standard pots 31
    Low containers 32
    Bulb pots 32
    Other shapes 32
    Hanging baskets 32
Accessories, at Your Service 32
    Saucers 33
    Elevation 33
A Pot for Every Plant 34

Part II: How to Plant *35*

Chapter 4: Soil Mixes **37**
Why Soil Mix Matters 37
A Quick Primer on Soil 38
    Soil — up close and personal 39
    The structured life of soil 40
    Sweet or sour soil? A word about pH 40
In Pursuit of the Perfect Container Mix 41
    The dirty truth about garden soil 41
    What container plants need 42
        Fast water infiltration and optimal drainage 42
        Plenty of air space 42
        Moisture retention 43
        Lack of contamination 44

Bring On the Soil Mixes (For Peat's Sake) 44
  Shopping for a soil mix 46
  Where to buy soil mixes 47
Mixing Your Own 47
  Doctoring up the mix 48
  Foolproof mixes from scratch 48
    Basic peat mix (Cornell soil-less mix) 49
    Variations on the peat theme 50
    Two specialized blends 51
    A mix from NOFA (Natural Organic Farmers Association) 51
    An organic mix based on soil 51

Chapter 5: When Plant Meets Container **53**
What You Need to Know Before Planting 53
  Planting seasons 54
  How plants are sold 54
  How to choose healthy plants 55
    Annuals 56
    Shrubs and trees 57
Your Well-Stocked Planting Tool Kit 57
Basic Planting Steps 58
  1. Getting the container ready 58
  2. Addressing the drain hole 59
  3. Dealing with the plant 60
  4. Planting the plant 61
  5. Watering 63
  6. What else? 63
If at First You Want to Seed 63

Part III: The Plants **65**

Chapter 6: Annuals **67**
What's an Annual? 67
Why Grow Annuals in Containers? 68
Strategies for Growing Annuals in Containers 69
Shopping for Annuals 70
Planting Annuals in Containers 71
  Choosing containers 71
  Actually planting something 72
The Caretaking of Annuals in Containers 73
Foolproof Annuals for Containers 74
  Old reliables for sunny spots 75
  Annuals for shady locations 77
Combining Annuals in Containers 77

Chapter 7: Perennial Pleasures **79**

Defining Perennials 79
Deciding to Pot Your Perennials 80
Matching Plants with Pots 81
Planting Perennials in Containers 82
Caring for Perennials in Containers 83
    Cutting back 83
    Fertilizing 83
    Winter care 84
Sooner or Later: Repotting 84
Choosing Perennials for Containers 85

Chapter 8: Lighting Up Containers with Bulbs **93**

We're Not Talking Lightbulbs, Here 93
Containers and Bulbs: A Great Partnership 94
    Shopping for bulbs 95
    Chilling out 96
    Choosing the container 97
    Preparing the soil 97
    Planting the bulbs — step by step 97
Force the Issue with Your Bulbs 99
Spring Favorites for Containers 100
The Bulbs of Summer 102

Chapter 9: Big Shots of the Garden: Shrubs and Trees **103**

Performance Payoff: Shrubs and Trees at Work in Container Homes 104
Planting and Care 104
    Planting 104
    Soil 105
    Container 105
    Feeding 105
    Watering 105
    Pruning 105
    Repotting 105
    Pests and diseases 106
Shrubs and Trees for Containers 106
    Aucuba 106
    Azaleas and rhododendrons 106
    Bamboo 107
    Boxwood 108
    Camellia 108
    Conifers: Pines, firs, junipers, and the rest of the clan 109
        False cypress (Chamaecyparis) 110
        Fir (Abies) 110
        Juniper (Juniperus) 110
        Pine (Pinus) 110
        Redwood (Sequoia sempervirens) 111
        Spruce (Picea) 111
        Thuja 111

Cotoneaster 112
Crape myrtle (Lagerstroemia indica) 112
Daphne 112
English laurel (Prunus laurocerasus) 113
Fatsia, or Japanese aralia (Fatsia japonica) 113
Ferns 113
    Big statuesque ferns 114
    Small ferns 114
Flowering fruit trees 114
Fuchsia 114
Gardenia 115
Harry Lauder's walking stick (Corylus avellana Contorta) 115
Heavenly bamboo (Nandina domestica) 115
Hibiscus 116
Holly 116
Hydrangea 116
India hawthorn (Rhaphiolepis) 117
Japanese barberry (Berberis thunbergii) 117
Japanese maple (Acer palmatum) 117
Lantana 118
Lily of the valley shrub (Pieris japonica) 118
Myrtle 118
New Zealand flax (Phormium tenax) 119
Norfolk Island pine (Araucaria heterophylla) 119
Oleander 119
Palms 120
Pittosporum 120
Pineapple guava (Feijoa) 121
Podocarpus 121
Pomegranate 121
Privet (Ligustrum) 122
Pyracantha 122
Rose 122
Sago palm (Cycas revoluta) 123
Strawberry tree (Arbutus unedo) 124
Sweet bay (Laurus nobilis) 124
Sweet olive (Osmanthus fragrans) 124
Six Vines for Containers 124
    Bougainvillea 125
    Clematis 125
    English ivy (Hedera helix) 126
    Mandevilla 126
    Star jasmine (Trachelospermum jasminoides) 126
    Wisteria 127

Chapter 10: Vegetables and Herbs **129**

What Container Vegetables and Herbs Really Need 130
    The right container 130
    Soil mix 130

Fertilizer 131
Water, water, water 131
Sunlight 131
Favorite Vegetables for Containers 132
Beans 133
Beets 133
Cabbage and kinfolk 133
Carrots 133
Corn 133
Cucumbers 134
Eggplant 134
Lettuce 134
Onions 134
Peas 134
Peppers 135
Potatoes 135
Radish 135
Spinach 135
Squash 136
Swiss chard 136
Tomatoes 136
Herbs in Containers 136
Basil 138
Chives 138
Oregano 138
Parsley 138
Rosemary 138
Sage 139
Savory 139
Tarragon 139
Thyme 139

Chapter 11: Fruits and Berries **141**

A Bowl of Fruit Facts 142
Pollination 142
Rootstocks and dwarfs 142
Fruit thinning 143
What to Grow In Containers? 144
Small size 144
Climate adaptation 144
Easy maintenance 144
Soil, Pot Size, Planting, and All That 145
Fruit and Berries for Containers 146
Apples 146
Growing tips 146
Adaptation 147
Apricots 147
Growing tips 147
Adaptation 147

Blackberries 147
 Growing tips 147
 Adaptation 148
Blueberries 148
 Growing tips 148
 Adaptation 148
Citrus 148
 Growing tips 149
 Adaptation 149
Cherries 149
 Growing tips 149
 Adaptation 149
Figs 149
 Growing tips 149
 Adaptation 149
Peaches and nectarines 150
 Growing tips 150
 Adaptation 150
Pears 150
 Growing tips 150
 Adaptation 150
Plums 150
 Growing tips 151
 Adaptation 151
Raspberries 151
 Growing tips 151
 Adaptation 151
Strawberries 151
 Growing tips 152
 Adaptation 152
And Just A Few More 152

Chapter 12: Cactus and Succulents 153
Rules of the Game 154
Growing Cactus/Succulents in Containers 154
 Choosing containers 155
 Selecting soil mix 155
 Planting 155
Maintenance 157
Which Cactus and Succulents? 158
 Cactus for containers 159
 Succulents for containers 160

Chapter 13: Indoor Container Gardening 163
Determining Your Plant Preferences 163
Choosing Containers 164
Getting the Right Soil Mix 165
Keeping Your Plants Alive 166

Watering 166
Temperature 166
Light 166
Fertilizer 167
Pests and diseases 167
Pruning 167
Knowing Your Plants' Needs 168
Plants that get along in low light 168
Plants that grow in medium light 168
Plants that need lots of light 170

Part IV: Designing and Decorating 171

Chapter 14: Matchmaking, Container-Style 173
Why Mixed? 174
Plants as a Palette 174
Fun with Form, Texture, Proportion 175
Container Compatibility: Picking the Right Pot 177
The Show Can Go On 178
One Final Note 180

Chapter 15: 12 Tested Recipes for Mixed Plantings 181
A Dozen Designs 181
Early spring bouquet 182
Nature's bounty 183
Autumn romance 184
Suspended animation 185
A new outlook 186
Terra-cotta collection 187
Timeless beauty, old world charm 189
Scented sensations 190
Shade-lover's delight 192
Next on the menu 193
Reflective beauty 194
Entryway elegance 195

Part V: Special Effects 197

Chapter 16: Hanging Baskets 199
How and Where to Display Baskets 199
What You Need to Plan Your Planting 201
Traditional wire 201
Wooden box 202
Solid and open-sided plastic 202

Plastic towers 202
Self-watering basket 203
Pre-formed fiber or peat pots 203
Looking at liners 203
Selecting a soil mix 203
Hanging the basket 204
The Business of Basket Design 204
Shoot for the Stars — Selecting Plants 205
Meet the cast 206
Trailing plants 206
Upright plants 207
Fillers 207
Steps for Sure-Fire Success 208
Planting an open wire basket 208
Planting a wire basket with a flexible liner 210
Planting a solid basket 211
Tricks for Trouble-Free Maintenance 211
Six Hanging Basket Designs 212
Color connection 212
Scented sensations 213
Edible aerials 214
Shady delight 215
Textured treasures 216
Wall basket collection 217

Chapter 17: Containers with Extra Character **219**
Window Box Basics 220
Planting and caring for your window box 221
Picking the (plant) winners 222
Annuals 222
Permanent plants 222
Water Garden Wisdom 223
Pocket Planting in Strawberry Jars 226
Troughs and Stone Sinks 227
Timeless Classics: Urns 229
Saucers — Not So Shallow After All 230
Whimsical One-of-a-Kinds 231

Part VI: Maintenance **233**

Chapter 18: Thirst Quenching **235**
Why and When Containers Need Water 235
Climate 236
Weather 236
Pot type 236
Pot color 237
Rootboundedness 237

Soil variations 237
Location, location, location 237
Genetic disposition 238
Ways To Water Container Plants 238
Hand watering 238
Sprinklers 239
Drip irrigation 239
Self-watering pots 241
How Often to Water? 242
How Much Water to Apply 243
Water-Saving Ways 244
Who Waters When You're out of Town? 245
Wick water 245
Use soil polymers 245
Other Container Watering Tips 246

Chapter 19: Feeding **247**

Preparing a Good Diet — Plant-Wise 248
Translating the Chemistry Listed on Labels 249
Granular fertilizers 249
Liquid fertilizers 250
Fertilizer lingo to know 250
Shopping for Fertilizer Bargains 251
Preparing a Fertilizer Plan 252
Discovering Organic Fertilizers 253
Recognizing Too Much of a Good Thing 254

Chapter 20: All the Other Chores **255**

When It's Time to Move On: Replanting 255
What to repot? 256
When to repot? 256
Where to put the plant? 256
How do you repot? 256
What is root pruning? 257
Container Cleanup 257
Humpty-Dumpty Duty — Repairing Broken Pots 258
Well-Preserved Wood Containers 260
Large Containers Looking for New Locations 260
Where to Store All the Goods 261
Maintenance Musts: Sanding, Painting, Staining 263
Metal or wire plant stands, brackets, hanging baskets 263
Wood 264

Chapter 21: When Bad Things Happen: Pests and Diseases **265**

Preventing Pests and Diseases 266
Smart gardening to prevent pests 266
Plant in the right location 266
Grow healthy plants 267
Choose resistant plants 267

Encourage and use beneficial insects 267
Keep your garden clean 267
Know the enemy 267
Encouraging good insects 267
When trouble begins 269
Using synthetic insecticides 271
Insects That Prey on Container Plants 272
Aphids 272
Borers 272
Caterpillars and worms 273
Geranium budworms 273
Japanese beetles 273
Mealybugs 274
Cutworms 274
Scale 274
Snails and slugs 275
Spider mites 275
Thrips 276
Whiteflies 276
Preventing Diseases 277
Seven Dastardly Diseases 278
Black spot 278
Botrytis blight 279
Damping off 279
Powdery mildew 279
Root rots 280
Rust 280
Salt burn 280

Part VII: The Part of Tens *281*

Chapter 22: More Than Ten Container Plants for Special Situations 283

Annual and Perennial Flowers for Shady Spots 283
Shrubs, Trees, and Vines for Shady Spots 284
Fragrant Plants 284
Easy Plants 285
Specimen Plants (Substantial Enough to Stand Alone) 285
Gift Plants (Nice Enough to Pot and Present) 286

Chapter 23: Ten Container Plants for Spring, Summer, Fall, and Winter 287

Spring 287
Summer 288
Fall 288
Winter 289
Living Christmas Trees 289

Chapter 24: Ten Handy Tools for Container Gardening 291

Chapter 25: Almost Ten Words about Bonsai 293

Appendix: Additional Resources *297*

Mail-Order Suppliers of Seeds and Plants for Containers 297
Mail-Order Sources of Fruit Trees 302
Mail-Order Sources for Water Gardening Plants and Supplies 303
Mail-Order Sources for Container Gardening Tools,
    Supplies, and Structures 304
How to Reach — or Become — a Master Gardener 306
Web Sites about Container Gardening 308
Books about Container Gardening 311
Magazines That Include Some Information about
    Container Gardening 313

Index *315*

Introduction

∙∙∙

*L*ook up container gardening in some reference book and you'll probably find out that the ancient Romans grew laurel (for their wreaths) in marble urns, or that Moses carried a pot-full of rushes with him everywhere on his long travels. Fair enough. But the real origin of growing plants in containers as we know it today goes back to southern California, specifically Pasadena in the early 1950s, I seem to recall hearing, when a man sitting by a kidney-shaped swimming pool thought, "Wouldn't it be even nicer if I could reach over to a handy fragrantly-blooming tree and pick a lemon to squeeze in my drink?"

The good life in the garden is what growing plants in containers is about. You don't grow container plants to put food on the table — but as you'll find out later, some container-grown tomatoes may be nice in a salad. You don't grow container plants to prevent erosion or even to keep your front yard green and mud-free so that your lawn-proud neighbors won't gripe. You grow plants in containers for fun.

In this book, we want to share with you the many pleasures of container plants. The fun comes in discovering the amazing number of plant possibilities and the equally amazing variety of containers. You can get immense satisfaction from growing something beautiful, in creating interesting combinations of plants, in experimenting with new plants, in getting to know plants much more intimately than you can know the same plants in the ground.

But what about all the work involved, you say? We'll be talking about that too: how to plant, how to water, how to feed, how to repot, and all that. And we should also mention that stuff isn't work if you enjoy growing container plants — which you will.

How to Use This Book

You can use this book very successfully if you have never grown a plant before. If that's you, better read the first two chapters first to get a sense of what's involved in growing container plants and what your climate and garden will allow and encourage.

Whatever level your gardening skill happens to be, feel free to skip around and look for ideas when you need them. If you want ideas on plants to try, check out Chapters 6 through 13. If you want to find out about more advanced containers, you'll find them farther along in the book (see Chapter 17). If you have your containers and plants already to go, better turn to Chapters 4 and 5 and start planting. If something is mysteriously afflicting your geraniums, turn to Chapter 21 right now.

What We Assume about You

We don't expect you to know much at all about gardening. As we just mentioned, this book is useful for both novice and experienced gardeners. We expect that you enjoy growing plants and will do the work that's necessary to plant and maintain them.

How This Book Is Organized

The book is divided into seven major parts that are intended to lead you through all stages of container gardening. The book's first three parts deal with the basics: getting excited about the possibilities, figuring out what your garden's conditions allow, choosing containers and plants, and doing the actual planting. Then we move on to a bit more advanced work: designing mixed plantings and working with more specialized containers. Whatever you grow in containers, pay attention to Part VI, which addresses all the things you need to do to keep your plants healthy and productive.

Part I: Container Plants: To Know Them Is to Grow Them

Want some good reasons to grow plants in containers? Here are just a few: the ease of moving them around, the way they allow you to experiment with plants, and the satisfaction of creating beautiful things. We touch on design and come back to the subject in later chapters. Right away, you find out some of the realities of container gardening — particularly the opportunities and limits your climate and garden conditions create for you (Chapter 2 is important!). Another important fundamental, of course, is knowing a bit about containers — materials, sizes, shapes, and how to match them with plants.

Part II: How to Plant

It goes without saying that soil mixes are important to container plants — what you provide in the pot is all that the roots will ever have. Want to buy ready-made mix or make your own? We offer details on both options. After you have the soil mix, you're ready to plant, and there's more to it than sticking the plant in the pot. It helps to understand how plants are sold, how to choose them wisely, and how to plant different types. If you want to save money and gain a certain amount of satisfaction by starting your own plants from seed (annual flowers most likely), you find step-by-step advice.

Part III: The Plants

This is your palette from which to create container plantings, and it is a huge and colorful one. We start with the most familiar flowering plants (annual flowers, bulbs, and perennials). Then come the permanent outdoor plants that can have year-round impact in your garden — the shrubs and trees. We also include less familiar container plants like vegetables, fruit trees, and cactus, as well as a chapter on indoor plants. In all cases, you find why each of these plants is a great choice for a container, how to plant them, and how to take care of them.

Part IV: Designing and Decorating

There's a chapter here for you if you're the type of person who can sit still for some theory about design — color, form, texture, and proportion — and then wants to create your own mixed plantings. Or if you just want to get out there and plant some terrific combinations, choose one of our dozen designs and follow our planting advice.

Part V: Special Effects

Call this part slightly more advanced container gardening. Hanging baskets are tricky but very rewarding — big enough to deserve a whole chapter on types of baskets, the best plants for baskets, plus info on how to plant and maintain them. You'll also see designs for six smashing basket designs. Beyond baskets, there's a whole world of other special containers: window boxes, strawberry jars, water gardens, urns, troughs, and one-of-a-kinds. We explain how to plant each and offer planting suggestions.

Part VI: Maintenance

Now comes the hard part or the satisfying part, depending on how strong your nurturing instincts are. Container plants do need more care than plants in the ground, and these chapters lay it all out: watering, feeding, repotting, root pruning, and such. Sadly, your plants may encounter troubles beyond your control; Chapter 21 tells how to recognize and deal with pests and diseases.

Part VII: The Part of Tens

Want a container plant for shade? Or something that looks great in fall. Or fragrance? This part has handy lists of such things. And if you want to know something about the authors' own favorites, read the last chapter.

Icons Used in This Book

When we provide a tidbit of advice that will save you time, save you trouble, or help keep your plants healthy, we use this icon.

This icon flags information that you ought to read carefully so that you retain it.

We use this icon to indicate that what we're about to say will save your life, or at least the life of your plant.

What and Where Next?

How about some inspiration? Turn to the color section to get an idea of how much you can do with container plants. Then take a look at the table of contents to see what topics catch your fancy.

Part I

Container Plants: To Know Them Is to Grow Them

The 5th Wave® By Rich Tennant

"That should do it."

In this part . . .

So, how does *your* garden grow? If your response is a slightly wry, "In the ground, of course," you may want to hold that thought until we dig a little deeper into the possibilities. Plants and the ground certainly go hand in hand — or root in botanical feeding station, to be slightly more scientific. But plants have far more to offer than can be sown and seen in a tract of land. Enter: the joys of container gardening.

Your favorite selections — whether they promise you the pleasures of blooms, herbs, fruit, flowers, or simple sensory delights — can take on fresh charm when presented in container homes. And better yet, your plants' new digs don't have to stay put; you can pick up and move your mobile gardens, for their benefit or yours.

This part opens the doors to exploration beyond the garden path. Your personal style, along with local climate and conditions, can guide your picks of plants, pots, and growing spots.

Shake loose an adventurous spirit and imagine all the ways that you can put down roots in places that are grounded in your own great taste.

Chapter 1

Neat Things to Do with Container Plants

In This Chapter

▶ Making the case for container plants

▶ Designing a good look

▶ Putting it all together

*A*re you just a little timid about growing plants in containers? What's more persuasive than the sight of a container full to the brim with spring's bounty of red tulips, the lip-smacking appeal of ripe strawberries dangling from a hanging basket, or the inspired zaniness of cactus rising from an old cowboy boot? Containers can provide a healthy, happy home for an array of indoor and outdoor greenery, and the attraction reaches beyond simply pairing a pot with a plant.

✔ Growing plants in pots, baskets, tubs, barrels, or other containers up to and including discarded footwear can be fun in a garden of any size and shape. If your gardening space consists of a small deck, a porch, or unfriendly soil or weather, container gardening may be your ticket to growing something green or colorful.

✔ Growing plants in pots is easy. Witness the neglected geranium outside the front door of your dry cleaner, which gets watered about as often as the cat gets fed — and how does that cat stay so healthy?

✔ And growing plants in pots can be as challenging as anything in gardening. Witness the art of bonsai and imagine how much dedication and skill is involved in the pruning and pampering.

Whatever your skill level and garden situation, we want to help you grow terrific plants in containers — to match the right plants with the right containers and to give them the kind of care that produces beautiful results.

Taking the Container Plunge?

We don't want to take all the suspense out of chapters that follow, but we can introduce you to some of the key concepts that run through this book — and offer at least four good reasons why you may choose to grow plants in containers.

1. You can grow plants in impossible places

Container plants are portable: They can grow where you don't have a conventional garden. Your chosen location may be a rooftop, a small condominium deck, the porch of a mobile home, or the deck of a houseboat. As you consider where to place your plantings, keep in mind how much water and light to provide, and all the other practical considerations that are covered later. And think about what purpose you want the container plants to serve. A spot of greenery? Some bright flowers? You can also use several plants to create a privacy screen or hedge.

Even if you have only a tiny space available, you may want to picture your container plants as a "garden" with different plants complementing one another. For example, if you have room for only three plants, choose containers and plants of different sizes and styles; perhaps a 4-foot Japanese maple (lacy, fall color, leafless in winter), a 1-foot Mugho pine (mounding, evergreen), and a bowl of colorful pansies in spring.

Container plants' transportable nature offers other advantages. You may learn a few things in the process: Maybe your begonias didn't enjoy their relocation from San Diego to Buffalo in winter nearly as much as you did!

Or just move containers around in your own garden as the seasons change. In December, put a potted spruce on the front porch, and after the holidays, move it to the side of the house where it can bask in good light and water; put a pot of spring bulbs on the porch as the weather warms up.

2. You can make plants look good

Even if you have acres of gardens, you still may want a container plant or two. Highlighting a plant by growing it in a pot brings out qualities not noticeable in a garden bed or in a block of plants at the garden center. Notice how the containers enhance the look of the plants in Figure 1-1. Take one of the more boring of all plants, Bar Harbor juniper, which is usually massed as a ground cover. Try planting a juniper in a rustic terra-cotta pot and see the instant transformation — your ordinary evergreen looks like a miniature weathered Sierra patriarch.

Figure 1-1:
Various
plants in
various
containers.

Maybe you prefer one special plant. Plan to devote some extra attention to it, even spoil it a bit like an only child, because you're not taking care of a lot of other screaming plants with dirty diapers and mouths to feed. Make the most of your chance to dote on a fussy but gorgeous azalea or a rare striped bamboo.

One pleasure of growing container plants is observing them up close. A 10-foot sunflower may look stunning against the back fence, but close-up viewing can be disappointing — what you see is several feet of bare stem. Better to grow something like a lace-cap hydrangea, whose intricate flower formations can absorb your attention on a summer day as you sit nearby with a cool lemonade in hand.

3. You can grow plants that you think you can't grow

Containers allow and encourage experimentation. You can give plants the exact conditions that they need — which may be missing from your garden. You can provide the preferred soil mix (acid type for azaleas, sandy for cactus, for example). You can provide water in preferred doses (abundant for azaleas, light for cactus). You can move plants around for best exposure (part shade for azaleas, full sun for cactus).

Containers let you grow plants with different soil and watering requirements side by side, which isn't possible in a garden.

Containers can be moved into protected spots during winter. Where can you find oranges growing in Minneapolis? In containers.

Containers invite you to become friendly with certain plants — you discover what they like and don't like, what they respond to, and how they change during the seasons.

4. You can do stupid container tricks

What makes otherwise rational people grow living plants in all kinds of things? Old shoes, old toilets, old boats. Whatever the motivation, container gardeners can exercise spunk without polluting the atmosphere. Yes, some people may raise questions of taste, but an indiscretion or two is a small price to pay for fostering the creative spirit in all of us.

Remember the most important rule, which we describe in more detail later: Provide drainage.

Enjoying an Out-of-Garden Experience

Before you take another step toward container gardening, make sure that you acknowledge and respect this concept: A container is not a natural place for a plant to grow.

A plant growing in the ground develops a network of roots to take in water and nutrients, gaining moisture from rain as well as your hose or sprinklers. If the plant gets too much sun or not enough, it clearly shows the effects with lanky growth, sunburned leaves, and, possibly, a painful death.

On the other hand, a container is confining, and without natural insulation, its contents dry out quickly. Nutrients wash out rapidly. The root system requires water and food in adequate doses. Roots run out of space and demand repotting. But think positively. You can improve the soil for a container far more dramatically than you can in the ground — your soil mix may not even contain actual soil (more on this in Chapter 4). Plus, if the plant doesn't respond well to its conditions, you may be able to move it to a spot it likes.

Container plants usually involve more of a time commitment than the same plants in the ground, but the rewards may exceed the investment.

What grows well in pots? Theoretically, just about anything for a while if the container is large enough. After all, nurseries sell giant sequoias in 5-gallon cans. But actually, not all plants are good candidates. Some look funny (corn keeps tipping over). Big shrubs and trees may look fine for a year or two. Some plants just take too long to reach their mature shapes and performance levels. Why grow a fruit tree (except a dwarf type) in a container? You can expect little more than a large green stick for the first few years.

Advantages of plants in pots

- ✔ You can give exactly the right soil the plant needs (sandy for cactus; high-acid for azaleas).
- ✔ You can move the plant around when weather doesn't suit it — into more or less shade or out of the cold.
- ✔ You can protect plants from pests. You're able to isolate them if you want to spray and use just the right control without having to worry about neighboring plants.
- ✔ You get to know them better. With container plants, you discover how to care for individual plants as they respond to your care.

Advantages of plants in the ground

- ✔ The soil provides a greater reservoir of water and food.
- ✔ The soil offers more insulation for roots during hot or cold weather.
- ✔ Less maintenance generally is involved.
- ✔ Permanent plants can grow to their full size and reach their highest level of performance (fruit or flowers, for instance).

Designing with Container Plants

Does the term "design" sound a bit pretentious for the container gardening process: picking plants to put in pots, mixing different plants in the same pots, or combining different pots — all to make things look as nice as possible? We're open to another word, but at least you can relate to what we're talking about. Bottom line: Your designs really depend on maintenance considerations — planning placement of plants, whether in the same container or in several containers grouped together, according to their shared requirements for care.

One plant in a container standing alone can be stunning — good news if that's all you have space for. But combining several or many container plants gives a greater effect — almost like a garden growing in the ground. Containers can do all the things that a whole garden can: announce the seasons, flash bright color, and create miniature slices of nature.

Thinking about style

Style issues can be especially perplexing because you aren't going to find any cut-and-dry rules — unlike, say, how deep to plant tulips. Here are a few general-direction reminders to keep in mind when creating container plantings:

- Work with what you already have. Use container plants to complement your home or garden. In an informal setting, for example, you may want to use tubs of mixed summer annuals. Cactus in shallow bowls lend a dramatic note to a contemporary setting.

- Think about color. Using mostly green or white creates a cooling effect. Bright hot colors (zinnias, for instance) heat things up.

- Consider the different shapes of the plants you're using — whether they're in individual containers, mixed plantings, or multiple containers. Start to think about the shapes of the plants that you're choosing and use them to complement and contrast with each other. Sample shape categories include

    - Tall spiky plants: snapdragons or New Zealand flax

    - Round mounded shapes: impatiens or lavender

    - Trailers: lobelia or ivy

- Want formal or casual? Topiary is formal. So are symmetrical plants — picture two boxwoods in urns flanking the front door or tree roses lining a walk. Containers with flowers all in the same color are formal. Mixed-color annuals are more casual, as are groups of containers of different sizes, materials, and shapes.

✔ Remember the value of repetition. Repeat the same colors or plants. For example, use yellow marigolds in a cluster of pots near the beginning of a front walk and then again on the front porch.

✔ Scale is a big subject. Big spaces demand large containers, at least 20 or 24 inches in diameter. If you cluster pots, make sure to include at least one good-sized container with a taller plant in it.

Growing that one special plant

This book covers hundreds of plants — annuals, cactus, fruit trees, even eggplant — that can make special showings in individual pots. Presenting a star calls for one plant in one pot or several plants of the same type (four pansies, for example) in one pot.

You always want to choose a container that's the right size for the plant (see Chapter 3 for advice on sizes). You're also wise to look for something of the right scale.

As a general guideline for goods looks, the plant needs to be at least as tall as the container; this is particularly true of annuals. Put 12-inch-tall snapdragons in a pot that's at least 12 inches tall. Don't put 6-inch pansies in a 12-inch pot — their friendly faces may be overwhelmed by all that space.

That rule of height doesn't apply to succulents or bonsai, where mound-shaped plants often are grown in taller containers. Don't follow the rule with big shrubs and trees, which can be much taller in proportion. The advice on proportion also doesn't apply to the bamboo just outside our window: The ornamental grass is 8 feet tall in a 15-inch-tall pot.

Combining plants in containers

Mixed annuals, annuals with perennials, perennials with bulbs, bulbs with eggplant (better quit while we're ahead) — plants can be combined in the same container in so many ways. You can read specific design suggestions in Chapter 15, but there's a basic strategy.

Start with one dominant plant (Japanese maple, snapdragons, delphiniums, and so on), then work around the main attraction with compatible mounding or trailing plants (lobelia, impatiens, and many others).

Making arrangements: How to combine containers

Arranging groups of container plants is like hanging pictures or moving furniture — complete with possible backaches. Don't be afraid to experiment, to move plants around again and again. Remember the most important thing: You're satisfying *your* taste.

Container groupings generally look best with at least three plants; dozens can be accommodated.

A few basic rules apply for grouping container plants:

- Start by using matching types of containers, like terra-cotta, in different sizes. Make one or two pots a lot larger than the others. If you want, throw in a maverick, like a glazed pot.

- For a big deck or expanse of paving, use lots of pots and mix sizes, styles, and shapes.

- Mix plants of different textures, colors, and heights. Think about the basic categories of shapes described earlier.

- And, of course, do just the opposite and group identical pots with identical plants. Nothing looks more smashing in spring than three 14-inch terra-cotta pots stuffed to the gills with red tulips.

- Raise some containers higher than others; provide a lift with a couple of bricks underneath or use plant stands. You can add emphasis as well as put the plants at better viewing levels.

- Be careful with small plants: They tend to go unnoticed. Clumsy people trip on them (we know from personal experience).

- Try to place containers where people gather. A seating area, for instance, offers opportunity to view plants up close and appreciate their fragrance.

- In large gardens, place containers near the house where you can notice them. Container plants scattered selectively along garden paths can provide a pleasant surprise. Another good placement is in the transition zone between a patio and lawn or between a lawn and wild garden.

Putting It All Together

As you think about the possibilities of designing with containers, here are some suggestions for growing and displaying them effectively in your garden — making use of the principles discussed earlier in the chapter:

- ✔ Put a single golden barrel cactus in a low 12-inch bowl. Slowly and magnificently, the cactus can fill the pot.

- ✔ Circle a small tree, where roots don't allow anything to grow, with eight or so terra-cotta containers overflowing with white impatiens. Plant eight impatiens seedlings in each 12-inch container.

- ✔ On a balcony, create a privacy screen with containers of bamboo or English laurel.

- ✔ By your front door, where shade makes growing conditions tough, use a pair of topiary ivy balls in matching containers to greet visitors in a formal way.

- ✔ Announce spring with a window box full of sun-loving, early-blooming pansies and snapdragons. See Chapter 17 for window box ideas.

- ✔ For the holiday season, buy gallon-can-size spruce, pine, or other conifer trees available in your area, transplant them to terra-cotta or glazed pots, and decorate them with tiny glass balls for tabletop decorations. They can do well indoors for a few weeks.

- ✔ If you live where Japanese maples thrive, there's nothing better for a striking specimen tree in a container. For all-year good looks, choose colorful-leaf types (like Oshio Beni), or even colorful-bark varieties (such as Sango Kaku).

- ✔ Lead the way up front steps by flanking them with big pots of white marguerites — one plant per each 14-inch pot.

- ✔ At the edge of a sunny patio overhead, hang baskets of bougainvillea — normally a vine, but a vivid-blooming trailer when allowed to free fall.

- ✔ On a blank shady wall, attach wire half-baskets — at least three, staggered at different heights — filled with blooming begonias and impatiens, plus ferns for greenery.

Down-to-Earth Advice

Before you head off to the nursery, we offer a few nitty-gritty reminders — with many more such details later on:

  ✔ Containers can be messy on a deck, patio, or balcony. They may drip water and stain surfaces. Use saucers as described in Chapter 3.

  ✔ Container plants don't always maintain their good looks. Patience is in order before annuals start blooming, when bulbs are drying out after bloom, and when deciduous shrubs are leafless. Maybe you need a staging area or infirmary elsewhere in your garden where you can keep container plants when they're not at their best.

  ✔ Remember your climate and the limits it puts on all plants, especially container plants. If you live in cold region, be prepared to move prized plants into protection when winter arrives. See the next chapter for more on climates.

One Last Thing: Plant Names

You'll see a lot of plant names in the pages coming up, and we want to make sure you know why we use the names the way we do. Every plant has a two-part botanical name, identifying its genus and species. The botanical name always appears in italics with the genus name (which appears first) capitalized. For example, *Tagetes erecta* is the botanical name for American marigold. The genus name (*Tagetes*) refers to a group of closely related plants found in nature — all the marigolds. The species name (*erecta*) refers to a specific member of the genus — such as the tall orange-flowered American marigold.

Of course, most plants also have common names. But common names can vary from place to place and from time to time. *Nemophila menziesii* will always be the botanical name for the same plant, no matter where in the world you find it. But when it comes to this plant's common name, some people call it California bluebell, while others know it as baby blue eyes. To add to this confusion, different plants may share the same common name. For example, various kinds of butterfly flowers exist, in addition to butterfly bush and butterfly weed. Sometimes, the common name *is* the botanical name. For example, the botanical name for the petunia is *Petunia hybrida*.

Some specialized plants have an additional name tacked on to its botanical name, which indicates a *variety* (also called a clone or cultivar), which is much like the species, but it differs in some particular way, such as flower color. *Tagetes erecta* Snowbird is a white-flowered variety of the tall American marigold.

You can see why people who want to be precise stick to botanical names, but for most of us and for most of the time, common names work fine. And that's what we're going to use in this book. In case there may be confusion over a common name, check out the botanical name, usually given in parentheses.

Chapter 2

Cultivating Your Little Corner of the World

In This Chapter

▶ Zoning in on your climate

▶ Surviving winter

▶ Finding your plant's place in the sun — or shade

▶ Considering other conditions in your garden

*W*hat can you grow in containers in your garden — your little corner of the world? The question may be pretty straightforward, but the answer isn't at all clear-cut. Bear with us: You can expect words like "factor," "macro or micro," and "local conditions" to sneak up in our discussion. That's because we're talking about what goes on with climate and nature and all their wondrous permutations and variabilities.

At the macro level, your choice in plants depends on your area's climate. Just as important are the microclimates in your own garden — factors like sun, shade, and wind — and the limits and possibilities that they create for growing plants. To grow container plants really well, you need to consider both the macro and micro sides of things.

Portability expands the climate tolerance of container plants. You can bring them indoors for protection from the cold, move them into more sun if they're not getting enough, or move them into a shadier spot if they're getting sunburned. But life in a container also makes a plant more vulnerable to extremes of weather. A container plant just doesn't have the insulation against cold and heat enjoyed by that same plant in the ground.

Before you bring the joys of container gardening to your own backyard, you need to figure out what kinds of plants your climate can support.

A Climate to Call Your Own

Although all kinds of conditions determine what plants can grow in a certain region's climate, cold — not heat or humidity — is usually the key consideration. All plants have a certain tolerance to cold temperatures. Below that temperature, a plant's tissues are damaged or destroyed; if cold temperatures are prolonged, the plant may die. A plant's ability to withstand a certain minimum temperature is called its *hardiness* (you say, for instance, that a fuchsia is hardy to 28°F). Individual plant hardiness can vary depending on growing conditions and climatic factors in addition to cold, but the hardiness numbers are the most useful figures we have.

The United States Department of Agriculture publishes useful maps showing plant hardiness zones. The zone boundaries are based on average winter minimum temperatures collected from 125,000 weather stations. North America is divided into 11 zones, the warmest (zone 11) having an average winter minimum temperature above 40°F. Each succeeding zone down to zone 1 averages 10 degrees colder. Zones 1 through 10 are further divided into "a" and "b" in order to distinguish zones where average winter minimum differ by 5°F.

Any attempt to divide all of North America into zones is bound to have limitations. Despite their limitations, zone systems based on average minimum temperatures are also available for Western Europe, South Africa, Australia, New Zealand, Japan, and China.

Plants mentioned in this book are identified by climate zone according to the lowest winter temperatures that they can withstand. For example, a tree that is recommended as hardy for USDA zone 5 can be reliably grown in that zone and milder ones (higher numbers) — areas where temperatures do not fall below -20°F. As you read elsewhere and often in this book, these climate zone recommendations need to be interpreted differently for plants in containers — remember how exposed they are to the elements.

If you make comparisons between climates within the same USDA zones, you can see some of the weaknesses of the hardiness zone system. For example, zone 9 is in both Florida and California. Both have average winter minimums in the 20- to 30-degree F range, but Florida gets considerable rainfall, mostly in summer, while much of California is near-desert with most rain falling in winter. Plants notice the difference, to say the least.

You can often find zone maps on seed packets. Also, you can find zone maps for North America and Europe in *Gardening For Dummies* (IDG Books Worldwide, Inc.).

Bottom line

USDA zone recommendations are handy, but you often need more to go on when choosing plants for your area. Check on heat tolerance and other factors with a local nursery. Most nurseries carry only the plants that perform well locally. But remember that many nurseries gamble with the seasons (such as selling annuals when frost can still kill them) because customers demand them.

Bottom bottom line

And here's the biggest caveat of all when growing plants in containers: Plants in containers are exposed to more of the elements than when they're grown in the ground, and to be cautious, expect that plants in containers may not be as hardy as in the ground. If you want to be on the safe side, figure that if you live in zone 5, you can subtract one or two zones, and choose plants that are hardy to zones 3 or 4. Of course, all of this advice changes if you can and are willing to move container plants into protection during cold weather.

Climates and Container Plantings

When you garden in containers, certain climatic factors are more important than when you grow plants in the ground; the reverse is also true — some climate considerations are less important for container plantings. For instance, the absolute minimum temperature in your area doesn't matter that much if you move a container-grown geranium indoors for the winter. On the other hand, the typical last frost date is even more critical because that's when you can safely move the geranium back out into the garden.

Here's how climate affects a few basic container plant categories:

Seasonal performers

Our focus on annuals includes tender perennials that are treated as annuals. You generally expect one season from them. For example, plant petunias when warm weather comes, and throw them away when they get tired or hit by cold weather. With annuals like petunias, you need to pay particular attention to the last frost date of your climate. To a petunia, it doesn't really matter that Frostpak City, North Dakota, drops to -50°F in winter, just that the last frost is expected around June 10, and you can start planting then. Growing plants in containers, of course, allows you to take some liberties. You can plant petunias before the last-frost date if you can move them under cover when you expect cold nights.

In mild climate locations like southern California, there's a whole other planting season for annuals in fall — more on that in Chapter 6.

Permanent plants: A few words about winter

We're talking mainly trees, shrubs, and vines — many climatic factors affect their projected success in your area.

Year-round container plants are a way of life in mild climates — as common as cell phones in California. But container gardening in cold-winter climates has its limitations. The reason, in one word, is *winter*. Even plants that most of us think of as hardy — pine trees, for example — can't survive really cold winters in containers exposed to the elements, although they thrive in the same climate in the ground. Their roots freeze, lacking the insulation provided by the ground, or they dehydrate as deep frost draws the moisture out of the soil.

For example, can you grow shrubs and trees all year in container plants in climates as cold as Minnesota in zones 3 and 4? "Forget it," says Deb Brown of the Minnesota Extension Service. She recommends that you stick to containers of annuals and perennials during warm seasons only.

Mike Hibbard of Bachman's Garden Centers, also in Minnesota, describes some extreme measures employed by energetic gardeners who want to carry treasured container plants through the winter. He cites the "tip and bury" method that can be used on deciduous plants that are normally hardy only to zone 7 (such as Japanese maple): Tie branches of the plant together after it loses its leaves, lay it on its side in a trench that is 14 inches deep and wide enough to hold the plant, cover the plant with burlap, and then cover the plant, container, and all with soil. When the soil starts to thaw out in April or later, dig out the plant, stand it up, start watering, and see if it responds. Yes, this is extreme. We leave it to you to figure out if it's worth a try.

Of course, if you have a greenhouse (or conservatory), you can keep tender plants safe for the winter. Other ways exist to winterize individual plants, none of them simple, none of them foolproof:

- Bury containers in the ground (watch that they don't become water-logged).
- Wrap the plant with an insulating blanket of straw and chicken wire (pictured in Figure 2-1).

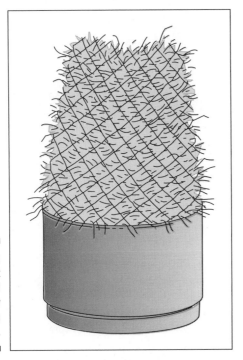

Figure 2-1:
A plant insulated with straw and chicken wire.

Again, you need to decide if these methods or other local strategies are worth the effort.

Simpler techniques work well in areas where container plants are marginally hardy. In climates like these, try to move frost-threatened container plants under an overhang on a cold night.

As you know by now, figuring out which plants can survive winter in your area is a bit tricky. Check with a knowledgeable local nursery or cooperative extension service before investing much in permanent container plants.

If you live in a cold climate, also remember that winter temperatures can affect your containers as well as your plants. If left outside, terra-cotta pots with soil in them can crack when moist soil expands as it freezes; move pots into protected areas for the winter.

Your Garden's Microclimate

Your own outdoor spaces have particular conditions that you need to take into account when planning to grow container plants.

Sun or shade?

Plants have natural attributes that cause them to perform better in different amounts of sunlight. Think about a plant's heredity for a few seconds. What is the best garden location for a vine that's native to the jungle? The logical response: where it's likely to receive some protection from the sun like it gets in nature from a high canopy of trees. Give the plant too much sun and it burns like an Irish redhead on the beach in Cancun. Or think about a plant with a sunny heredity. Zinnias, originally from Mexico, thrive in full sun. In too much shade, they grow spindly and develop mildew on their leaves.

Most annuals and vegetables do best in full sun, usually meaning about seven hours of sunlight during the middle of a summer day. If a spot in the garden gets its seven hours during the morning or late afternoon when the sun is not as intense, you're probably looking at a shortage of required sunlight. For those situations, think about growing shade lovers.

Permanent plants differ widely in their needs for sun or shade, ranging from cactus with a fondness for full sun to ferns that can get along fine in total shade.

Try to notice the pattern of sun and shade in your garden. Expect changes with time and the seasons, as the sun moves higher and lower in the sky, as trees grow taller and develop and lose leaves, as neighbors build or tear down buildings.

Here are some points to keep in mind:

✔ A northern exposure probably is blocked from the sun all day. This is *full shade*.

✔ The east side of your house, unless it's blocked by trees or buildings, receives sun in the morning and shade for the rest of the day. This is a typical *part shade*.

✔ A southern exposure gets the most hours of sun. This is *full sun*.

✔ A western exposure may get shade in the morning and full sun in the afternoon — this is usually considered a *sunny* location because of the intensity of the light (count on shade plants to cook in this location).

Pay attention to the sun/shade requirements specified for each plant or recommended by your local nursery. And watch plants for responses to existing conditions. A sign of too much sun is brown, burned spots on the leaves, as shown in Figure 2-2. A giveaway for too much shade is spindly foliage growth and weak blooming. If you notice those signs, experiment with different plants next time.

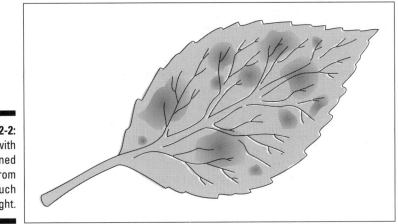

Figure 2-2:
A leaf with burned spots from too much sunlight.

Definitions of sun and shade also depend on your climate. Near the coast, where it's cool and often overcast, plants generally need more sun than in inland regions. There, sun-loving plants like zinnias may not get enough light even growing right out in full sun, and the result may be mildew. In cool coastal climates, normal shade-loving plants like begonias can flourish right out in full sun.

Wind

What about wind exposure in your garden? Wind can dry out the soil quickly and rob plants of moisture. Stiff breezes can topple tall plants and break brittle ones. Not much you can do, except make sure that you water carefully. Plant shrubs or trees to provide a windbreak if possible. Or find a more protected spot.

Slope

Hilly terrain can affect weather conditions. A sunny south-facing slope can provide a milder situation — cold air drains away. You may find a hillside garden to be several degrees warmer and several weeks ahead of the neighbor's garden at the bottom of the hill. Low spots collect cold air and can be decidedly chillier than nearby sloping spots.

Reflected heat

Paving, house walls, and other reflective surfaces can warm up a garden. Yes, warming effects can be considered a positive, but we generally become aware of reflected heat when plants burn up from conditions that are too bright — often from paving around a swimming pool. Even sun lovers like cactus can burn a bit.

Flexibility for Flourish

Experiment by moving plants around to see what they like. Move flowering plants that aren't blooming well into more sun; move foliage plants that look burned into more shade. Be careful, though, about moving conifers like pines or spruce into shade; they show their disinclination for shady places by losing needles.

Be ready to change with the seasons. Annual flowers, for example, can start out in the bright full sun of early spring when the weather's still kind of coolish. Your plants may benefit from a move to part shade when the weather heats up.

Chapter 3

Containing Your Excitement

In This Chapter

▶ Container composition

▶ Size and shape alternatives

▶ Types of containers

▶ Great plant-pot combinations

*A*mong the joys of gardening is the opportunity to combine aesthetic challenges and satisfactions with practical science-y stuff.

Your definition of beauty and function comes into play when you start choosing the containers and matching them to plants. Whether you buy containers, make them yourself, or improvise, your attention to materials, colors, shapes, and cost can yield a great statement about your personal taste.

Also make sure that you approach the process with a horticultural-science frame of mind. Your chosen containers need to be good for the plant's health — the right size, material, and shape.

None of this is difficult. And it's kind of fun.

Types of Materials

Containers are available in a huge variety of materials —especially if you start making your own or finding unusual planter prospects. As you look, be sure to consider at least two key factors: porosity and drainage.

✔ **Porosity:** Some materials used for containers are more porous than others and allow moisture and air to penetrate more readily. Unglazed terra-cotta, wood, and paper pulp dry out faster but also allow soil to cool by evaporation and to "breathe" (roots need oxygen); porosity has the effect of drawing away excess water, preventing waterlogged soil. Non-porous materials like glazed terra-cotta, plastic, and metal hold soil moisture better, which can be both good and bad — depending on the importance of drainage or water retention to your particular plants (more about this real soon).

✔ **Drainage:** For healthy root development, soil must drain water properly and have enough space for air. Soil that is too heavy or dense can slow drainage; so can lack of a drain hole or a blocked drain hole. If drainage is slow or nonexistent, water may collect at the bottom (it can even stagnate and smell bad); roots can smother and the plant can die. Look for drain holes when selecting containers.

The following materials are used most often for containers these days. Each has its strengths and weaknesses.

Terra-cotta or unglazed clay

Picture a flower pot, and you probably see a plain clay container — the kind Peter Rabbit tipped over while he was sneaking into Mr. McGregor's garden. Unglazed clay or terra-cotta (baked earth, in Italian) is usually reddish-orange in color but is available in other colors as well — tan, cream, black, and chocolate brown. Pots come in many shapes and sizes. Figure 3-1 shows some in various sizes. Higher quality pots, with thick walls fired in high heat, last longer. Pots fired at low heat have a grainier texture and weather away more quickly — not a bad effect if you want a pot that looks like it was made by ancient Romans.

Unglazed clay pots generally offer good value for the money. Their earthy colors and natural surface make the pots look comfortable in almost any garden situation, rustic to formal. Unglazed clay's porosity allows plant roots to breathe and excess moisture to evaporate — all desirable for many plants. Porosity also means that the soil dries out quickly.

Remember that unglazed clay pots are on the breakable side. Durability depends on how they're fired, ingredients in the mix, and thickness of the walls. Simply by hefting the pots, you can pretty much tell the more durable, thick-sided ones.

Remember that in cold climates, terra-cotta pot sides can split when moist soil freezes and expands inside the pot.

Glazed clay

Usually inexpensive, these pots come in many more colors than unglazed pots — bright to dark, some with patterns. Many are made in Asia and fit nicely in Japanese-style gardens. They're great in formal situations or to liven up a grouping of plain clay pots. Glazed pots are less porous than unglazed and can hold moisture better. They are breakable.

Figure 3-1:
Some terra-
cotta pots.

Wood

Square and rectangular boxes and round tubs are sold in many styles and are usually made of rot-resistant redwood and cedar. They're heavy and durable, and stand up well to cold weather. Appearance is usually rustic, at home on decks and other informal situations. Wood containers provide good soil insulation, keeping roots cooler than in terra-cotta. Evaporation is also less than with clay pots. Thicker lumber is better — at least $7/8$ inch. Bottoms may rot if they stay too moist; raise containers at least an inch off the ground with stands or saucers as described later in this chapter. To make wood last longer, treat the insides with wood preservative.

Half barrels are inexpensive large containers. Recycled oak whiskey and wine barrels once filled the bill; now, rustic-looking wooden vessels are made specifically for garden purposes. Because of their healthy dimensions, barrels can accommodate small trees or larger vegetables (beans, tomatoes, squash).

Bushel baskets also offer a homespun look. To encourage longer basket life, treat them with wood preservative and line them with plastic.

Figure 3-2 shows some wood containers along with a few others you're likely to encounter.

Plastic

Many plastic pots are designed to imitate standard terra-cotta pots. Plastic is less expensive, easier to clean, and lighter than terra-cotta. It's also nonporous and doesn't dry out as quickly as terra-cotta, so be careful that you don't overwater. Watch for poor quality plastic pots, which can fade in the sun and become brittle.

The plastic look isn't for everyone. You can camouflage plastic pots in a group of more decorative pots. Or sink a plastic pot with a plant into a larger pot for an instant facelift without even transplanting.

Other materials

You're less likely to encounter containers made of the following materials; but each has its own appeal and reason for being:

Figure 3-2:
Big wooden
containers,
a trough,
and a
glazed pot.

✔ **Cast concrete** is durable, heavy, and cold-resistant.

✔ **Paper pulp** is compressed recycled paper that degrades in several years. You actually can plant pot and all directly in the ground, and the roots grow through the sides as the pot decomposes. Inexpensive and lightweight, but not particularly handsome, these also are candidates for slipping into larger, more attractive containers. Use them where looks don't matter. They're excellent for vegetables.

✔ **Metal** is a favorite choice for antique and Asian planters. Look for brass, copper, iron, aluminum, and other metal containers at boutiques and antique shops. Make sure drainage is provided.

Improvised containers

Turning mundane items into plant containers is fun — as long as you don't mind hearing from more "sophisticated" gardeners. In Chapter 17, you can read about how to choose, prepare, and plant wheelbarrows, wagons, and other found objects. Figure 3-3 shows some interesting improvisations.

Raised beds

Planting beds built into gardens — made with lumber, brick, or many other materials — actually are a form of container, most likely filled with planting mix rather than garden soil. We're not going to discuss raised beds specifically, but much of the advice for watering and feeding container plants applies.

Containers of your own making

You can also make your own containers — most likely of wood. Check with a local building supply store for plans and materials. Another simple material is hyper-tufa; see Chapter 17 for how-to directions.

Container Sizes and Shapes

What's good for the plant? What looks nice? You need to deal with both.

A pot that's too small crowds roots, cutting off moisture, oxygen, and nutrients that are vital for healthy growth. If the pot is too big, the superfluous soil may stay too wet and can smother the roots.

Figure 3-3:
You can turn all kinds of stuff into containers for plants.

Rules for ideal container size differ a bit for permanent plants and seasonal plants.

For permanent plants like Japanese maple or conifers, think longer term and choose a pot that looks in scale with the plant when you buy it and allows room for a year or two of root growth. As a rule, when buying a nursery plant, transplant it to a container that is 2 inches deeper and wider than its nursery container. Don't be shy about taking the plants you're buying to the container section of a store to find the best match. Or if you own the container, take it into the nursery to match it up with plants.

Seasonals like annuals and bulbs can be crowded together more closely than plants that you grow in the ground, providing much more impact quickly. Crowded conditions can't persist for long, but you can satisfy the tight-quarters demands for extra water and food over your plants' short seasons. You can find advice on spacing in the sections on annuals and other plants (Part III). As a rule, figure that if the recommended spacing for ground planting is 10 to 12 inches, container planting translates to 6 to 8 inches apart. As a general rule of scale, if the annuals normally grow 10 or 12 inches tall, provide a pot with a diameter of at least 8 inches. If the plants grow 2 or 3 feet tall, better go for a diameter of 24 inches or a large container like a half barrel.

Container shapes vary. Some are designed for practicality, and others, we can assume, look the way they do because someone likes their appearance. The tapered shape of terra-cotta pots, for example, allows plants to slip out more readily for repotting. Makes sense, right?

Standard pots

Most standard pots — the familiar terra-cotta with rim or plastic versions of the same — are taller than they are wide, allowing the roots to grow deep. This works for most plants.

Small containers, up to 8 inches in diameter, can hold a few annuals or perennials, and a single young permanent plant (a small conifer, for example).

Standard pots up to 12 inches in diameter can hold half a dozen annuals or small perennials or medium-sized shrubs or vines.

Use larger pots (at least 18 inches in diameter) for bigger shrubs, small trees, bamboo, and mixed plantings of annuals and perennials.

Low containers

Sometimes called azalea or fern pots, these containers are wider than tall, typically sold in diameters from 4 to 14 inches. Use them for shallow-rooted plants — may we suggest azaleas and ferns? Terra-cotta is the most commonly used material.

Bulb pots

Usually made of terra-cotta and sold in 6- to 12-inch diameters, these shallow containers are not much deeper than saucers. You can get away with planting bulbs in such a small amount of soil; they have shallow roots, need little soil, and are grown for only one season. Shallow bowls can be used for smaller annuals, but make sure that you provide enough soil for growth, and water and fertilize carefully.

Other shapes

Many other styles are also available: bowls, tapered Spanish pots, and bonsai pots (which are shallow). With all of these, remember to check for drainage and space for roots.

Hanging baskets

For the sake of lightness, hanging baskets come mainly in wood and wire. The wire baskets, lined with sphagnum moss or synthetic material to hold in soil, offer room on the sides for inserting plants — producing a look of overflowing abundance. Pick a diameter of at least 9 or 10 inches, preferably 15 or 16 inches. The most common shape is round, but half baskets to attach to a wall are also available and useful.

Accessories, at Your Service

You may want to consider a few other container-related items to help grow container plants successfully.

Saucers

These items help keep water from going where you don't want it — onto a deck or patio, for instance. Unwanted water, of course, can damage surfaces; in addition, water draining from containers can carry stains from the soil mix.

A saucer looks better if it matches the container, and you can find the shallow dish in terra-cotta or plastic. Clear plastic saucers are inexpensive and fairly inconspicuous. Saucers come in standard sizes, designed to match pots. Select a saucer that's at least an inch wider in diameter than the bottom of the pot.

Saucers also can be converted to hold soil and plants. See Chapter 17.

Elevation

Lifting containers off the ground has several advantages. A tall stand, either purchased or made, can lift plants up for eye-level viewing (see Figure 3-4). But just raising the container up several inches allows water to flow more freely out of the container and promotes better air circulation underneath. Wood rot is reduced and insect hiding places are eliminated.

Figure 3-4:
Stands raise plants to eye level and promote circulation.

So how do you raise the containers? You can buy decorative "pot feet," sold in many catalogs. You can use three bricks or wood blocks. For just a little lift, you can use hose washers on masonry surfaces.

Feel like improvising? Consider borrowing ideas like a container stand made from an old stool or a water heater base. Take your plants to a higher level with a touch of creativity!

A Pot for Every Plant

For starters, here's a sampling of proven plant-and-container combinations that promise a great look. The containers also deserve note because they're the right size and shape for healthy growth. Read on in this book and you may come up with many other ideas of your own.

- A 10-inch-high golden barrel cactus in a 14-inch-diameter terra-cotta bowl

- English lavender, sweet peas, geranium, sweet alyssum, and catmint in an 18-inch wire basket stuffed with sphagnum moss

- Six water plants (including water lily and Japanese iris) in a water-tight half-barrel filled with water

- Tomato, parsley, and basil in a 16-inch plastic pot

- Dwarf Washington Navel orange tree in a whisky barrel

- Eight dwarf dianthus in an 18-inch ceramic bowl

- A 7-foot black bamboo in a terra-cotta pot that's 12 inches high, 14 inches wide

- Miniature rose and English ivy in an old work boot, size $10^1/_2$ D (We're not kidding!)

Part II
How to Plant

The 5th Wave®   By Rich Tennant

"The seeds fell out of Walt's pocket six years ago and since then every August we just sit somewhere else."

In this part . . .

Plants really don't ask for much. A place to call home and a decent diet usually keeps these earth-bound guys going strong through the seasons of their lives.

But as we know from our own human experiences, comfortable lodging and well-prepared meals are a step up from a basic existence. And that's what this part can give you — not an estate with a chef, but a boost to your understanding about starting your container plants out on solid ground, and then growing with the flow.

Your reward: What price happy, healthy plants — even if they can't claim a permanent residence?

Chapter 4

Soil Mixes

· ·

In This Chapter

▶ Getting to know soil

▶ Understanding what container plants really need

▶ Searching out the good soil

▶ Shopping for soil mixes

▶ Making your own foolproof soil mix

· ·

This is the most important chapter in the book! Go ahead, skip this chapter.

Wondering what's going on? The explanation's really pretty simple.

If you want to do all your container planting with bags of soil mix bought at the garden center — without having any idea what's in the blend — you can count on reasonably good results. You really don't need to read this chapter.

But if you want to understand what plants need and why — and you may discover that it's fascinating — the place to start is at ground level. A warning: The road to knowledge can be littered with lots of technical stuff. But when you understand how to provide just the right soil for different plants, you open one of gardening's most interesting doors. Make your own soil mix, and you can save money as you customize to create perfect growing conditions for each container plant — and you may enjoy results beyond your wildest imaginings!

So what are you going to do? Read on, or see you in Chapter 5.

Why Soil Mix Matters

Finding or preparing the right soil mix — one with a perfect crumbly texture that provides plenty of oxygen, plant nutrients, and moisture but that also drains well and is free of diseases, insects and weed seeds — is the most important thing you can do to ensure the success of your container plants.

Because no matter what you plant, whether it's an exotic shrub or a simple pot of geraniums, the key to making it work is making sure that your plants are happy beneath the surface.

Why is soil so critical? Because of roots. While we sit back and applaud the flowers and foliage that grow above the rim of the pot, it's the roots underground that are really supporting the show and that deserve our accolades. Roots make up more than half of every plant, and they're working constantly to find the right amount of air, moisture, and nutrients to fuel the flowers and foliage above.

Plants in containers are especially dependent on the soil or growing mix in which they develop simply because there's so much less to choose from in the confines of the pots. So to keep your plants happy and healthy, you need to first take care of the roots. And that means growing them in the right stuff.

Finding the ideal soil mix for container gardening isn't difficult — if you depend on the experts. Fortunately, a whole lot of people study just what plants in containers need. You can go into just about any nursery or garden center and find an aisle with packages marked "growing mix." But to make sense of all the different soil mix products on the market today, or to try your hand at mixing up a batch of your own custom concoction, you must understand what your plants need in order to grow. In this chapter you can dig a little deeper into the underground life of plants and find out just what this pursuit of the perfect potting mixture is all about.

A Quick Primer on Soil

Soil, whether you're discussing the stuff that we walk on and garden in or the bagged commercial products for container growing, provides plants with a means of support — a way to hold the plant up — and a storehouse for the balance of nutrients, oxygen and moisture needed by the plant's roots. But not all soils are created equal, and it's not even recommended that you use outdoor garden soil for container gardening, as we discuss in more detail later. That's right, your good old garden-variety dirt can actually be *bad* for your container plants. However, before you discover the particulars of a good planting mix for container growing, look at what makes up a typical garden soil, just to get some of the lingo down. After you understand the terms, you can move on to the potting mixtures. So sit still for a short course in soil science.

Soil — up close and personal

Healthy garden soils contain a mixture of water, air, and solids (mineral particles and organic matter, or *humus*). The relative percentages of the mineral particles — sand, silt, or clay — determine the soil's *texture*. Here's a closer look at all three components, which are shown in Figure 4-1:

✔ **Sand:** This gritty stuff is larger in size than the other two soil particles. A soil with 70 percent sand particles is classified as *sandy*. Such soils drain well and dry out quickly, but they're unable to hold nutrients. One way to recognize a sandy soil: Take a pinch of it and it won't hold together.

✔ **Clay:** These particles are so fine that they can be seen individually only with an electron microscope. Clay soils — classified as containing at least 35 percent clay particles — are sticky to the touch and drain slowly. Clay feels slippery to the touch when you squeeze it together in a ball, and it holds its shape. Clay soils are very high in nutrients, but the nutrients often occur in forms that are unsuitable for plants.

✔ **Silt:** Silt is similar to clay, but the individual particles are much larger, moderating its characteristics. If moist, silt holds its shape fairly well when squeezed together and feels smooth but not sticky. Dry silt feels like flour. Silt holds water and nutrients longer than sand, but not as tightly as clay.

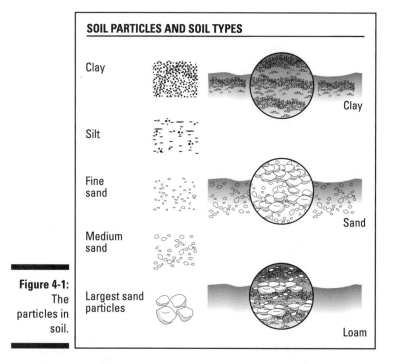

SOIL PARTICLES AND SOIL TYPES

Clay

Silt

Fine sand

Medium sand

Largest sand particles

Clay

Sand

Loam

Figure 4-1: The particles in soil.

Most outdoor garden soils are composed of a combination of all three particles, in varying proportions. *Loam,* which is considered an ideal soil for typical backyard gardening, contains a mixture of sand, silt, and clay as well as plenty of humus. Loam retains water without becoming waterlogged and contains a balance of the nutrients necessary for plant growth. Formulas for soil mixes presented later in this chapter allow you to create an ideal texture and balance of nutrients for growing plants.

The structured life of soil

The way in which a soil's mineral particles group together determines the *soil structure.* The size and arrangement of these groupings influence the drainage capacity of the soil and its nutrient availability. A very sandy soil, for example, can't form good aggregates (the basic structural units of soil) because its particles are too coarse, and a heavy clay can't form good aggregates because its particles are too fine, causing the soil to be too compact and thereby excluding water and air. Without good drainage, a soil becomes wet and low in oxygen, causing your plant's roots to rot. Drainage is not only important to backyard gardening but is also a *critical* in container growing — more on this in a moment.

When a soil has good structure, it has plenty of spaces for air and water, and lots of room for plant roots to grow in the spaces between the soil aggregates — remember, it's those roots that we're trying to please. In a soil with good structure, the tiny root hairs are able to absorb the air and the nutrient-rich water that help produce the stems, leaves, fruit, and flowers that we cherish so.

Unfortunately, few gardens have true loam soils with an ideal structure. You probably have to make do with a mixture that's too high in clay or sand, and correct it by adding organic matter such as *compost* (garden and kitchen waste that's decomposed to the texture of a crumbly dirt) and nutrients (in the form of compost or fertilizers). Adding organic matter helps form humus, which enables small silt or clay particles to stick together to form larger aggregates; in sandy soils, the humus acts like a sponge to catch and hold moisture and nutrients. Doctoring up the dirt is called *amending the soil.* The repair work makes bad soil better for growing your plants, better for those — you got it — all-important roots.

Sweet or sour soil? A word about pH

No discussion of soil science can be complete without a mention of pH, or the relative sweetness (alkalinity) or sourness (acidity) of the soil. The pH is measured on a scale of 1 to 14, with 7.0 being neutral. A soil pH below 7.0 is considered acidic, while one above 7.0 is alkaline.

The reason a soil's pH is important for plants is that some nutrients are available for uptake by a plant's roots only when the pH is within a specific range. The ideal pH for most plants is 6.0 to 7.0, though a few plants (such as acid-loving rhododendrons, azaleas, blueberries, and some perennials) prefer a slightly lower pH.

Kits for determining pH are readily available in most garden centers, and they're all you probably need for testing soil or your own potting mixes. For the definitive word on a soil's chemistry and makeup, you can order a professional test. Check with your local Cooperative Extension office for more information or for addresses of reputable soil-testing labs.

When buying commercial soil mixes for container plants, you don't have to worry about pH. Mixes in bags are formulated to the correct pH for most plants. Special mixtures are available for ferns, azaleas, or woodland plants that prefer a more acidic soil.

If your garden soil has a pH that is too high or too low, you can correct it. Unfortunately, such a discussion is a bit complex and is really beyond the scope of this book. We can tell you that adding lime counteracts acidity. If you choose to blend your own soil mix, look for recipes later in this chapter that include lime to bring the pH to the right level.

In Pursuit of the Perfect Container Mix

Now that you have some of the soil science lingo under your belt, you can begin to navigate the sea of container mixes. There's a whole slew of blends on the market, under a variety of brand names and companies. Some are formulated specifically for starting seedlings, while others are geared for potting up transplants or growing nursery stock. But if you take a look at the ingredients, one of the chief things that you may notice is that there's very little real soil, if any, listed.

What gives? Why not use garden soil to grow your prize plants in containers? After all, many of the plants that we raise in containers outside on our patios and decks also grow successfully in the open ground. Why don't we just take a shovelful of soil and dump it in a pot and call it a done deal?

The dirty truth about garden soil

Although it seems to make sense that a good soil in the garden has all the right stuff to make it a good soil in a pot or planter, it just isn't so. Soils that are terrific in the field are not so great when put in containers. When the soil is lifted, it loses its structure. And as garden soil settles in a shallow container (much different from the natural depth of the soil in a field), it forms a dense mass that roots can't penetrate, making it drain poorly, saturating the roots. As a result, not enough oxygen reaches the root zone, and the roots suffocate. Plus, garden soil harbors disease-causing organisms that can devastate container plantings, as well as the probability of unwelcome weed seeds.

What container plants need

Plants in containers have different soil and water requirements than plants in the ground, and they need a special soil mix that meets those needs.

Fast water infiltration and optimal drainage

In garden soil, water is pulled down to the roots by gravity, capillary action, and the attraction of the small clay particles. The water keeps moving through the soil in a continuous column, acting in the same manner that a hose siphon works, or a blotter of ink. Each drop needs another drop of water behind it to continue the flow. Because the soil in a container is so confined, it needs to have a loose, open structure to encourage this flow of water. Plants in garden soil, for example, can grow fine when the rate of water infiltration is as little as $1/2$ inch per hour, but to survive in a container, the same plant needs a water infiltration rate of 5 to 10 inches per hour. How fast a soil drains is known as its *total porosity,* and the higher the number, the faster the drainage.

You know that common advice that calls for putting a layer of pea gravel or other potting shards in the bottom of your container to improve drainage? Don't do it! Although it may sound logical, using pea gravel in the bottom of a pot actually results in less air for the plant's roots and more water in the bottom of the pot. Instead, fill the entire container with the same soil mix, covering the drainage holes at the bottom with hardware cloth or screen to hold in the soil as needed. Or put the smaller soil-filled pot in a larger decorative pot that has gravel in the bottom.

Plenty of air space

Open air goes hand-in-hand with good drainage, and providing breathing space is actually the most important requirement for a good container mix. Container plantings must have plenty of air in the soil after drainage be-cause they require air for growth and respiration (it's those roots again!). A proper container mix has both small and large pores *(micropores and macropores)*. When the mix is watered, the water is held in the micropores but drains quickly through the macropores, enabling air to follow. A soil mixture of sphagnum peat moss and *perlite* (a naturally occurring mineral that's used in commercial soil mixes), for example, has more than 20 percent air space after drainage. A typical garden soil may have little space between the soil particles, allowing less than 5 percent air space after drainage.

Determining exactly how much air you need in your potting mixture after drainage depends on the type of plant you're growing. Some plants get by with less, others demand an airy environment. Ferns and azaleas, for example, need at least 20 percent air space. Rhododendrons, begonias, snapdragons, and most foliage plants also require high aeration. Vegetables, such as carrots and lettuce, do best with a lighter soil as well. Camellia, chrysanthemums, and poinsettias do fine in an intermediate soil, while carnations, geraniums, ivies, and most conifers can tolerate a heavier mix. And for large shrubs or small trees, you need a mixture that has enough weight to keep the container from falling over and retains enough water to support the larger root systems, yet still drains well and provides adequate air spaces.

Moisture retention

Hey, hold it now, you're probably thinking. You just said that container plants need plenty of air and good drainage. Doesn't that message go against holding onto moisture? The logic can be a little tricky. This last requirement — *water retention* — is a tradeoff, because the soil mix that holds onto the most water and drains slowest has less room for air.

Table 4-1 shows how the materials in container mixes vary according to how fast they drain and the amount of water and air left in the soil after drainage. The numbers for water retention and air space are given in percentage by volume; total porosity is a measure of the speed with which a soil drains.

Table 4-1	Characteristics of Container Soil Components		
Material	*Total Porosity*	*Water Retention*	*Air Space after Drainage*
Clay loam	59.6	54.9	4.7
Sphagnum peat moss	84.2	58.8	25.4
Fine sand	44.6	38.7	5.9
Redwood sawdust	77.2	49.3	27.9
Perlite ($1/16$"–$3/16$")	77.1	47.3	29.8
Vermiculite (0–$3/16$")	80.5	53.0	27.5
Fir bark (0–$1/8$")	69.5	38.0	31.5
Fine sand/fir bark (1:1)	54.6	37.4	15.2
Fine sand/peat moss (1:1)	56.7	47.3	9.4
Perlite/peat moss (1:1)	74.9	51.3	23.6

Lack of contamination

Container mixes need to be free of diseases, insects, weed seeds, and harmful chemicals. Garden soil loses out on all counts for container planting. Along with all the clay, silt, and sand that we find in garden ground, a multitude of disease-causing organisms can infect your prize plants. At the time of germination, seedlings are extremely vulnerable to the organisms that cause damping-off and root-rot diseases. But soil contamination can be a factor for larger plantings as well. If you use diseased soil to grow tomatoes, for example, you can expect to end up with a patio of rotted fruit rather than a container bursting with vine-ripened beauties. The alternative, pasteurizing the soil with heat, is not an easy task and definitely not something that you want to do in the house — the odor produced by the process is not pleasant.

With garden soil, you're also getting insects in various stages of development and weed seeds from harvesting, which can flourish in the environment of many container plantings. Although the weeds may not be such a big deal, bringing insects indoors or into a container area can wreak havoc on the rest of your plants. Finally, it's possible that herbicides or other plant-harmful chemicals may be lurking in field or garden soil, and when transferred to the delicate ecosystem of a container garden, the caustic substances may kill the very plants you're attempting to grow.

Rather than use backyard garden soil, commercial nursery growers (and most gardeners) now turn to soil-less mixes as a basis for their container potting mixtures.

Bring On the Soil Mixes (For Peat's Sake)

The movement away from real soil in potting mixes in this country began more than 60 years ago, in an attempt to eliminate the soil diseases that were plaguing the nursery industry and to find an alternative to topsoil, which was being lost to urbanization and herbicide contamination. The first mixes were made of sand or sandy soil mixed with milled sphagnum peat moss. But these concoctions still had to be sterilized because of the natural disease organisms present in the sand, and the mixtures were heavy. Then in the mid-1950s plant pathologists at the University of California (Go Bears!) developed U. of C. mixes that were uniformly lightweight and disease-free. On the other coast in the early 1960s, researchers at Cornell University, in Ithaca, New York, produced their peat-lite formula — a half and half mixture of milled sphagnum peat and vermiculite (a natural mineral) — which became the basis of today's commercial soil-less growing mixes. The dozens of companies that now market soil-less mixes each has its own variation of this basic formula, customized for uses running the gamut from seed-starting to nursery plantings. You can find them under the names Fafard Mixes, Jiffy-Mix, Metro-Mix, Pro-Gro, Pro-Mix, Redi-Earth, and many others.

Referred to as growing media in the professional nursery trade, the mixes that you find on the shelves of your local nursery, garden center, or superstore today are based on a combination of organic components like *sphagnum peat moss, composted pine bark or fir bark,* or other wood by-products, and a mineral fraction such as *vermiculite* and *perlite* (two naturally occurring mineral elements that pop like popcorn when they're exposed to very high temperatures, making them extremely lightweight and porous). Some heavier mixes include sand, which has been washed and screened to remove the fine particles. Most mixes also contain a small amount of *ground limestone* (usually dolomite) to correct the acidity of the organic component and to buffer alkaline or acidic water supplies, and they may include a *wetting agent* (to help moisten the naturally water-resistant peat) and a dose of *fertilizer* (to get your plants off to a good start).

Mixes containing high-quality compost and perlite, plus other ingredients like composted manure, are now making their debut as well. Proponents of compost-peat mixtures claim that the naturally disease-suppressive qualities of high-quality compost actually help inhibit soilborne diseases.

Other ingredients used in some commercial mixes include rice hulls, rock wool (a soil-less amendment made from basaltic rock), and coconut coir pith (a coarse outer-husk fiber used as an alternative to sphagnum peat moss).

The following list gives a sampling of what you may find in different mixes:

- **Charcoal:** Used to absorb toxic agents in the mix.

- **Compost:** Decomposed vegetative matter. Adds nutrients, microorganisms, and weight. Holds moisture. Can be highly variable in quality.

- **Composted fir or pine bark, redwood sawdust or shavings:** Lightens the mix by providing better porosity. The ingredients used in commercial mixes are stabilized so that they won't deplete nitrogen.

- **Dolomitic limestone:** Added to peat-based mixes to correct the acidity of the peat. Supplies some calcium and magnesium to plants.

- **Fertilizers:** Chemical fertilizers give plants an initial boost, and are included in many soil-less mixes under the term *starter charge.* Seaweed fertilizers are sometimes used for a quick fix in organic mixes, while slower-acting amendments like bone meal or blood meal provide longer-lasting nutrients.

- **Manure:** May be found in organic potting mixes, usually available in bags. Well-aged, composted, commercial type originates with cows.

- **Perlite:** A granite-like volcanic rock that pops like popcorn and expands to 20 times its original volume when heat treated at 1500° to 2000°F. Does not absorb water like vermiculite. Aerates and lightens soil mixes; improves drainage.

- ✔ **Sand:** Washed, screened sand (often called builders' sand). Primarily adds weight to the mix and aids water flow.

- ✔ **Sphagnum peat moss:** High-quality peat that acts like a sponge when moistened, retaining water while also aerating the mix and improving drainage. Basic component of soil-less mixes.

- ✔ **Topsoil:** May be found in soil-based potting mixes. Usually a select loam soil with 3 to 5 percent humus. Adds weight to mix; provides nutrients; contains microorganisms that may cause disease. Bagged topsoil is best; avoid garden loam.

- ✔ **Vermiculite:** Processed mineral flakes that expand to 20 times original volume under heat treatment. Retains water and aerates the mix. Breaks down more quickly than perlite.

- ✔ **Wetting agent:** Used to help wet peat moss, which is naturally water-resistant when dry.

Shopping for a soil mix

Picking the most appropriate mix for your planting needs depends on knowing what you want to grow.

For starting your own plants from seed or growing very small (under 4 inches) potted plants, for example, you're best off buying a straight soil-less mix based on peat, vermiculite, and perlite, labeled *seed starting mix* or *germinating mix*. These mixes are screened to be very fine, which makes them ideal for starting small seeds. But they're not a good choice for growing plants in larger containers through the season because they hold too much water and eventually compact, providing too little air for good long-term root growth.

For container gardening in hanging baskets or medium-size containers, you need a coarser mix that has better porosity, labeled *general-purpose mix*. The formulations often include composted pine bark for better drainage.

Larger containers that can hold large shrubs or small trees require an even heavier mix (to anchor the pot), but one with adequate drainage and air space for root growth. Such mixtures, sometimes labeled *nursery mix,* often have sand and composted bark mulch added to the peat mix.

Also look for soil mixes formulated for plants that require specific conditions: African violets, bulbs, cactus, orchids, and others.

Fortunately, most reliable suppliers describe the contents of their various mixes clearly, with the most common ingredient listed first (often with the percentage), followed by the lesser ingredients in descending order, so that you know what you're getting. If you're still unsure about what to buy, visit your local nursery or garden center and ask the experts which product they suggest.

Where to buy soil mixes

Soil mixes for container growing are sold in plastic bags, either loose (in a size range from 1 quart up to a 40-pound bag) or in compressed bales (weighing about 70 pounds). Compressed bales yield almost twice the volume on the label when you dig out the mix and fluff it up. If you have a large number of plants to pot, it can be more economical to buy the bales than to purchase individual smaller bags of mix.

You can find soil mixes at most places that sell potted plants. Superstores with gardening sections offer a wide choice of brand names, often at bargain prices. Local nurseries and garden centers have a full line of soils, likely at more expensive prices, but you can get some advice on what to buy. At a retail nursery that propagates and pots up some of its own plants, you can expect the narrowest selection, but potentially the best choice: the mixes the professional growers use themselves. You may be able to buy a soil-mix bag or a bale at a cost above the wholesale price, but less than retail if the grower is willing to sell you some. At the very least, you can ask those experts what they recommend, and then match your mix to that recipe (see "Doctoring up the mix," later in this chapter).

Whatever you buy, keep the bag tightly closed (so that it doesn't dry out or become infected with disease organisms) and protected from rain (to prevent saturation and rot). The plastic covering on commercial-size bags and bales is usually treated with ultraviolet light inhibitors, giving the material about a one-year shelf life when stored out in the open. You can store the mix in an enclosed shed or in a dry, well-aired basement, though, if you want to keep it for more than one season.

Mixing Your Own

With a little knowledge of what to look for, you can't really go wrong with buying a commercial mix. And if you plan to grow only a few containers out on the patio or pot plants for indoors, you can purchase a container mix, plant your pots, and then sit back to enjoy the gardens that result. With commercial mixes, you're most likely to get a consistent product that's free of disease — a significant advantage with container plantings. If you want a sure thing, that's the way to go. And in some cases, relying on a tried-and-true formula is actually the most economical thing to do.

If you can't find a growing mix that suits your needs, however, and you really want to get down and dirty, you can mix your own blend. If you decide to take this route, be aware that you may need to experiment (using the general recipes that follow) to achieve just the right mix. Or you may be able to whip up exactly what you want by slightly modifying a commercial mix.

Doctoring up the mix

Professional nurseries, who generally have plenty of the raw materials on site, often buy wholesale mixtures of a general peat-based growing mix, then customize it to meet their needs. Some growers, for example, find the commercial soil-less mixes too dense when used as is and want to lighten the mix with amendments like perlite. Other experts determine that the mixes are too dry for their intended container plants or too light to support larger plantings like trees or shrubs, so they add composted bark mulch, compost or leaf mold (partially decayed leaves), sand, or even high-quality bagged topsoil to the brew. Fertilizers, generally in slow-release forms that are temperature- and water-sensitive, such as Osmocote, are often added to provide nutrients throughout the growing season.

If you add topsoil or other soil-based ingredients to your potting mixture, you run the risk of introducing disease-causing organisms to your container mixture. For best results, use only bagged, commercial topsoil, not the backyard garden fare.

If you're growing large shrubs or even trees in containers, a sterile potting mixture is not as critical as it is for seedlings or small pots. But you're still taking a chance. Also, when you add any amendments to a commercial soil mix, you upset the balance of ingredients that are carefully formulated by the soil mix experts who produce the blend. Perhaps the best course to take if you want to amend a mix is to visit your local nursery or garden center and find out what the folks there recommend for the specific plants you're intending to grow.

Foolproof mixes from scratch

If you've read this far, you probably fit the description of a do-it-yourself gardener — someone who wants to get to the nitty-gritty of all this soil science stuff. Or maybe you're hoping to save some money by mixing your own brew in bulk. Whatever the reason, the following recipes can start you on your way to developing your own custom concoction. All sorts of combinations are possible in your experimentation; you need to decide if you want a purely soil-less (peat-based) mix or an organic type that contains real soil.

Overall, you're aiming for a mix that has an ideal texture, crumbling easily in your hand, providing good drainage and air spaces while retaining adequate moisture. The right stuff also has the correct balance of nutrients and matches the appropriate level of lime or acidity for your chosen plants — slightly acid for most plants, moderately acid for azaleas and other acid-loving plants. The mix needs to be uniform from batch to batch, and free of diseases, insects, weed seed, and harmful chemicals.

A simple combination of peat moss and vermiculite (or perlite or sand), such as the Cornell mix described next, can be used for virtually all types of plants. Choose the ingredients that best suit your planting program. For outdoor containers that receive frequent rains, for instance, use perlite rather than vermiculite. If the mix is to be used for shrub or tree containers, add $^1/_3$ part sand and $^2/_3$ ground bark or peat moss for a heavier mix.

Whichever mix you use, follow the same basic method for mixing (described next), and store any leftover mix in plastic bags or a tightly sealed plastic garbage can.

Basic peat mix (Cornell soil-less mix)

This recipe creates one cubic yard of mix. First combine the following:

$^1/_2$ cubic yard of sphagnum peat moss

$^1/_2$ cubic yard of vermiculite

Dump the ingredients in a pile on a smooth, clean surface like a concrete patio or driveway, or on a plastic tarp where you won't contaminate the mix (for smaller proportions, use a wheelbarrow or garden cart). Break up the peat moss as needed so that it isn't clumped. Mix, adding warm water as necessary to lightly moisten the material, and continue mixing until thoroughly combined.

Now add fertilizers:

5 pounds of dolomitic limestone

1 pound of superphosphate

2 pounds of 5-10-5 fertilizer

Mix by shoveling all the ingredients into a cone-shaped pile (see Figure 4-2). Repeat the cone building at least three times. See Chapter 20 for explanation of 5-10-5 and other fertilizer terms.

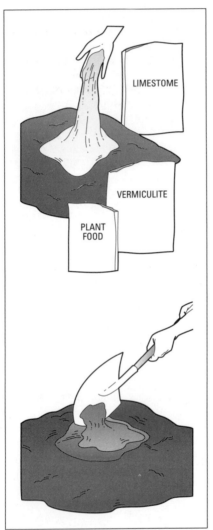

Figure 4-2:
Combine the ingredients by shoveling them in a cone-shaped pile.

If you don't plan to use the mix immediately, store it, tightly closed, in plastic garbage bags or in a clean plastic garbage can.

Variations on the peat theme

For a very lightweight mix for seedlings and small pots, use equal parts of peat moss, vermiculite, and perlite (roughly 9 cubic feet of each).

For a heavier mix for seedlings and pots, use 1 part peat moss (about 14 cubic feet), $^{1}/_{2}$ part sand, and $^{1}/_{2}$ part perlite (7 cubic feet each).

WARNING

Hold those packing peanuts!

Tempted to use those polystyrene packing peanuts in your custom mix? Better not. They're too large, coarse, and lightweight to use in a soil mix. To get them to the right size, you'd have to shred them into ¼-inch pieces or smaller, and the particles are so light that they would migrate to the soil surface and blow away. Stick to perlite instead.

For shrubs and trees, use 1 part peat moss, 1 part composted bark, and 1 part sand (9 cubic feet each), or a mixture of 2 parts composted bark and 1 part sand.

Two specialized blends

If you prefer to work with organic materials, consider either of these two all-purpose mixes.

A mix from NOFA (Natural Organic Farmers Association)

(Makes 1 bushel of mix)

> 16 quarts of sphagnum peat moss
>
> 16 quarts of vermiculite
>
> 7 ounces of bonemeal
>
> 3½ ounces of dried blood meal
>
> 3½ ounces of ground limestone

An organic mix based on soil

> 2 parts vermiculite
>
> 2 parts perlite
>
> 3 parts bagged, commercial high-grade topsoil
>
> 3 parts sphagnum peat moss
>
> 2 parts bagged, composted cow manure
>
> ½ part bonemeal

Chapter 5

When Plant Meets Container

In This Chapter

▶ Planning your plants

▶ Organizing your planting tools

▶ Getting down to business

▶ Starting plants from seeds

*Y*ou have your container (look back to Chapter 3) and your soil mix (Chapter 4). What's next? Go ahead and stick the plant in the pot. Well . . . there's actually a little more to container gardening if you want to give your plants the best possible start in life — sort of the equivalent to sending them to preschool and kindergarten before elementary school and on their way to medical school.

Exactly how and when you plant depends on the plants that you choose. In the chapters that follow, we recommend hundreds of plants to grow in containers. Here we cover the basic planting techniques that work for most annuals, perennials, shrubs, and trees. For more specialized plants, please refer to their sections: bare-root perennials (Chapter 7), bulbs (Chapter 8), and cactus (Chapter 12). We also offer planting advice for specific types of containers: hanging baskets (Chapter 16), and water gardens, strawberry jars, and window boxes (Chapter 17).

What You Need to Know Before Planting

Before you consider sticking a plant in a container, try to digest a fair share of basic planting advice. If you're already familiar with the fundamentals, feel free to skip ahead a few pages in this chapter.

Planting seasons

With containers, you follow the same seasonal rhythms that direct planting in the ground. Table 5-1 offers general guidelines for planting timing in two basic broad climate types.

Table 5-1	When to Plant Various Plants	
Plant Type	*Cold-Winter Climates*	*Mild-Winter Climates*
Perennials	Spring and late summer	Spring, fall, and late winter
Annual flowers	Spring and summer	Year-round
Hardy bulbs	Fall	Fall
Tender bulbs	Spring	Spring
Shrubs and trees	Spring and fall	Year-round
Bare-root (shrubs, trees, fruit trees)	Spring	Winter
Vegetables (cool-season)	Fall, winter, spring, summer	Early spring
Vegetables (warm-season)	Late spring	Summer

How plants are sold

Most people buy plants in convenient nursery packs and pots, transplanting their purchases into various sizes and shapes of containers. But several other excellent ways to purchase plants exist. Here we touch on all of them:

  ✔ **Seeds:** Mail-order catalogs and nursery racks offer seeds of countless varieties of annuals and perennials, and even an array of larger permanent plants. Growing plants from seeds takes time, and because you're unlikely to want huge numbers of the same plants for container gardening, you generally can't take advantage of the money-saving economy of scale provided by seeds. But if you want to cut costs by growing 200 white impatiens for a wedding, follow our seed-starting advice later in this chapter. In that same section, you also find a few plants that are easy to grow from seeds started directly in a container. For a list of seed sources, see the Appendix.

- ✔ **Bulbs:** They're great for containers. Order from catalogs or check your local nursery in fall and spring. See Chapter 8 for details.

- ✔ **Bedding plants:** We're talking about annual and perennial flowers for summer bloom — and other seasons, too — as well as many vegetables. Seedlings are usually grown by large wholesalers and sold at your local garden center in flats (wooden boxes, almost obsolete now), small cell-packs or six-packs, and small pots (up to 3 or 4 inches or so) — a top choice for most people who plant containers with summer flowers or vegetables.

- ✔ **Container-grown plants:** Shrubs and trees, along with some larger annuals and perennials, are offered in familiar 1-gallon, 5-gallon, and 15-gallon cans — more often plastic than metal these days. Paper pulp pots, made of compressed recycled paper, are also used for many shrubs and trees but primarily contain larger annuals and perennials.

- ✔ **Bare-root:** Deciduous trees and shrubs, especially fruit-bearing types and roses, are typically sold when they're dormant and leafless. (Many perennials also are sold bare-root, particularly by mail-order companies.) The plants are dug from growing fields, and their roots are washed of soil — don't worry, survival rate is high as long as the roots don't dry out. Bare-root is one of the more economical ways to buy good-sized plants, and it's a sure way to start plants off right; you can ensure that roots are properly spread out in the right growing medium. After you buy bare-root plants, make sure that you keep the roots moist until planting time by covering them with damp peat moss or other organic matter. As you're planting, immerse the roots in a bucket of water to keep them moist.

- ✔ **Balled and burlapped:** Here's another traditional method that we see less of today. Evergreen shrubs and trees, along with deciduous types that can't be successfully handled bare-root, are dug from growing fields with a ball of soil around the roots, then wrapped with burlap. You can find balled-burlapped plants during the dormant season, often in very large sizes.

How to choose healthy plants

The longer you garden, the better you become at recognizing healthy plants that are ready to take off for a long and productive life in a container. Here are some obvious signs that you already may be aware of, but just in case:

- ✔ Younger is better than older, smaller better than bigger. The longer plants stay in nursery containers, the more likely they are to develop a root-bound condition.

- ✔ Deep green is better than yellow or a dull color — realizing, of course, that we're not talking about plants that naturally have yellow foliage or dull leaves.

✔ Bushy is better than sparse.

✔ Green lively branches are better than woodier growth.

The following specific pointers can help you select healthy specimens from the two big categories of plants used for containers:

Annuals

Look for bedding plants that are a good green color, appear to have been watered regularly, and are relatively short and stocky.

Plants in small containers cost less than those in larger ones, and you may get more — or less — than you bargained for. Larger plants with more extensive root systems have a head start over smaller plants, but sometimes there's a disadvantage to buying large, fully developed bedding plants. In any container, a plant's roots tend to grow into a thick spiral. If the root situation is extremely crowded, the roots may refuse to spread outward after transplanting. At the nursery, don't be shy about tipping the plant out of its pot or pack and inspecting its roots. Avoid plants with thick tangles of roots searching for a place to grow — like out the bottom of the container's drainage hole.

What about annuals in bloom? To make seedlings as appealing as possible for sale at the nursery, plant breeders tinker with genes to develop flowers that pop a blossom or two at an early age, and then downshift for a few more weeks of vegetative growth before they start blooming again. In other words, precocious blooming may slow down growth and flower production in the long run. If you buy plants already in flower, pinch off the blossoms when you set out the plants. This preemptive pinching encourages the plants to get on with the business of growing buds and branches.

Seedlings purchased straight from a greenhouse benefit from a short period of hardening off — that simply means acclimating the seedling to its new surroundings, the difference between the comforts of a greenhouse and the cold or heat of an exposed garden bed. As soon as you get seedlings home, place them in a bright, protected place in partial shade, and water them well. After a few days, move them to full sun, and add a little fertilizer to the water. By this time, they're nicely accustomed to direct sun and wind and are tough enough to transplant. If your new seedlings have already spent some time outdoors at the nursery, they can skip the hardening off and go straight into the garden.

Shrubs and trees

Again, avoid the temptation to buy the largest size. Instead look for thick branching and sturdy, well-rounded shape (not one-side growth). Inspect for vigorous new growth at the branch tips and healthy bark (no splits).

The biggest thing to avoid is a root-bound plant — where the roots fill up the container, poke through the drain holes, and don't allow sufficient water to soak in. If a seriously root-bound plant is all you can find, better choose another variety.

When shopping for bare-root plants, check for plump, firm, moist roots. Avoid shriveled, dry, and brittle roots.

With balled-and-burlapped plants, check for splits in the ball of soil – which can cause roots to dry out. Make sure that the soil ball hasn't dried out; remoistening it thoroughly can be difficult.

Your Well-Stocked Planting Tool Kit

Here are a few reminders and a quick checklist to make sure that you have all you need before you start planting:

- ✔ **Container:** Is it the right size (see Chapter 3)? You have to prepare it as described in Step 1 in the following "Basic Planting Steps" section.

- ✔ **Potting soil:** Make your own or buy it. Include complete fertilizer if you haven't already added it. See Chapter 4.

- ✔ **Drain hole cover:** Screen or pot shards — see Step 2, which follows this section.

- ✔ **Shears and knife**: You may need to cut up root-bound roots or trim top growth a bit.

- ✔ **Scoop:** Use this to move soil mix. A trowel or shovel (for big jobs) also works.

- ✔ **Gloves:** Handling soil dries out your hands, and you may want leather or cloth gloves to protect them.

- ✔ **Water:** Your plant needs it as soon as you plant it. Use a watering can or hose (a bubbler attachment helps soften the flow).

- ✔ **Miscellaneous:** Stakes, plant ties, trellis, snail bait — anything else you may need right after planting.

Basic Planting Steps

Follow these steps for most shrubs, trees, annuals, and perennials. Check specific chapters for details on other types of plants and containers (cactus, hanging baskets, and so on).

1. Getting the container ready

Make sure that the container is the right size for your plants — see Chapter 3. A few quick reminders: For permanent plants, choose a container that's 2 inches wider and deeper than the nursery container, as shown in Figure 5-1. Bare-root plants need a container that's several inches wider and deeper than the stretched-out, trimmed-up roots — after they're pruned, if necessary, at the nursery. Annuals and perennials can be crowded together more closely than if they're planted in the ground.

Some containers need a bit for preparation. Traditional advice for new terra-cotta pots is to soak them in water for 10 or 15 minutes before planting to prevent clay from absorbing moisture from the soil mix.

If you're using old pots, you may want to clean them as described in Chapter 20 to remove salt deposits and reduce chances of disease. And, as logic dictates, it's easier to apply preservative (also Chapter 20) to wood containers before you plant than afterwards.

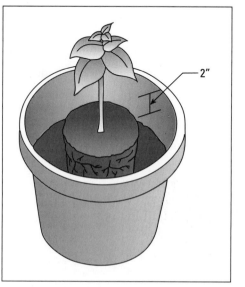

Figure 5-1: Give your plant about 2 inches more in depth and diameter than its nursery container.

2. Addressing the drain hole

Most commercially made pots have drain holes to allow water to flow out of the container. Don't ask why, but these holes usually are too big, allowing too much water to escape.

You need to partially cover the drain holes to keep soil mix from slipping through. Use a piece of fine-mesh metal screen large enough to cover the hole — don't worry about the screen's shape or looks since no one but sowbugs will see it. Or use a time-honored method and cover the drain holes with pot shards (pieces of broken pot), as shown in Figure 5-2. If you don't

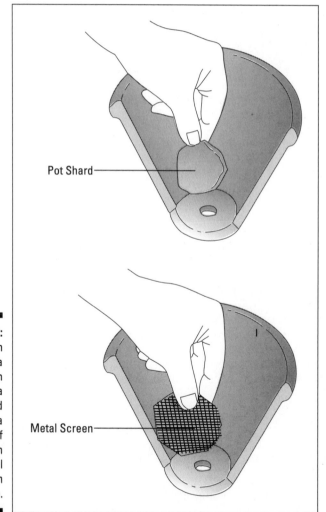

Pot Shard

Metal Screen

Figure 5-2:
You can cover a large drain hole with a pot shard (top) or a piece of fine-mesh metal screen (bottom).

have any pots you want to smash, use a rock with an uneven shape that doesn't block the hole (a flat stone over the hole stops all drainage).

If your container lacks a drain hole, you need to make one. Drilling holes in a the base of a wooden box is easy: one $1/2$-inch hole for a box up to 12 inches square; two to four $1/2$-inch holes for larger boxes or a half barrel. For clay pots, use an electric drill with a masonry bit. Support the pot on a block of wood, and start drilling with a smaller bit, eventually reaching the final size of $1/2$ inch; adding water to the drill hole may help.

3. Dealing with the plant

Whatever the plant's original residence — nursery can, cell-pack, or paper pulp pot — you need to pay attention to a few key matters before you start the actual planting.

First make sure that the nursery plant's soil is moist enough to hold the roots together when you plant. If the soil is dry, give it a good soaking and let it drain for at least an hour. Soil in the confines of the nursery pack, pot, or can absorbs water better than when it's in a newly planted container — a plant's dry root ball surrounded by fresh soil mix sometimes repels water. (If you're planting bare-root, keep roots moist until the last minute, and just before planting or the night before, immerse the plant in a bucket of water.)

Remove the plant from nursery container, and inspect the root ball. Is it root-bound? Do roots protrude from the drain hole? Or are roots twined around into a dense mass that repels water? For small plants, such as annuals, that may be a bit root-bound, gently loosen the mat of roots with your fingertips. For larger plants, such as 1-gallon or 5-gallon shrubs, use a knife to score some vertical scratches in a tight root ball.

✔ **Larger containers, such as 1- and 5-gallon cans:** Have the nursery cut open metal cans for you; if you use tin snips, be careful of jagged sharp edges. Tip plastic containers upside down, taking care not to break branches, and let the root ball slip out, catching it with one hand, as shown in Figure 5-3. Tap the rim of the container upside down on a hard surface if the root ball doesn't slip out easily. Wetting the soil makes the process go more smoothly. If the soil mass really resists, hack apart the plastic with shears, but don't damage the roots. Paper pulp pots can be treated like plastic — they're easy to cut apart if plants resist slipping out.

✔ **Small pots:** Usually, small plastic pots can be held upside down and gently shaken to release root balls. Tap upside down on a hard surface if needed.

✔ **Plastic cell-packs:** Turn pack upside down and wiggle the base of each cell. Gently tug, but don't break the stem or loosen the root ball.

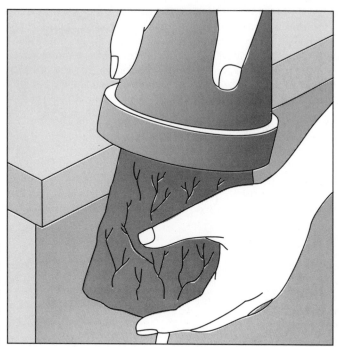

Figure 5-3:
Getting a
plant out of
a plastic
container.

4. Planting the plant

Does your store-bought or homemade soil mix include fertilizer? Check the label or your memory. If fertilizer is a part of the mix, don't worry about feeding for at least four to six weeks after planting. If fertilizer is not in-cluded, incorporate a complete food now, as suggested in Chapter 4.

Check to see if the soil mix is moist. Bagged material may be moist enough already, but if the bag is open or old, the soil may be too dry. Test soil by squeezing it into a ball. Soil mix is easy to wet while it's still in the bag: Add water and stir or knead soil until it reaches the desired level of moisture. Or pile up soil mix and squirt it with the hose, turning it over until it's wet enough.

Add soil mix to your container. Fill to an inch below the rim of the container for small plants, 2 inches or more for large containers — the idea is to create enough space to hold plenty of water. The amount of soil you add depends on the type of plant:

✔ **For small plants in packs or little pots:** Fill the pot to the level that you want to end up with. With your hands or trowel, scoop out a little hole for each plant, slip in the plant, and firm down around its edges with your fingers. If soil level starts to rise too high, remove some soil. Match the soil level to your plants' previous growing conditions — don't bury too deep or allow root balls to rise above the soil level. Figure 5-4 shows the ideal.

✔ **For plants in gallon cans and larger:** Size up the root ball by placing it in the empty pot. Add enough soil mix to raise the top of the root ball to the desired level in the pot, from 2 to 4 inches below the rim. Set the root ball on top of the soil mix and then fill in around it and tamp it down with your hands, a trowel, or a shovel handle. Tamping down is important to establish firm contact between the root ball and new soil mix. Keep adding soil mix until it levels up with the top of the root ball.

Figure 5-4:
This one's planted just right.

✔ **For bare-root plants:** First trim off the root tips as recommended by your nursery or have it done for you (also ask about pruning the top growth back, especially for fruit trees). Mound the soil mix at the bottom of the container, spread roots over mound, and adjust level of mound until the plant's former soil line (usually indicated by a faint discolored ring around the trunk) matches up with the desired soil level in the container. Fill around the roots until the soil reaches the plant's former soil line.

✔ **For balled-and-burlapped plants:** Place the root ball on soil mix at the bottom of container as for plants grown in 1 or 5-gallon nursery cans. Cut away the twine holding burlap in place at the top of the root ball. Fold back and trim away the top several inches of burlap with heavy scissors or a knife — the lower, buried part gradually decomposes. Fill with soil mix around root ball as recommended for container-grown plants.

5. Watering

Pay attention. Watering a just-planted container is trickier than you may imagine. Water tends to follow the path of least resistance and drains quickly through the loose soil mix, bypassing the denser root ball. You walk away thinking that your watering job is done. Days later, you realize that the root ball never really got wet and the plant is desiccated. Protect against this by watering thoroughly the first time.

The secret to successful watering is a slow and gentle stream. Use a watering can, a hose gently trickling, or a hose-end bubbler to soften the flow. Slowly fill the pot to the rim, and repeat several times. Probe with your fingers to find out if the root ball has absorbed water — if you can't detect moisture, try soaking it again.

6. What else?

The laundry list grows on: A number of other necessities require attention:

✔ Apply a mulch to shrubs and trees that have a lot of exposed soil, improving appearances and helping to conserve water. Use stone or bark chips, or other organic matter. Make sure that mulch size is in scale with the container and the plants — no boulders or big chunks for wood.

✔ Stake and tie trees or tall annuals or perennials.

✔ Add a trellis to the container for vines that need support.

If at First You Want to Seed

Just a few types of plants do well if started from seeds sown directly in the containers where you want them to grow. Better stick with fast-growing, easy-care types like marigolds, zinnias, and lettuce; follow seed packet directions for sowing in the ground.

Most seedlings grow better if they're started in small containers and then "moved up" — transplanted into gradually larger containers. Seedlings just don't perform well if grown in an excessive amount of soil mix.

If you want to grow large quantities of annuals from seed, you can easily start them indoors and gradually transplant up to your final containers. Seed-starting kits and equipment are available at garden centers and in catalogs. Mainly, you need trays or flats, cell-packs, or other small containers, along with special seed-starting soil mix.

1. Fill containers to the top with sterile soil-less mix (see Chapter 4), level the top by sweeping across it with your hand or a table knife, and use your fingertip or a pencil to make small depressions for seeds. Seeding depth need not be exact, but try to plant seeds about three times as deep as the seeds are wide. Drop one or two seeds into each depression, cover with pinches of seed-starting mixture, and dampen thoroughly with plain water. To keep from flooding out the planted seeds, either use a pump spray bottle to mist the containers repeatedly, or place the containers in small pans or trays and fill the pans with 1 inch of water. The containers absorb the water from the pans in about an hour.

2. To keep the surface of the planted containers from drying out, cover them lightly with plastic wrap or enclose the whole tray in a large plastic bag. Keep the containers in a warm place, and start checking for germination after three days. As soon as the first sprouts emerge, remove the plastic and move the seedlings to good light.

3. Most of the time, you end up with way too many seedlings. If left alone, they become so crowded that they can't grow well, so you must retain only two or three seedlings in a container that's 2 inches across. To thin seedlings, either pull out the extras with your fingers or tweezers, or dump out the container on its side, tap the mass of roots to make them fall apart, and gingerly transplant the tiny seedlings to individual containers filled with sterile soil-less mix. As long as you handle young seedlings by their leaves and never, ever touch their tender stems, they transplant very easily. If anyone asks, the process of pulling apart and transplanting very young seedlings is called pricking out.

4. When seedlings are about two weeks old, they're ready for a little fertilizer. Use a fertilizer that can be mixed with water, and mix it at half the strength recommended on the package. Fertilize seedlings about once a week, or every other time that you water them.

5. After four to six weeks, your seedlings become big enough to move outside. To help them get ready for the big move, spend a week or two letting them gradually become accustomed to outdoor sun and wind. Set them outside for a few hours at first, then for all day, and then for several days before you transplant them to outdoor containers. This process, called hardening off, makes a huge difference in how well seedlings grow right after they're transplanted.

Part III
The Plants

In this part . . .

When you make the move to container gardening, you start to look toward proud exteriors — and the residents who look best at that address. Your choices are all over the map. You can create a neighborhood with plants that last one season, perennials that pop up year after year (with attentive care), permanent strong-stemmed sorts, resourceful desert types, or any in a range of edibles and purely enjoyables. Options are ripe for the picking, but one warning: Instructions are not included with every plant that you select. In this part, we arm you with enough knowledge to get growing. We bet that as soon as you set foot on success, your next stop may be a new welcome mat — perhaps, the first floral scratch-and-sniff?

Chapter 6

Annuals

- -

In This Chapter

▶ Painless botany

▶ A little seasoning

▶ Annuals for sale

▶ Groundwork for planting annuals

▶ Foolproof annuals for containers

- -

*W*hat's the first thing that you think of when you picture container plants? Probably a geranium, or maybe a petunia — both annual flowers. What's the first colorful container plant right out of the chute in early spring in cold-winter climates? Probably a pansy, again an annual. Bring to mind some of the spectacular container gardens in public spaces, like the hanging baskets in Victoria, British Columbia, or the year-round colorful containers at Disneyland or Disneyworld, and you may focus on the fact that the flowers are annuals — impatiens, marigolds, lobelias, and other familiar garden friends.

Annuals flowers — popular, fun, easy to grow, and universally loved — are just the right plants to consider when talking about container gardening. They're apt to be the first plants that you grow in containers. Yet annuals are so varied and abundant, you may never get tired of growing them.

In this chapter, we point out the many reasons to grow annuals in containers, describe the special care needed that's a bit different from growing the same plants in the ground, and then look at annuals that are particularly well-suited to container life.

What's an Annual?

First, the requisite botany book definition: An annual is defined as a plant that propagates itself by seed and undergoes its life cycle in one growing season. For example, a marigold seed sprouts in May, grows quickly, blooms all summer, dies when frost hits in fall, and scatters seeds that sprout the next year to repeat the process. Compare an annual with a perennial, which usually blooms in its second year and lives for at least a few years. And technically there also are biennials, which usually bloom in the second year and then scatter seed and die.

The nursery definition is more practical: Annuals are one-season plants, typically sold in six-packs and small pots, planted in spring for bloom in that spring, summer, and fall. (In mild climates, you can plant annuals in fall and winter — more on this later.)

Some plants labeled as annuals actually are perennials, but they typically bloom that first season then die when cold weather hits. The geranium is a classic example — it's sold as an annual in cold-winter climates but can live over from year to year and become shrublike in mild climates. And some biennials, such as foxgloves that can bloom the first season, are also considered to be annuals.

At most nurseries, you may not even see the word annual used. More likely, the plants are tagged as bedding plants because of their traditional role in planting beds. Don't pay too much attention to the bedding label — most of these plants grow just fine in pots, as well as in beds.

Why Grow Annuals in Containers?

You may want to grow annuals in containers for a variety of reasons, among them:

- ✔ Annuals are just plain fun to grow. They have the brightest, most appealing flowers, which attract children, butterflies, and just about anyone who wanders past.

- ✔ Annuals are movers. They grow fast and bloom when young, even while they're still in the nursery packs, which is not always such a good thing (more on this later).

- ✔ Annuals give you the longest season of abundant bloom of any plants.

- ✔ Annuals are relatively inexpensive, especially if you buy small plants. If you make mistakes, you can pull out the plants and may even have enough time to replant.

- U Annuals are responsive. You start to feel like you can read their minds. Provide them with good care and you see the results — lush leaves, lots of flowers, a long bloom season. Give them too little water and the plants dry up right away. Give them too little food, and leaves start to turn yellow. You can correct all these conditions nearly as quickly as you created them — as long as you haven't gone so far as to kill the plants.

✔ With containers, you can put your favorite annuals where they can be best appreciated: sweet peas (yes, even sprawl-prone sweet peas) where you can smell their fragrance; Johnny-Jump-Ups where you can view their tiny splotched faces.

✔ With containers, you can keep annuals out of sight when they're not doing much — as they grow up before blooming or dwindle away after blooming.

✔ You can rotate blooming containers of flowers by the season. Start with spring bloomers like pansies, follow with summer petunias, and then try fall asters. In mild-winter climates, you can also grow containers of annuals that bloom from fall through spring — Iceland poppies are a great choice.

✔ Nothing dresses up a deck or patio faster for a party than blooming annuals brimming from decorative pots.

Strategies for Growing Annuals in Containers

Nothing's simpler than planting annuals in pots: Go to the nursery, put whatever looks good in the shopping cart, buy a pot and a bag of potting mix, take it all home, and put it together. That's often plenty good enough.

But do try to pick up tips about what annuals to look for, when, where, and how to plant them, and how to combine different varieties. You may be surprised at how much you enjoy the process and the results.

Timing is everything with annuals. In typical cold-winter climates, the season for growing annuals is spring to early fall. In mild-winter climates, annuals can thrive year-round. So when do you shop for annuals and plant them? That depends on your climate and whether the annuals are hardy or tender.

Hardy annuals can stand a varying amount of frost, from a little to a lot; some types, in fact, are quite hardy and are actually perennials that live over the winter in many areas. Hardy annuals considered as cool-season annuals perform best when temperatures are mild, days are short, and soil is cool, typically in early spring and early fall. Their enemies are hot weather and long days, which cause a decline in performance and seed setting — ending the bloom season. Examples of cool-season favorites are calendulas, pansies, and snapdragons. You can usually plant hardy cool-season annuals safely a few weeks before the average date of the last spring frost in your area.

Freezing temperature damages or downright destroys tender annuals. Many of these tender types thrive in hot summer weather and are considered warm-season annuals; examples are celosia, marigolds, vinca rosea, and zinnias. Plant them after the date of your last frost — and when soil and air temperatures are warming up. Count on them to reach their peak in midsummer.

Cool-season and warm-season are, of course, relative terms. Where summers are cool, like along the foggy California coast or other overcast climates, you can grow cool-season annuals all summer. Where winters are warm and nearly frost-free (as in low-elevation Arizona and much of California), fall through spring is an ideal stretch for growing cool-season annuals like Iceland poppies and even some warm-season annuals like petunias.

Annuals can be grown all year in several locales — places that boast climates where winter temperatures rarely drop much below freezing.

In mild-climate regions, you can plant cool-season annuals like pansies and Iceland poppies in late summer or early fall (after summer cools off). Blooms may appear before Christmas and peak in late winter and early spring. After growth and flowering slows down in spring, replace them with warm-season annuals.

In these climates, cool-season annuals can also be planted through the winter and early spring. The plants miss out on fall's warm weather to push them into growth but they surge as soon as temperatures start to warm in late winter and early spring.

Truly tropical climates like those found in Hawaii and southern Florida are in a separate category and have their own special rules for growing annuals. Better check with local nurseries for exact timing.

Shopping for Annuals

A fair bet is that you decide to plant containers with nursery transplants rather than seeds. Transplants make it easier for you, and they're not expensive when used in the quantities that most people buy for containers. (Actually, some annuals are easy to start from seeds sown right in containers if you're so inclined; good choices for seed sowing are cosmos, marigolds, and zinnias.)

Nurseries typically offer the greatest variety of annuals in six-packs containing a half-dozen seedlings or in 4-inch pots containing single plants. Look for plants that have a good green color and are relatively short and stocky. Start with small plants — their root systems adapt quickest to growing in new conditions. If you want color right away, buy larger, blooming plants in pots, gallon cans, or even larger containers. Just be sure that the roots haven't filled the nursery container to the point of shedding water. At the nursery, don't hesitate to tip the plant out of its pot or pack so that you can inspect the roots. Avoid plants with a thick tangle of roots.

Many small transplants sold these days already come with flowers — thanks to clever plant breeders successfully developing annuals to bloom precociously and tempt you into buying them rather than the more laggardly all-green seedlings. Blooming as a youngster actually impedes future blooming. Snip off the flowers before or just after you plant.

Planting Annuals in Containers

An annual grown in a container needs the same things that a plant in the ground does — mainly water, air, and nutrients. Please remember that roots in a container are confined and can't forage. Careful watering and feeding are essential. Equally important is starting off with a good soil mix — not dirt dug up from your garden — whether you buy it in a bag or mix it yourself. See Chapter 4 for more information on soil mixes.

Choosing containers

What kind of containers are recommended for annuals? Anything goes — that's especially true with annuals. There are so many kinds of annuals, so many colors, shapes, and sizes, and so many different kinds of looks that your container choices are truly wide open.

Here are a few possibly obvious, certainly worthwhile rules:

- ✔ Put tall annuals (gloriosa daisy, cosmos) in big pots.
- ✔ Grow sprawling or spreading types (impatiens, petunias) in low bowls.
- ✔ Terra-cotta pots look great with annuals in almost all situations.

Glazed pots can add even more brightness. Thinking about putting pink petunias in a bright orange glazed pot? Works for us, but don't expect *Garden Design* magazine to come calling.

Now, on to more concrete advice on the practical matters:

✔ To grow healthy annuals, the container needs to be at least 6 inches deep.

✔ As a general rule of scale, if the annuals normally grow 10 or 12 inches tall, provide a pot with a diameter of at least 8 inches. If the plants grow 2 or 3 feet tall, better go for a diameter of 24 inches or a large container like a half barrel.

✔ Seasonal plants like annuals can be crowded together more closely than is suggested for ground planting. Cramped conditions can return a much greater impact quickly. Annuals can't grow in crowded conditions for long, but their season is short, and you can satisfy the demand for extra water and food that the tight quarters create. If the recommended spacing for ground planting is 10 to 12 inches, in a container you may space the plants 6 to 8 inches apart. Again, as a general rule, you can safely plant most annuals 4 to 6 inches apart.

Actually planting something

Are you ready to plant? Have you assembled your containers, soil mix, and seedlings? Time to get started:

1. **Before removing plants from their nursery containers, make sure that their root balls are moist.**

   If soil feels dry, soak plants at this point; a root ball can absorb water in the confines of the nursery pack better than in the wider expanse of your planter. Watch for signs of root-bound seedlings: small white roots woven together so tightly that they repel water. Gently loosen roots at the bottom and sides of the root ball.

2. **Deal with drain hole as described in Chapter 5.**

3. **Fill the container to within 2 or 3 inches of its rim with moistened soil mix (wet enough to form a ball when squeezed, but not dripping).**

   Smooth soil level with your hands.

4. **With a trowel or your hands, scoop out a planting hole for each seedling, as shown in Figure 6-1.**

   Make the hole deep enough so that the top of the seedling's root ball is at the same level as the soil in the container.

5. **Place the seedlings in the holes you made, as shown in Figure 6-2.**

   Use your fingers to tamp down soil around each seedling, again ensuring that the root ball's soil level matches the soil level in the container.

6. **Water gently with a watering can or hose until the soil is thoroughly moist.**

Most annuals benefit from full sun, but even sun-lovers can use partial shade right after planting. Keep the containers in partial shade for at least a few days after planting — until they toughen up a bit.

The Caretaking of Annuals in Containers

More than anything else, remember that annuals like to set a fast pace with no pit stops: Running out of water or food can set them back for weeks or abruptly end their seasons.

Watering is much more critical with annuals grown in the confined spaces of containers. Never let the soil dry out. You may want to install a drip system (discussed in Chapter 18) if you have many containers.

Feeding container-grown annuals is also more critical than nourishing the same plants grown in the ground. Start feeding a few weeks after planting. One proven method is to use liquid fertilizer at half the recommended rate and twice the frequency (every two weeks instead of monthly, for example).

Figure 6-1:
Scoop out holes for each seedling.

Figure 6-2:
Place the
seedlings in
the holes.

Pinching and deadheading are important chores. This caretaking keeps new flowers coming for as long a season as possible. Start pinching back tip growth to encourage bushy growth as soon as you plant, or even right before. Cosmos, marigolds, and zinnias are among many annuals that respond noticeably to pinching; they also produce many more blooms if you constantly remove dead flowers.

Foolproof Annuals for Containers

When choosing plants for containers, pay special attention to their eventual sizes and growth habits. In general, compact varieties perform better in containers (sunflowers are perhaps the most extreme example, with the 10-foot Russian Giant out of the question and the 24-inch Teddy Bear perfect for containers). Look for special varieties developed for containers. Names often provide a clue to container performance. Cascade petunias, for example, are designed to spill from pots.

Some annuals look great when planted alone; others are mixers that work well when used in combinations with other annuals, perennials, or bulbs.

Old reliables for sunny spots

Here are some favorite annuals to grow in containers alone or combined with other annuals. Of course, annuals are versatile, so feel free to try other ways to use them.

- **Ageratum:** A full pot of ageratum may not be your cup of tea, but it's a great plant to edge a container of mixed annuals. Puffy little flowers most typically are blue, but white and pink also are available. Plants range up to 2 feet tall. Look for dwarf varieties such as Blue Mink.

- **Calendula:** Here's a great choice for containers early in the year. Sturdy plants and bright orange or yellow blooms stand up well to cool weather. Dwarf varieties are best suited to containers.

- **Cineraria:** This one's a spectacular choice for cool-summer climates. Plants are nice and compact, up to 15 inches tall, with clusters of daisy flowers that look like perfect pre-assembled bouquets.

- **Cosmos:** Lacy and elegant, tall cosmos (up to 4 feet) stand out in borders and can also perform in large containers (half barrels, for example). For smaller containers, look for more compact or dwarf varieties. The daisy flowers come in a range of purple, pinks, and whites.

- **Dahlia:** You want compact bedding dahlias, not the tall pot-toppling varieties (unless you grow them in a huge container). Dwarf dahlias grow about 12 to 15 inches tall, with 2 or 3-inch flowers in bright clear colors: orange, pink, purple, red, white, and yellow.

- **Dusty Miller:** This is a role player if there ever was one. Its role is to make other plants look good. Silvery gray foliage circling a container's outside edge beautifully sets off purple petunias, red impatiens, or many other annuals and colors. Plants grow about 15 inches tall.

- **Geraniums:** We can't think of any geranium that isn't a candidate for good healthy living in a container. Ivy geraniums are a favorite choice for hanging baskets; Summer Showers is specifically designed for hanging. Scented geraniums are fun in pots placed where their foliage can be pinched off for sniffing.

- **Iceland poppy:** A cool-season stalwart, its crinkly flowers in bright oranges, pink, yellows, and other shades stand tall on long slender stems, but the plants are low and unprepossessing — best mixed with spreading plants that can provide some camouflage. Pansies are good container companions.

- **Lobelia:** Call on the compact edging types (Crystal Palace) to tuck into mixed plantings. Use the trailing types (Sapphire) to spill from hanging baskets or pots. Flowers in light to deep blue, as well as white and lavender, lend themselves to color-combining with many other annuals.

- **Marigold:** The tall types are best left in the ground, but the more compact French marigolds and signet marigolds (12 to 20 inches) are indispensable container classics. Fill a pot with a single variety or combine marigolds with other annuals. Colors include yellow and orange, by all means, plus mixes of orange, yellow, maroon, dark red, and more.

- **Nemesia:** Feel good about trying nemesia if you live in a cool-summer climate. Otherwise it's pretty fussy. Flowers are richly and vividly colored in red, yellow, white, and pink. Plants grow 8 to 18 inches tall — great near the rims of containers where they can spill over the sides.

- **Ornamental kale:** Grow it for striking multicolored foliage — not flowers — early in the season when color is hard to come by. Show off a single plant in an 8-inch pot, or put several in a larger container.

- **Pansy and Viola:** Hardy and carefree, these are often the first annuals you notice in containers each spring. Pansies have big, blotchy flowers. Violas are usually solid colors — yellow, blue, purple, and more. Combine pansies or violas with bulbs or fill pots with single or mixed colors.

- **Petunias:** Standouts for containers are big-flowered Grandiflora types, especially Cascade and Supercascade strains (they're great spillers). Or try much more compact, smaller-flowered Millifloras such as Fantasy. If plants get too rangy in containers, cut stems back by about a third.

- **Salvia:** Scarlet sage, with its bright red spikes of bloom, is an attention-getter in borders or containers. More useful is *Salvia farinacea* Victoria, 24 inches tall, with deep blue flower spikes; this is an ideal choice to plant at the center of pots and surround with lower-growing annuals.

- **Snapdragons (dwarfs):** Tall types are too big for most containers. Look for dwarfs such as Little Darling and Royal Carpet — bushy types that grow about a foot tall, with flowers on short stems (unlike long stems on tall types). Don't plan on cutting flowers for bouquets. Snapdragons bloom best in cool weather.

- **Sunflowers:** Really. Bushy dwarf varieties grow only 1 or 2 feet tall and are terrific in containers. Two top choices: Dwarf Sungold and Teddy Bear. Sunflowers are easy to grow from seeds started directly in the containers.

- **Sweet alyssum:** Low and spreading, this is a dependable choice for filling in among mixed annuals in a pot or spilling over edges of a pot. Sweet alyssum is easy to grow from seeds or transplants. Familiar white is a great complement in mixed plantings, but rose and purple varieties are also available.

- **Sweet pea:** The familiar tall, climbing sweet peas quickly grows out of bounds in a container. Bush types, such as Bijou, make a fairly re-strained container plant, growing only 12 to 30 inches tall. Flowers come in the usual pastel shades — with a heavenly fragrance.

- **Transvaal daisy (Gerbera):** Look for this elegant, deeply colored daisy sold blooming in pots. Transplant a few into a larger container, put them on the front porch or wherever you can appreciate their beauty, and let nature take its course. This is a beautiful temperamental plant; don't take it personally if the daisy fails on you.

- **Vinca rosea:** Take a lesson from shopping centers and other public spaces where you see vinca rosea in the hottest spots. This is one tough, heat-loving annual for containers that must face hot sun. Foliage always looks sharp and glossy. White and pink flowers bloom over a very long season.

- **Zinnias:** Mix the colors or use single colors for bright containers in full sun. Compact dwarfs, such as Peter Pan, work best in containers. Avoid tall, lanky types. Zinnias come in hot colors and do well in hot weather.

Annuals for shady locations

Color is harder to come by in shady spots, but a handful of annuals thrive in containers and will bloom well in light to medium shade.

- **Bedding begonia:** For a neat, well-groomed look, fill pots with solid-colored begonias. Or use them to edge large pots of mixed annuals. Flowers come in red, pink, and white; glossy leaves may have tints of bronze or red.

- **Browallia:** This is a beautiful blue trailing plant. A number of new varieties are available specifically for hanging baskets. Look for Blue Bells Improved.

- **Coleus:** Colorful foliage can brighten up dark parts of your garden, and provide a tropical look. Combine with shorter shade-lovers like impatiens.

- **Impatiens:** Tall or compact, single or double, just about all impatiens perform brilliantly in containers, including hanging baskets. Flower colors include red, pink, rose, violet, orange, white, and bicolors. Double-flowered varieties are especially nice in containers where you can admire the blooms up close. Plant just one color to a pot for the boldest look. Impatiens combine beautifully with ferns, coleus, begonias, and other annuals in mixed plantings.

Combining Annuals in Containers

Combining different annuals in the same container is an easy way to create rainbows of color. The possibilities are infinite. Following are a dozen suggestions for combinations made up of basic plants that look terrific together and have compatible needs. The plants bloom at the same time, their colors contrast or complement each other beautifully, and they're in scale with one another.

- ✔ Blue ageratum and pink petunias
- ✔ Blue ageratum and yellow marigolds
- ✔ Red impatiens and gray dusty miller
- ✔ White cosmos and blue lobelia
- ✔ Yellow violas and white sweet alyssum
- ✔ Blue salvia (*Salvia farinacea* Victoria) and yellow dwarf marigolds
- ✔ Coleus and impatiens
- ✔ Pink bedding begonias and blue lobelia
- ✔ White impatiens and red begonias
- ✔ Yellow marigolds, gray dusty miller, and blue lobelia
- ✔ Blue salvia, dwarf marigolds, and nemesia
- ✔ Pink geraniums, purple violas, and white sweet alyssum

Chapter 7

Perennial Pleasures

● ●

In This Chapter

▶ Identifying perennials

▶ Planting for repeat performances

▶ Maintaining this year's crop

▶ Finding cool containers

▶ Choosing outstanding perennials

● ●

*W*hy bother with perennials when annuals, which you have just read about, bloom for a much longer season and have less demanding lifestyles?

As much as we hate to resort to such a vague and overused word, we have to say that perennials are *interesting.* And that's the main reason why you grow them. They're interesting in the range of their flowers – from tiny fragrance-packed lavender to towering blue delphiniums. They're interesting in their sheer numbers and variety — thousands of available kinds, including grasses, shade plants, foliage plants, plus some of our more spectacular blooming plants (chrysanthemums and primroses, to name just two). And perennials are interesting in the challenges that they present: how to cut back, how to divide, what to do with them in the winter — you don't just relegate them to the compost pile at the end of the season as you do with annuals.

We do a bit more PR soon on behalf of perennials, but first can we get some of the less exciting nuts and bolts out of the way?

Defining Perennials

Right up front you need to know that we're talking about a specific type of perennial: herbaceous flowering perennials. These perennials have soft fleshy stems (as opposed to a sturdy woody trunk like an oak tree), bloom with worthwhile flowers, and live for several years under the right conditions. Perennials represent a huge and storied population of plants — the subject of their lives now reaches beyond magazine racks and library shelves to the World Wide Web where they're covered in an abundance of Web sites, discussion groups, and electronic ordering opportunities.

Some of these perennials are deciduous. They lose their leaves at some point in the year, usually in winter, or they die back completely to the ground.

Other perennials are evergreen, especially in mild climates. Some stay evergreen in mild climates but die way back – or just plain die — in cold climates, where they're considered annuals. One example is the geranium, which is grown as an annual in most parts of the country. In mild places, such as Southern California, geraniums thrive like permanent shrubs — so much so that they're known by the nickname "rats of the garden." So is the geranium an annual or perennial? In this book you can locate the universally popular plant in Chapter 6.

Perennials generally have one main bloom season, usually in spring or summer, that can be as brief as a few weeks or as long as a couple of months. Again, evergreen perennials in mild climates can be the wild cards — blooming every month of the year, as a marguerite daisy does.

Enough of the botany class! Now the fun part — what can *you* do with perennials?

Deciding to Pot Your Perennials

Ask a gardener why he or she loves perennials in containers, and here's what you can expect to hear:

- ✔ **Time, money, and labor:** Many gardeners prefer to fill their pots with perennials simply because the plants can last a long time. With perennials, there's no need to replant pots every few months as you often must do with annuals.

- ✔ **Size counts:** Perennial plants tend to grow larger than annuals and bulbs, so they can fill large spaces if that's what you want.

- ✔ **Usefulness:** Do you have a spot under the eaves where nothing ever grows? A long wooden staircase that needs some livening up? A blank wall with no soil at the base for planting? In any of these situations, you can use a pot of annuals for bright, perhaps short-lived flowers, but if you want something with interesting flowers, foliage, or fruit over several seasons or years, try perennials.

- ✔ **Growing the unusual (or temperamental):** If your garden beds are too sunny for hostas or your soil too cold and wet for lavender, try growing them in containers so that you can customize their environments.

Alas, there *are* a few downsides to growing perennials in pots:

- ✔ **Down time.** Just as we all look a little ratty from time-to-time, a perennial plant sometimes seems out of season — like when it's not blooming or when its leaves fall off. Don't toss (or compost) the unsightly plant. Simply move it, in its pot, to a location hidden from view but where you can still provide the necessary care until it returns to presentable shape.

- ✔ **A bit more care.** Perennials in pots require more monitoring than annuals do. You must provide year-round care including fertilizing, moving plants to protected spots for winter in cold-climate areas, and periodic repotting. We cover this information more thoroughly a bit later in this chapter.

Matching Plants with Pots

Imagine those daylilies brightening up your front porch, their silky trumpets heralding a soft summer breeze — but what kind of pot to show off their multicolor magic?

And how about that gorgeous Asian urn you discovered at a garage sale, what can you grow in it? Sometimes we start with the plant, and sometimes we start with the pot — either way can work.

Along with the aesthetics of matching the plant to the right pot, perennials demand that you consider another factor: the plant's size now *and* its size at maturity. For example, a 4-inch daylily may ultimately spread out to a 2-foot diameter — eventually, you need a very wide pot. But right now, introducing the 4-inch plant to a 24-inch pot doesn't make much sense — especially because you risk making your plant very unhappy when all that extra soil creates inhospitably soggy conditions. Remember that in a pot, a perennial may not get quite as big as a ground-grown plant, but it may come close.

So how do you choose the right size pot for now and for later? You have two choices: Put that little plant into a 6-inch (or 10-inch) pot and repot it to larger size pots as it grows or put it in a pot that can accommodate its ultimate size, and add annuals to fill the empty space for now (expect them to die before the daylily needs the extra space). Make sure that the pot you decide to use is large enough to accommodate the ongoing root growth while remaining topple-free as the plant matures. (We use daylilies as an example here, but the same holds true for any perennial.)

Planting Perennials in Containers

At nurseries and garden centers, you find that perennials are sold mostly in 2-inch, 4-inch, and larger pots, including gallon cans. To plant these, follow the basic steps outlined in Chapter 5. Choose or make a potting mix that matches the perennial's normal soil requirements (if your plant's fussy about such things as acidity and alkalinity); make sure that the mix contains plenty of sand or perlite to ensure that it drains quickly.

If you buy perennials by mail order, they're likely to arrive as bare-root plants.The roots are exposed and devoid of any potting soil — a handy, lightweight way to ship perennials and a healthy way to start new plants.

So you open the box of perennials that came in the mail, and you find a bunch of small plants with their roots embedded in paper or wood shavings, all loosely held in a plastic bag. Or you may find what look like only roots. Are they alive? Are they dead? What do you do with them? Here are the basic planting steps:

1. **Remove the plastic wrapping.**

2. **Gently extricate the plant roots from the paper or wood shavings.**

   Alternatively, if the material is biodegradable, you can just leave it on the roots and plant it with your plant. The wrap protects the roots from any unnecessary disturbance.

3. **Soak the plant in tap water for an hour or so before you're ready to plant it.**

4. **Prepare your pot. Be sure to moisten the potting mix thoroughly and let it drain to settle the soil until it feels about as damp as a wrung-out sponge.**

5. **Dig out a hole in the potting mix for the plant. Make the hole an inch or so deeper and wider than the longest root on the plant.**

6. **Gently spread the roots so that they fan out in all directions from the base of the plant.**

   Separating the roots may be difficult if the plant has a particularly intertwined system. Just be sure that the roots are not all clumped together beneath the plant.

7. **Carefully fill in the hole with potting mix, covering the roots as you work your way toward the base of the plant.**

   Add potting mix until the base of the plant is just below the surface of the soil. Do not cover any of the green, growing parts with potting mix.

8. **Firm the mix around the plant and water it well to eliminate any air pockets in the potting mix.**

   Label the plant with its name and the date that you planted it. You may be surprised how interesting and helpful those labels are when you start to collect more than a few plants.

Caring for Perennials in Containers

Perennials, like all good plants, expect their owners to satisfy their special requirements — but these guys, in truth, are not terribly demanding. Keep in mind that the only plants that don't require some care are dead plants.

Flowering perennials share a common goal with all other plants — they live to make more plants. When you see a perennial whose flowers are fading, remember that you're seeing a natural process — after it flowers, the plant produces seeds. Your goal, on the other hand, is probably to enjoy the flowers. When the blooms fade, if the plant is still growing strong, you can encourage a new flush of flowers by *deadheading*. To deadhead, pinch or cut off the fading flowers right where the flower stalks join the stems. After you deadhead, the plant doesn't have to put its energy into setting seed; instead, the plant can concentrate on making more flowers — just what *you* want.

Cutting back

Some plants grow stronger and bloom better after you cut them back. If you cut back leggy stems as much as halfway, they usually come back fuller and bushier with more blooms. Some plants are best cut back in fall, others in spring. Recommendations for cutting back perennials in pots are the same as for perennials in the ground. Check with a local nursery for advice on timing and how much to cut a particular plant back in your area.

Fertilizing

Since perennials and annuals grow differently, you need to fertilize them differently. Annuals have a quick growth spurt, and then poop out — they need a fertilizer that's available quickly and over a short time period. Perennials grow more slowly and over a far longer period of time. Hence, they need a fertilizer that lasts longer — the nutrient needs for annuals and perennials are otherwise pretty much the same.

To feed perennials, some gardeners use only slow-release synthetic fertilizers. Others swear by natural products like bonemeal and blood meal. One good strategy for proper nourishment is to mix slow-release fertilizers into potting soil before planting, and supplement weekly with fish emulsion and other natural products during the plant's major growing season; add more slow-release fertilizer as the old runs out.

As a rule of thumb for fertilizing perennials in containers, find out what the specific varieties need in your area, and feed just a bit more than you'd deliver to the same plants in the ground. The extra food accounts for the loss of nutrients washed out during watering of container plants. For more details on fertilizing in general, see Chapter 19.

Winter care

In cold-winter climate areas, container-grown perennials cannot be left out in the elements — even if the same plants growing in the ground are perfectly hardy. Check locally to find out exactly which plants survive outdoors all year where you live; you'll also learn by trial and error.

Gardeners in cold climates *overwinter* their plants (keep them in a protected spot) to shelter them until the milder temperatures of spring arrive. Like everything else gardeners do, each individual has his or her favorite method of overwintering. Here are two:

- ✔ Before cold weather strikes, place more tender perennials, in their pots, in an insulated garage or basement where they can lose their leaves and go into a dormant state. Continue to water once a month through winter to be sure that they don't wither and die. Move plant back into the garden in spring, after frost danger has passed.

- ✔ For hardy perennials, wait until the first hard frost. Then cut foliage back to just a few inches above the soil. Bury each plant, still in its pot, in the middle of your compost or mulch pile, or place in your basement or an insulated garage. When the weather warms in spring, monitor the pots until you see signs of life from the stub of each plant. When plants start to grow, move them back to their spots in the garden.

Sooner or Later: Repotting

Because perennials tend to grow larger — in some cases *much* larger — than annuals, you may find your plants outgrowing their pots. (Sure signs: roots filling all available soil space, bulging out at the top. An even surer sign: roots bursting the sides of the container.) At times like these, you need to cut back your plants, divide the roots, and repot in the same container or repot into a larger container.

Some perennials, like coral bells and hosta, spread by underground roots. In pots, they can eventually grow so crowded that they no longer look good or grow well. When your plants enlarge to this size, think about dividing the clump. The ideal time to divide a plant is when it's in its most dormant state, which may be in fall or spring, depending upon your climate and the particular type of plant.

To divide a perennial:

1. **Ease the plant from the pot.**

2. **Wash off as much soil as possible — you need to be able to see the roots.**

3. **Using a trowel, garden knife, or whatever tool seems to work for you, gently tease apart the root mass into two or more clumps. These clumps are called "divisions." Be sure that each division has a healthy set of roots to support it.**

Repot each clump into a new pot using the bare-root potting procedure described earlier in this chapter. You can also plant some or all of the clumps to give you new plants in the ground. Or share or swap divisions with your friends and neighbors.

Choosing Perennials for Containers

The following popular perennials qualify as good candidates for container gardening. Everything on the list blooms for a fairly long season and is relatively easy to grow. Most of these plants can work alone in containers or can be combined with annuals or other perennials. (Perennials that are grown as annuals in many parts of the country are not listed here, but in Chapter 6.)

✔ **Agapanthus, or lily of the Nile:** This South African native has long, strappy leaves that grow from 1- to 3-feet long. In spring and summer, the plants send out tall, onionlike clusters of flowers in shades of blue-purple or white. A single agapanthus easily fills a 24-inch pot and doesn't need to be divided for 5 or 6 years. This is a great all-year, easy-to-grow long-blooming plant in mild climates — and, of course, needs overwintering (in basementlike conditions) in a cool climate. The dwarf variety, Peter Pan, grows only to 12 inches tall, an ideal size for smaller containers.

Hardy to zone 8. Provide full sun or part shade. Keep soil moist but not wet. Divide when roots fill up container.

✔ **Alstroemeria or Peruvian lily:** Not a true lily, but just as beautiful and graceful. Intense hybridization has created a myriad of lily-like multicolored flowers: shades of white with pink, pink with white and yellow, lilac and purple, orange-yellow, and many more color combinations. Leafy stems range from 2 to 5 feet tall.

Hardy to zone 8. In mild-winter areas, Peruvian lilies bloom much of the year. In colder-winter areas, bloom season may be May through summer. Provide full sun or part shade, depending upon variety, high-quality soil mix, moderate amounts of water. Roots are rather brittle; when you plant, set fairly deep, with only the top of the root cluster showing. Roots prefer not to be disturbed, so plant in a container with plenty of room to grow.

✔ **Asparagus fern *(Asparagus densiflorus):*** Overall effect is long, billowy clouds of green, sometimes studded with red berries. Arching stems 18 to 24 inches long have 1-inch long, flattened leaves that look a bit like needles. This is an asparagus, not a fern, and it's easy and fast-growing in containers — a great choice for baskets, alone or with shade-loving companions.

Hardy to zone 9. Provide full sun or part shade. Keep well-drained soil just barely moist. Overwinter in colder areas of the country. Trim out old dead branches and repot overcrowded plants or divide old clumps.

✔ **Blanketflower *(Gaillardia):*** Tough, native American plants have a ruggedly handsome look with daisylike flowers in beautiful shades of yellow to red, orange, and burgundy in different patterns and combinations. Plants grow 2 to 4 feet tall, and spread into a dense mound of blooms.

Hardy to zone 3. Provide full sun, fast-draining soil mix, minimal water. When mature, plants can fill a container completely on their own — don't combine them with other plants in the same container. Cluster pots of blanket flower with other low-growing perennials, separate pots of annuals, or tall grasses.

✔ **Blue marguerite *(Felicia):*** Blue daisies with yellow centers are tiny but profuse. Main bloom season is summer, but in frost-free areas expect flowers in winter and early spring — especially if you remove faded flowers. Plants grow up to 2 feet tall, shrubby, and a bit sprawly. This is a tender plant grown as an evergreen perennial in mild climates, but as an annual where winters are cold.

Hardy to zone 9. Provide full sun. Constantly pinch, prune, and groom flowers to contain vigorous growth and control tendency to become a bit raggedy.

✔ **Chrysanthemums:** Familiar autumn flowers make chrysanthemums a garden favorite. So-called florist's chrysanthemum is sold year-round at supermarkets and everywhere else — typical use is as instant color, then thrown away. But look beyond the florist version to hundreds of other varieties, typically in shades of yellow, white, bronze, and red, in sizes ranging from 6 inches to 4 feet tall. Choose compact varieties for containers. Use taller, more upright types in center of large container plantings.

Hardiness depends on variety. Provide full sun and regular water. Pick fading flowers to prolong the blooms. Divide clumps every few years.

✔ **Coral bells** *(Heuchera):* Flower clusters on stalks as tall as 3 feet feature drooping, bell-shaped blooms in shades of red, deep pinks, coral, and white. Foliage is nice too — long, lobed leaves are green with shades of red and purple. Coral bells are not plants to feature alone in containers, but they combine beautifully with annuals like pansies and other perennials such as hosta.

Hardy to zone 4. Provide full sun in cool climates and part shade where it's hot. Plant groups of coral bells toward the rim of a large pot, next to taller and bushier plants that also require regular water. Plants need to be divided every few years when they start to look woody.

✔ **Coreopsis:** A container of blooming coreopsis can look like a pot of golden sunshine on your patio. *Coreopsis grandiflora* grows to 2 feet high and 3 feet wide with 2- to 3-inch bright yellow flowers.

Hardy to zone 3. Provide full sun and fast-draining soil mix. Keep blooms coming by cutting off the fading flowers. If a plant has too many faded blooms to cut individually, shear back all the stems at once — expect your reward to be another round of flowers.

✔ **Daylilies** *(Hemerocallis):* Choose from numerous varieties with flowers in yellow, orange, red, rust, or burgundy — and every imaginable color combination. Blooms rise regally above the leaves and face north, east, south, and west. Better yet, daylily is an easy plant to grow almost everywhere. Varieties can be either deciduous (better for cold climates) or evergreen. Plants have long strappy leaves that can grow 2 feet or taller. Dwarf daylilies — nice choice for containers —typically grow to only 6 or 10 inches tall.

Hardy to zone 4. Daylilies are tough. Provide full sun with a bit of shade in very hot summer areas. Make sure that you keep soil moist during bloom time. To prolong the flowering season, snap off spent flowers. Plants spread by underground rhizomes, and need to be divided every few years — dividing is easy. If you have a friend who grows daylilies that you admire, ask for a division next time he or she divides plants.

✔ **Delphinium:** Thumb through a gardening magazine, and you probably come across a picket-fence-enclosed garden planted with elegant blue-flowering delphiniums — the classic, photogenic perennials. Delphiniums grow as tall as 6 feet with stalks of blue, lavender, white, pink, or yellow flowers, mostly in summer. More compact varieties — only 2 to 3 feet tall — work best in containers: Try to find Connecticut Yankee or Blue Fountains.

Delphiniums grow in zones 3 - 7 and in parts of zone 9 where night temperatures are cool. Plant in rich, well draining soil mix that's not too acidic. Provide full sun and fertilize regularly. You may need to stake tall flowers.

✔ **Euryops:** This is a landscape and container mainstay in mild climates long blooming and very easy to grow. Shrubby daisy, from 2 to 6 feet tall, blooms heavily in late winter and early spring, then off and on throughout the rest of the year. *Euryops pectinatus* has gray-green leaves. *E. p.* Viridis has deep green leaves.

Hardy to zone 9. Provide full sun. Allow soil to dry out a bit between waterings. After main bloom period, cut plant back by about one-third.

✔ **Foxglove *(Digitalis):*** Usually thought of as a towering background plant, consider the compact varieties for containers: Foxy, Excelsior, and Gloxiniiflora are in the 2- to 3-foot range. Flowers from late spring to early fall are tubular, in shades of purple, white, yellow, with striped and speckled throats.

Hardy to zone 4. Provide full sun or light shade and regular water. A single foxglove can fill a pot 18 inches in diameter. When the flower stalk fades, cut it at the base — you may get a second bloom. Foxgloves are biennials not perennials, so don't expect year-after-year bloom.

✔ **Hosta, or plantain lily:** This is a great plant for containers in the shade. Grow hosta for its big oval or heart-shaped leaves, in deep green, chartreuse, and many other shades. Plants form mounds from 6 inches to 5 feet tall, depending upon species.

Hardy to zone 4. Hostas go dormant in the winter, requiring overwintering in colder climates. New leaves appear from the roots in early spring. Divide plants when they outgrow their containers.

✔ **Lavender *(Lavandula):*** English, French, and Spanish lavender are just a few types of this fragrant, favorite perennial. Shrublike plants grow 1 to 3 feet tall with slender stalks of purplish flowers at the tips. Lavender is an outstanding container plant — mostly because portability lets you move plants where you can easily snatch a few leaves or flowers and appreciate the fragrance. Dwarf varieties — Compacta and others — work especially well in containers.

Hardy to zone 5, but varies by species. Lavender is evergreen in mild climates, and dies back in cold places, where plants can be overwintered — or start with new plants each year. Provide full sun and well-drained, sandy soil. Let the soil dry out between waterings. Lavender works well by itself in pots — the perennial's preference for dry conditions makes it incompatible with most other plants. Cut plants way back (halfway or so) after first bloom period.

✔ **Marguerite** *(Chrysanthemum frutescens):* If you are like the rest of us, this may be the first perennial that you grow in a container — very easy, fast growing, long blooming, abundant. White, yellow, cream, or pink daisies bloom continuously over the summer. Shrubby plants grow into a dense mass 4 feet tall.

Hardy to zone 9, can be grown as a summer annual everywhere else. Provide full sun. To control size and force more blooms, pinch tips right from the beginning. In mild climates, cut back plants by at least one-fourth in early spring.

✔ **Penstemon, or beard tongue:** Penstemons abound in all parts of the country. They're shrublike plants, 2 to 5 feet tall, with spikes of tubular flowers in shades of white to coral, pink to red, and purple. Humming-birds love the flowers. Best bets for containers are *P. gloxinoides* hybrids, with bushy, compact growth. Combine with lower-growing, broad-leafed perennials like lamb's ear.

Hardiness depends on variety. *P. gloxinoides* can grow year-round only in mild climates; elsewhere treat it like an annual. Provide full sun, unless you live in a very hot climate where plants may need a bit of shade in summer. Keep soil mix very well-drained — too much water and too rich of soil can be deadly. For a strong second bloom, cut off all dead flower spikes.

✔ **Pinks and carnations** *(Dianthus):* This is a huge family, most of them carrying a familiar, wonderfully spicy fragrance — boutonniere-type carnations are the most familiar. For containers, consider compact types: cottage pinks, border carnations, and China pinks. Plants grow 8 to 16 inches tall, covered with a profusion of fragrant flowers in white to pink to magenta.

Hardiness depends on variety; most are hardy to zones 3 or 4. Plant in light, well-drained soils. Provide part shade in hottest summer areas. Water well, but do not overwater. Cut or pinch fading flowers to prolong bloom.

✔ **Primroses:** Their long, crinkly leaves and clusters of flowers in bright shades of blue, yellow, magenta, lavender, and white make them the perfect cottage garden accent. At least 500 different species and varieties, but you can't go wrong with English primrose (*Primula polyantha*); it's easy to grow, one of the first plants to bloom in spring. In the garden, primroses are usually planted at the edge of borders to draw attention to their beautiful flowers. Use that same principle in mixed flower pots, planting primroses at the perimeter of large pots; or fill containers with single colors.

English primroses are hardy to zone 3. Where winters are mild and summers long and hot (such as in California), grow primroses for bloom from fall through early spring. Provide full sun in cool climates (or if grown to bloom in winter), part shade in warm climates. Make sure soil mix is high in peat moss. Keep soil moist.

✔ **Purple fountain grass** *(Pennisetum setaceum Rubrum):* Grasses are strikingly beautiful in pots. This is one of the more striking, forming graceful mounds of purplish-brown leaves up to 2 or even 4 feet tall. In summer, fuzzy pink or purplish flower spikes form. If you prefer to control the spread of grasses throughout your garden, cut off seedheads before they mature.

Hardy to zone 8, but you can grow fountain grass as an annual in colder climates. Provide full sun and almost any soil mix. Combine with other perennials that require little water.

✔ **Sage** *(Salvia):* You may think of sage as a culinary herb, but the 900+ types of ornamental sages are plants of tremendous beauty and usefulness in the garden. Perennial salvias tend to be shrublike, ranging from 12 inches to 6 feet tall. Flowers grow on flower spikes, in shades of pink, red, white, coral, blue, and purple. Some salvias stand tall and upright, others cascade. Good choices for containers are mealy blue sage (*S. farinacea*), with foot-long spikes of blue flowers; and cherry sage (*S. greggii*), a low, bushy type that blooms from summer through fall.

The two types mentioned are hardy to zone 8. Provide full sun. Pinch frequently, starting when plants are young, to produce bushy growth. Cut plants way back in spring.

✔ **Yarrow** *(Achillea):* Available in many varieties, yarrows are ground-hugging perennials with feathery leaves and delightful flowers in shades ranging from yellow to pink, white to crimson red. Tall stalks are topped with flat clusters of flowers, 2 to 4 inches in diameter. Handsome foliage is green or gray-green, depending upon the variety. Yarrows spread easily by roots; a single 4-inch-pot plant quickly fills a container. Use low-growing, creeping varieties to fill blank spaces and spill over the edges of containers that include taller and bushier perennials. Use taller varieties (up to 3 feet) as the centerpiece of a mixed pot.

Hardy to zone 3. Provide full sun and minimal water. Divide in spring when the clumps grow too large or too raggedy. Keep overwintering dormant plants on the dry side.

Don't be limited by our list. Nearly any perennial can grow in a container if you're willing to work with it. Here are ten more to consider. When shopping, remember to look for compact, bushy varieties. Check locally for best growing tips.

- ✔ Artemisia Powis Castle — silver foliage plant, sun
- ✔ Aster — richly colored daisies, sun
- ✔ Astilbe — spikes of flowers, part shade
- ✔ Bellflower *(Campanula)* — blue flowers for baskets, sun or part shade
- ✔ Catmint *(Nepeta)* — little blue flowers, sun
- ✔ Diascia — pink, sun
- ✔ Erigeron — daisies in many colors, sun
- ✔ Gazania — festive daisies, sun
- ✔ Lenten rose *(Helleborus)* — foliage and blooming plant, shade
- ✔ Statice *(Limonium)* — purple, sun

Chapter 8

Lighting Up Containers with Bulbs

In This Chapter

▶ Finding out what bulbs are

▶ Planting bulbs in containers

▶ Identifying bulbs for spring and summer

*J*ust imagine a 2-foot-wide bowl of bright red tulips all abloom against a backdrop of dark green conifers. Or what about a single, intensely fragrant hyacinth perfuming your whole kitchen . . . in February! The most spectacular container gardening that you ever do may involve bulbs.

Of course, you have to pay a price for all this beauty (in addition to the sometimes considerable cash outlay, that is). Bulbs demand your careful attention to the calendar and to their specific planting needs. But don't let this requirement scare you away; bulbs are easy to handle, and after you plant your top choices, you can virtually forget about them for a few months.

We're Not Talking Lightbulbs, Here

What exactly is a bulb, you ask? Well, as with most questions, you can go for an extremely thorough, technically accurate, and often difficult-to-pronounce answer; or you can hope for a response during which you have at least a slim chance of staying awake. Guess which approach this book takes?

In case you really care, botanists define a true *bulb* as a short underground stem surrounded by fleshy leaves (like the layers of an onion). Bulbs store food for the plant that ultimately sprouts, triggered by seasonal changes in moisture and temperatures. Bulbs can reproduce underground by developing little offsets, or *bulblets,* which eventually grow to mature bulb size.

The discussion of bulbs in this chapter, and elsewhere in this book, includes types of plants that are not true bulbs, but that perform pretty much the same (corms, rhizomes, tubers, tuberous roots, and so on). All are underground storage systems that sprout foliage and flowers, die back to the ground, and can be dug up and replanted.

The bulbs that you're most likely to be familiar with are the classic spring bloomers, such as tulips, daffodils, hyacinths, and crocuses. Here's their routine:

1. You plant spring bulbs in fall.

2. Using stored food for energy, the bulbs sprout roots through the winter.

3. Top growth emerges in late winter or early spring.

4. Flowers burst into bloom in spring for a couple of weeks, and then dry up.

5. Foliage continues to grow, replenishing the underground bulb's food supply. (If you dig up a bulb at bloom time, you find it scrawny compared with the plump one that you planted.)

6. When the foliage is done growing and replenishing the underground food supply, the leaves turn brown and die back. The bulb is plump again with stored food and, if left underground, can sprout and bloom again the next winter and spring. At this stage, after foliage dies back, you can dig up the bulbs and store them for planting in fall. (As you find out later, typical spring bulbs grown in containers aren't good candidates for replanting in a container the next fall.)

Some less typical bulbs bloom at other times of the year, but are plenty worthwhile in their own right. For example, you plant summer bulbs (including calla lily, canna, and tuberous begonia) in spring for summer or early fall bloom. Plant fall-blooming bulbs, such as colchicum and autumn crocus, in late August or September; flowers appear just weeks later.

Some bulbs don't act like bulbs at all. Agapanthus and Clivia, for example, grow from bulbs but can become permanent plants, left in the same containers (or the ground, in mild climates) year after year.

Containers and Bulbs: A Great Partnership

Spring-blooming bulbs create a blaze of color just when it's most welcome — late winter and early spring. Nothing else announces spring more emphatically and lyrically.

Planting bulbs in containers allows you freedom of movement to meet your needs. Place the containers nearby at bloom time for close-up viewing (and smelling, in the case of the beautifully scented types such as hyacinths and narcissus!). Store the containers out-of-sight when your portable garden isn't very interesting — during the several months when nothing shows above ground and the several months after bloom, when foliage is growing and then dying back.

Shopping for bulbs

You can buy bulbs at a local nursery or garden center or by mail order. The nursery bins and bags give you a chance to personally inspect the bulbs for quality — always important! But perhaps more than any other plant, durable and compact bulbs lend themselves to mail-order delivery. When you order from reputable suppliers, you don't have to worry about the quality of the bulbs that you receive in the mail. Plus, mail order generally offers the widest selection of varieties.

TIP

Bulb strategy

How much thought can you possibly give to a dull and drab little lumpy thing? Knowing some strategy ahead of time can make all the difference in transforming your ugly bulbs into beautiful flowers worthy of the finest containers!

✔ To get the most for your money and effort, prominently display your containers of blooming bulbs. Keep the containers out of sight until the plants are ready to bloom and, when they finish blooming, move them out of the way where adequate water and sunlight is available for the rest of the growth period.

✔ Good timing is a must. You have to shop at the right time, plant at the right time, and follow directions for depth of planting and spacing. Yes, a bulb casually buried (even upside down) may perform, but not as well.

✔ The bloom season for most bulbs can be short, two or three weeks at best for daffodils and tulips. (But isn't that why we love bulbs — their fleeting burst of beauty in the spring garden?) If you want a longer bloom season, check out the bloom dates of bulbs you buy; varieties are sold as early-, mid-, and late-season. For an extended bloom season, plant varieties with staggered bloom dates in separate containers.

✔ Planting just one bulb variety per pot ensures that all the bulbs in the pot will bloom at the same time. Mixing varieties in a container, on the other hand, results in flowers coming at different times, which has much less impact. If you want different flower colors and bloom times, grow different varieties in *separate* containers.

The bulbs that you see for sale at nurseries have been dug up at their most dormant stage — with no root or top growth. Spring bulbs are dug in summer for fall planting. Nurseries begin selling bulbs right before their planting season (as soon as late August or early September for fall planting). Mail-order companies encourage you to order months ahead, in late spring or early summer; they then ship the bulbs to you at the proper planting time. With any source, try to buy bulbs as soon as you can to get the best choices.

Keep these tips in mind as you shop for bulbs:

- **Earlier is better than later.** When you pick out your bulbs as soon as they hit the nurseries or catalogs, you get a much better selection of varieties. And at this time, the bulbs aren't picked over, with just the runts remaining. If you're not yet ready to plant, keep your bulbs in a cool dark place, with good air circulation and temperatures ideally between 35°F and 50°F.

- **Bigger is better than smaller.** The size of the bulb indicates the amount of food stored for growth development. Bigger bulbs (graded number 1) usually produce bigger flowers, more flowers, and taller, thicker stems. Smaller bulbs at a good price may make sense if you plant them in the ground where they can develop over several years, but not for containers, where the bulbs usually can thrive only for one year.

- **Plump is better than scrawny.** Follow the same rule for choosing a bulb as you do for choosing a good grapefruit: The bulb should feel heavy for its size. A bulb that feels light may have lost moisture.

- **Firm is better than squishy.** To what in the world does this rule not apply? You don't want to buy rotting bulbs.

- **Two noses are better than one.** This rule applies primarily to daffodils and perhaps some Picasso paintings. Daffodil bulbs develop *noses,* or little bulbs attached to the main bulb, each of which can produce leaves and flowers. Try to buy big fat bulbs with two or three noses.

Chilling out

In mild climates (California, for example), you have to simulate the conditions that bulbs need and naturally enjoy in cold climates. Without a certain amount of chilling, bulbs (particularly tulips and hyacinths) produce small and insubstantial flowers. Check with your local nursery to see what chilling requirements are needed where you live. Bulb suppliers recommend bulb chilling in USDA zone 8 and milder climates. (See Chapter 2 for a discussion of climate zones.)

If chilling is necessary where you live, place bulbs in a paper bag in the refrigerator (not freezer) for six to eight weeks before planting. Make sure that you buy bulbs early enough in the season to allow time to chill them before planting in mid to late fall.

Choosing the container

Bulbs look fine in a wide variety of container shapes and styles. As a general rule, spring bulbs are planted in the ground at a depth three times their diameter, but that rule doesn't have to apply to short-term container growing. Choose containers that allow at least 2 inches of soil beneath the bulbs.

The traditional container in which to grow spring bulbs is a clay or plastic *bulb pan,* a shallow pot 10 inches or larger in diameter and only 5 or so inches deep. These pots don't hold much soil — which is perfectly okay for spring bulbs and their typical one-season stay in containers.

For other kinds of bulbs, especially those that can live in containers for several years, make sure that roots have enough growing space. Pick containers at least 12 inches deep for lilies and other more permanent bulbs.

Preparing the soil

For container-grown bulbs, you want a mix that's well-drained but that holds adequate moisture. Most commercial potting mixes work well, or you can mix your own soil, as suggested in Chapter 4.

For bulbs that grow only one season, you probably need to fertilize only at planting time. A complete fertilizer with proportions of 5-10-5 (see Chapter 19 for an explanation of fertilizer types) works well, as does fertilizer labeled *bulb food.* Stir fertilizer into the soil mix as you are planting bulbs in your container.

Planting the bulbs — step by step

Containers don't provide enough space, nutrients, or temperature control for most kinds of bulbs to come back successfully year after year. Figure that fall bulbs like daffodils and tulips are good for only one year in a container. You can try these bulbs in the ground after they bloom — although it may take the bulbs several years to rebuild their vigor and ability to bloom. Or give post-bloom bulbs to a more patient friend.

The following steps describe the typical way to plant fall bulbs, such as tulips and daffodils. Expect the results to be containers dense with flowers. (Remember that different bulbs may require specific conditions — see individual bulb descriptions for details.)

1. **Figure out which end is up.**

   If you plant bulbs upside down or sideways, you're asking them to waste time and energy taking a circuitous run to daylight. Examine your bulbs for root remnants at the base — that end goes down.

2. **Fill your pot partway full of soil mix so bulbs placed upright on top end up 1 inch below the rim of the pot.**

3. **As shown in Figure 8-1, space bulbs so that they're gently touching or no more than $1/2$-inch apart, and press base of bulbs into the soil to keep them standing straight.**

   Place any larger bulbs at the center of the group.

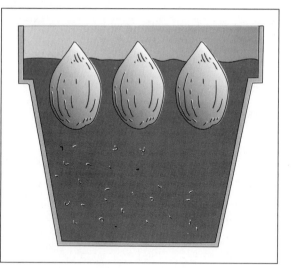

Figure 8-1: Your bulbs should be about $1/2$-inch apart and 1 inch below the rim of the pot.

4. **Barely cover tops of bulbs with soil mix.**

5. **Water gently with a watering can or hose set at a trickle until the soil mix is fully moistened.**

6. **To keep roots from sprouting too soon, keep them cool.**

   Move planted containers into a cool shady spot for 8 to 15 weeks, depending on your climate. In colder climates, keep containers where they won't freeze, such as in an unheated garage. In mild-winter climates, insulate with several inches of ground bark or other organic matter. Roots begin to grow before you see signs of top growth.

7. **Inspect stored containers every couple of weeks (or more often in warm, dry climates) to see whether soil is still moist or if it needs watering.**

    After six to eight weeks, start looking for signs of top growth.

8. **When you see small green shoots, remove any cover of organic matter and move the containers to a spot in the garden with filtered sunlight (under trees or a patio roof cover, for example).**

9. **When flower buds start to show color, move containers into their display positions.**

10. **Water bulbs as needed to keep soil moist throughout the whole depth of the container.**

Cut off flowers as they dry up. When blooming is over, move containers out of the way. Continue to water plants until the leaves dry up so that the bulb can become fully rejuvenated. When the leaves are dry, dump the bulbs out of pot. Remove all foliage and shake off excess soil. Store the bulbs in a dry place until planting time in the fall. Plant these bulbs in the ground — not again in pots. Don't use the same soil (it's worn-out) for container plants again.

Force the Issue with Your Bulbs

To brighten the dreariest winter days with sweet fragrance and spring colors, you can *force* (or trick) bulbs to bloom early indoors. Your best bets for forcing early blooms are crocuses, daffodils, hyacinths, and tulips.

Because you have to move containers indoors when you force a bloom, you probably want smaller pots than for outdoor use. For example, try half a dozen tulips or daffodils in a 6- to 10-inch pot; one daffodil or tulip or three small bulbs (such as crocus) in a 4-inch pot.

Follow the preceding steps for growing bulbs in containers. Start checking for roots and sprouts after two or three months (usually after New Year's Day). When stored bulbs show 2- to 6-inch sprouts, bring them indoors to a cool room (60 degrees or so) to speed up the bloom season. You may say that the bulbs think that spring is here! A week or two later, when sprouts have buds that show a little color, move the bulbs into normal room temperature (a room that's too warm shortens the bloom period) in a spot that gets as much sunlight as possible. Flowers should appear within the next week or so. Continue to keep the soil moist.

When the plant finishes blooming, move the container outdoors and make sure that soil is kept moist until the leaves are dry, as suggested for bulbs grown outdoors.

Spring Favorites for Containers

The most familiar kinds of bulbs are those that bloom in the springtime (tulips and daffodils), but equally welcome are such delights as sprightly crocus and fragrant freesias. You plant these bulbs in the fall, and they bloom for several glorious weeks in late winter or spring — exact dates depend on the specific variety that you choose. Many spring bulbs do well in containers; the following list includes the most reliable and rewarding spring bulbs for container gardening. (Unless otherwise noted, expect to get just one good year in a container from these.)

- **Amaryllis *(Hippeastrum)*:** Monster-size flowers, up to 8 inches across, sit atop 20-inch stems. This is a tender bulb, usually grown in pots indoors. Plant one bulb, with the top-half sticking out of soil, in an 8-inch pot. Complete directions for indoor forcing usually accompany bulbs sold by mail order or at nurseries.

- **Crocus:** Welcome as the first sign of spring in many places, the small goblet-like flowers come in many colors, including blue, purple, white, and bicolors. The look is most effective when you pack several crocus bulbs into a small container. Plant 2 inches deep, with small corms touching.

- **Daffodils *(narcissus)*:** Daffodils are the most popular spring bulbs, and for good reason. They're easy to grow and look smashing when crowded into a container. Hundreds of species and varieties are available, many colors and two-colors, but how can you pass up tried and true old yellows? King Alfred, big-flowered and bright yellow, is an all-time hero and still a great choice. Smaller types are usually referred to as *narcissus*. A dozen daffodil bulbs in a 12-inch-diameter clay pot make an impressive showing. Follow planting steps for typical spring bulbs, placing bulbs with their sides touching and tips level with soil surface.

- **Freesia:** With bright flowers in many colors, and sweetly fragrant, freesias are great for forcing and bringing indoors. Plant corms 1 inch apart, $1^1/2$ to 2 inches deep; you can squeeze about a dozen into an 8-inch pot. After the container season, move freesias into the ground where they may *naturalize* (grow wild).

- **Hyacinth:** Famously fragrant spikes of blue, white, or pink flowers can grow so large (12 inches long!) that they can tip over a small pot. Buy the biggest bulbs available. Plant in a shallow pot (about 5 inches), with sides of bulbs almost touching; cover lightly with soil mix. Don't expect much from the bulbs the next year, even if you move them into the ground. Be sure to chill bulbs in mild climates.

- **Iris:** Bulbous iris (not the familiar bearded iris) are good in containers. These include Dutch, English, and Spanish types, with flowers in many colors. Wedgwood is a favorite Dutch iris with big blue and yellow blooms. Plant bulbs 1 to 2 inches deep, 6 or 8 to an 8-inch pot. Move bulbs into the garden after bloom.

- **Ixia:** The long stems of this plant (which is also called African corn lily) carry pink, red, orange, yellow, cream, or white flowers in late spring. This is a tender bulb, not for areas where winter temperatures drop below 20°F. Plant corms close together 1 inch deep in a deep container.

- **Lily:** Large trumpet flowers, in almost all colors except blue, are an amazing sight in late spring and summer. With so many species, varieties, and hybrids and so many special growing instructions, lilies can be daunting to novice bulb growers — and to experienced gardeners as well. Trusty choices for containers are Enchantment and Pink Floyd (who says horticulturists are stuffy?). Plant bulbs in a deep container and leave them there for several years: 1 bulb in a 7-inch pot, 5 bulbs in a 16-inch pot. Grow in part shade. Pay attention to special lily advice for the variety you choose; look it up in a catalog, or check with a nursery.

- **Grape hyacinth** *(Muscari):* Often described as cheerful, the grape hyacinth heralds early spring with spikes of little blue or white flowers. The delicate flowers and foliage show off best in a small shallow pot (6- or 7-inch diameter, 5- or 6-inch depth). Plant the bulbs close together and cover them lightly with soil mix.

- **Ranunculus:** This plant produces beautiful, frilly flowers on long stems. The colors are bright and clear: pink, red, white, and a yellow so intense that it compares favorably with daffodils. Plant in fall in mild climates, in spring where temperatures drop much below freezing. Soak the hard dry tubers in water a few hours before planting. Provide a big pot, 12 inches deep at least. Plant tubers with clawlike part pointed down, 2 to 3 inches apart, 1 inch deep.

- **Tulip:** Tulips are probably the most impressive bulbs that you can grow in your containers. They're always classy, if a bit regimental when the whole potful blooms all at once, with the same height and color. Many, many colors and flower forms are available. Follow the directions for typical spring bulbs, and you find that tulips grow and bloom almost automatically in containers. But expect little from them in following years, in the ground or in containers. Tulips look best when bulbs are packed tight. Plant with sides nearly touching and tips just below soil surface. Be sure to chill in mild climates.

The Bulbs of Summer

You plant summer bulbs in late winter and spring for bloom during the summer. Some of them (especially begonia) need special care too detailed to describe here; we suggest that you inquire at a local nursery, or check out bulb catalogs and books.

- **Caladium:** With its big jungly-looking leaves splotched with pink, white, and red, this bulb adds a tropical feeling to a garden. Caladium can grow outdoors only in very mild climates. Plant tubers, one per pot, even with top of soil.

- **Calla *(Zantedeschia):*** Choose the common white or any of the many bright hybrids in yellow, pink, and red. All have the familiar cup-shaped flowers. Plant rhizomes 2 inches deep, 1 per 6-inch pot.

- **Canna:** Expect bright, flashy flowers and big, tropical-looking leaves. Most cannas grow tall, but for container gardening, look for dwarf varieties. Plant rhizomes 2 to 4 inches deep in containers at least 12 inches wide, 14 or 15 inches deep.

- **Dahlia:** This is a huge group of plants, from foot-tall dwarfs to strapping 6-footers, from quarter-sized flowers to dinner-plate dimensions for entering in the county fair. Dwarfs and intermediate types are best for containers; bigger plants require stakes. Plant tuberous roots 3 to 5 inches deep, 1 root to a 10- to 12-inch pot, 3 roots to a 14- to 16-inch pot.

- **Glory lily *(Gloriosa rothschildsiana):*** Beautiful red and yellow flowers bloom on a distinctive climbing plant. Provide a trellis to support this very tender bulb. Plant tubers 4 inches deep, 1 to each container at least 8 inches in diameter.

- **Tiger flower *(Tigridia):*** This flamboyant, heat-lover comes from Mexico. Plant the bulbs 2 to 4 inches deep, and 4 inches apart in a container at least 8 inches in diameter.

- **Tuberous begonia:** Great for containers (especially hanging baskets) in part shade, this plant is a favorite among hobbyist growers. Its richly colored flowers come in a variety of forms and sizes. For best results, follow the very detailed growing instructions (supplied by nurseries or catalogs) from planting time in winter or spring until bloom time in summer.

Chapter 9

Big Shots of the Garden: Shrubs and Trees

. . . .

In This Chapter

▶ The treasure of permanent pleasures

▶ How to care for your rich array

▶ A wealth of container plant choices

. . . .

*G*rown in containers, shrubs and trees (and we include a few vines in this chapter) are most appreciated when you have little or no ground space to grow them. These generous-size container plants can instantly transform a small open space into an inviting landscaped garden.

But any garden, old or new, large or small, can benefit from a handsome shrub or tree in a container. A container has a way of highlighting a plant that is otherwise pretty mundane. Mugho pine in a rugged terra-cotta pot evokes the sturdy dignity of the forest, while the same plant in the ground looks kind of like a green blob.

We don't mean to scare you off before you start, but growing permanent plants in containers calls for a different level of commitment than you bring to growing a pot of annuals for a few months. The particular needs of each plant are all-important: when to plant it, when to feed and prune it, how much sunlight it needs, and more.

You also need to consider the climate adaptability of the plants that you choose. Review Chapter 2, and remember that plants that are hardy in the ground in a certain climate may not be hardy in a container. (Roughly add two climate zones. If a plant is hardy to zone 5 in the ground, it may be hardy only to zone 7 in a container.) A fair prediction is that container plants in cold climates can't survive the winter outdoors. One final caution: The hardiness zones that we list are for plants in the ground (there is no firm data for container plants that we know of). Choose accordingly.

Performance Payoff: Shrubs and Trees at Work in Container Homes

Shrubs, trees, and vines can perform big-time in containers. Here are just a few things they can do for you:

- ✔ They can create a sense of scale in a garden. They can make a small terrace or balcony seem like a garden.

- ✔ They can produce seasonal displays: spring blossoms, fall color, winter berries.

- ✔ They can look handsome or dramatic in their own right, especially if pruned to emphasize structure. When we refer to a *specimen plant* or *accent,* that's what we're talking about — a container plant that's attractive enough to stand alone and be admired.

- ✔ They can work hard in a landscape: creating a privacy screen, a divider, or shade. They can provide a dependable green background for seasonal container plants like annuals and bulbs.

- ✔ They let you experiment. Try plants that are dicey in your area because of cold weather or bad soil. Try hibiscus outdoors for the summer, indoors in the winter.

Planting and Care

Permanent plants generally need less care and replacement than annuals or perennials, but they're not maintenance-free. Just keep in mind that you may not feel that bummed if you lose a pot of pansies that you forget to water, but it's a different matter when the casualty is a 7-year-old wisteria you just coaxed into bloom for the first time.

Special care required for different shrubs and trees is described in the section that follows. Here are a few reminders that apply to most permanent plants:

Planting

Planting schedules are the same for shrubs and trees in the ground and in containers. Generally, you plant in spring in cold climates, and in spring or fall in mild areas. The plants discussed here typically are available in gallon cans or larger, some sold bare-root, and some sold balled and burlapped.

Soil

Use soil mixes described in Chapter 4 or special mixes recommended for specific plants in the list that follows.

Container

Pay special attention to container selection because a permanent plant can live in the same container for a number of years. The basic rule applies: Start with a container that's 2 or 3 inches wider and deeper than the one in which the plant was grown.

Feeding

Permanent plants don't need the constant feeding that annuals do, but plan to feed at least several times during the growing season. See Chapter 19 for details on fertilizing. For best results, incorporate slow-release fertilizer into the soil mix at planting time.

Watering

No way around it, you have to water. Consider a drip irrigation system if you have a lot of containers.

Pruning

However flip it seems, if you grow a lot of different shrubs and trees, the best advice may be to buy a pruning book. Pruning is a big subject, and you need to prune your container plants just as you do garden plants. Our plant descriptions later in this chapter give some tips. Also check with the nursery where you buy your container plants.

Repotting

If you keep plants in the same containers for a few years, you can count on a round of repotting. Look for clues that it's time to replace your plant's happy home: when roots fill the pot or start to show at soil level; another clue is that the plant always seems dry. See the section on repotting in Chapter 20.

Pests and diseases

Unfortunately, container shrubs and trees are susceptible to the same problems as their cousins in the ground. See Chapter 21 for some pointers.

Shrubs and Trees for Containers

We don't plan to be purists here — not our style anywhere else in this book, right? Shrubs and trees are lumped together because so many of them overlap in size and function, especially when grown in containers. You may come across a few vines and some unclassifiables like bamboo.

The bottom line: All these are permanent plants that look great in containers and promise to grow well if you treat them right.

Aucuba

Bright red berries in fall and big shiny leaves (dark green or splotched with yellow variegation) are reasons why you grow *Aucuba japonica*. Aucuba also gets big enough — to 6 feet tall — to create a privacy screen or backdrop for smaller container plants. Oh, one more thing: Aucuba does well in shady spots where few other plants can thrive.

Provide part or full shade and ordinary soil mix. Soil can stay on the dry side. Prune back tips of new growth to encourage bushiness.

Hardy to zone 7.

Azaleas and rhododendrons

Consider yourself lucky if you live in an area where you can grow these magnificent spring-flowering shrubs — happily, containers can improve your odds.

Rhododendrons and azaleas are closely related and, along with their beautiful blooms and handsome year-round foliage, also share some rather demanding needs. What they need most are acid-type soil mix and just the right amount of sunlight — enough to bloom, not enough to burn the leaves. Exactly how much light depends on your climate, but containers allow you to move the plants around and experiment a bit.

You can choose from literally thousands of varieties (really). Check with local nurseries for varieties that do well in your area.

Evergreen azaleas, usually grown as small shrubs, are most reliable for containers. These include the compact Belgian Indica types (the kinds sold at florists), hardy only in the mildest climates. Southern Indicas, medium-sized shrubs or small trained trees (standards), are hardier, to zones 8 and 9; try Fielder's White and Formosa (purple). Kurume types are compact and bushy, 3 to 4 feet tall, hardy to zone 7; look for Coral Bells (pink) and Ward's Ruby (deep red).

Rhododendrons grow 4 to 6 feet tall in containers. Try to find small, compact types. Ironclads do well in containers and are hardier than most (to zone 5).

Exposure to sunlight and soil mix are the keys to healthy plants. In cool overcast climates, grow the plants in full sun or nearly full sun. Light shade is best in most places. In hotter climates, provide shade from afternoon sun and drying winds. Make sure that soil mix is on the acid side and fast draining (see Chapter 4); nurseries sell mixes specifically for rhododendrons and azaleas.

Plant gallon-can-size azaleas in 14-inch pots. Rhododendrons are usually sold in larger sizes; eventually they require a big container, usually a redwood box 16 to 24 inches in diameter. Don't plant too deep — level the top of the root ball with with top of the soil mix or even a fraction of an inch higher.

Never let the soil dry out. Rhododendrons and azaleas are difficult to grow in hot, dry climates, especially where water is alkaline. Start fertilizing when the blooming season ends; use an acid-type food (just choose one labeled for rhododendrons and azaleas) at the frequency recommended on the label or monthly through the growing season. After bloom, cut off dead flowers right away. Watch for brown leaf tips that indicate salt burn. Flush salts every few months with a couple of extra heavy waterings.

Rhododendrons and azaleas are plants to pamper. Move them out of the way when not in bloom, put them in your most prominent spot when they're flowering. If you are in a marginal climate, try to overwinter them as described in Chapter 2.

Bamboo

Statuesque in a container, bamboo actually is a giant grass. One reason to grow it in containers is to confine the running types that can take over a garden if let loose in the ground. Bamboo looks great as a single plant or combined with small pine or azaleas. Or plant several to create a privacy screen.

Many kinds are available. Golden bamboo, a notorious spreader, is easy; black bamboo is striking. Both grow to 8 feet tall. Provide full sun or part shade. Plant it in a container at least 15 inches in diameter. Treat it like a grass — don't let it dry out. You can bring bamboo indoors for the winter — make sure to provide lots of light.

Hardy to zone 7.

Boxwood

The first word in formality, boxwood is a shiny, dark green evergreen that lends itself to shearing in geometric shapes: globes, rectangles, and so on. Grow in urns, glazed pots, or other formal containers. Can't you picture boxwood sheared into round balls, growing in matching containers, flanking a front entry?

Provide full sun or part shade. Roots are shallow. Don't let soil dry out.

Hardy to zone 6.

Camellia

Here's a wonderful choice for containers if you live in a favorable climate, primarily the southern and western United States. Grow camellias for their beautiful flowers in late winter and early spring — white, pink, and red — and their glossy evergreen leaves. Plants are handsome year-round, and in containers can grow slowly to 5 or 6, or even 12 feet.

Thousands of varieties exist — check out nurseries and choose plants with appealing flowers. *Camellia japonica,* the most familiar species, has a number of varieties that make fine container plants: Glen 40 (deep red), Alba Plena (white), Guilio Nuccio (rose red), Elegans (pink), Shiro Chan (white). Also consider *C. reticulata* varieties with spectacular flowers on rangy plants. *C. sasanqua* varieties can spill from containers or stand upright, and the flowers come at a most welcome time — early fall.

Pay special attention to planting and care. Camellias are not fussy but do need special conditions for best growth. Put gallon-size plants in 12-inch tubs, larger plants in 16-inch containers. Provide part shade or full sun in cool climates. Soil mix should be fast-draining and acidic — if you want, just choose a mix labeled for camellias and other acid-loving plants. Plant on the high side with the top of root ball above soil level. Keep soil moist constantly. Pick up dead flowers to stop spread of petal blight. Move plants into protected spot during cold weather in marginal climates. Start feeding after bloom with camellia or acid food.

Hardy to zones 7 or 8.

Conifers: Pines, firs, junipers, and the rest of the clan

Call them evergreens if you like, these are shrubs and trees with needles and cones — among the more widely planted and dependable plants in all gardens in all climates. In containers, many do well where climatically adapted, but remember that just because a conifer is rugged and easily grown in the ground doesn't mean it automatically works in a container the same way. And although conifers are considered hardy, in cold climates you still have to provide winter protection (see Chapter 2). In really cold climates, you can't even grow any conifers outdoors in containers.

Conifers don't give us flowers (a few have colorful foliage), so why bother with them? A few excellent reasons:

- ✔ Conifers offer greenery all year, for background plantings, for privacy screens, and or quiet good looks.

- ✔ Some conifers make striking specimen plants — worth showing off individually — especially as they grow older and are pruned to expose more of the trunks and branches.

- ✔ Some conifers can make nice living Christmas trees — indoors for a few weeks and outdoors the rest of the year.

- ✔ As a rule, conifers are pretty easy to grow — not fussy about soil and relatively free of pests and diseases.

Here's some general container-growing advice that applies to the whole group of conifers:

- ✔ Plant in ordinary soil mix. Most conifers are pretty fussy about fast drainage and not much else.

- ✔ Provide a container that's a step up in size from the nursery container (2 or 3 inches larger). Some conifers can live for years in the same container. With most, figure on moving up plants to larger-sized containers by repotting every few years. You can also root-prune to keep the plant in the same container. After a few years, the plant may completely outgrow the container (top growth out of scale, roots filling up container); transplanting into the garden is the best idea.

- ✔ Grow conifers in full sun. A little shade may not hurt, but too much shade causes needles to drop and growth to become noticeably sparse.

- ✔ Keep soil consistently moist.

- ✔ Fertilize a couple of times during the growing season — once at the beginning of the season and again in the middle. You don't need to worry about encouraging fast growth or abundant blooms.

> ✔ Pruning can be minimal. As plants grow, you can cut off lower branches to reveal trunks; cut branches all the way back to the trunk — don't leave stubs. Thin out branches, again pruning back all the way to the trunk. Try to do your pruning in the winter or early spring before active growth begins. Be careful about shearing plants, which can leave dead branches that may not resprout.

Enough generalities! Conifers represent a huge and diverse group — now on to individual plants that offer you a wealth of growing opportunities!

False cypress (Chamaecyparis)

Many dwarf forms work beautifully in containers. Best bets are varieties of Hinoki cypress, such as *C. obtusa* Nana, with deep green foliage and very slow growth to 3 feet. Prune off lower branches to expose handsome trunk that looks a lot older than it is.

Hardy to zone 5. Hinoki cypress struggles in hot-summer climates. Watch for spider mites.

Fir (Abies)

The same trees used as cut Christmas trees can work as living Christmas trees in favorable climates. Noble fir (*A. procera*) and white fir (*A. concolor*) have the typical Christmas tree shape and grow slowly enough for container life.

Hardy to zones 5 to 7.

Juniper (Juniperus)

Boring to beautiful, ground-huggers to twisted spires, dozens of species and hundreds of varieties span a range of shapes and sizes.

Small compact types (*J. horizontalis* Bar Harbor or Wiltonii) can live in containers for years; use them as handsome individual plants in low containers. Big ones, like *J. chinensis* Pfitzerana, are useful as major specimen plants or backdrops. An old favorite (one way of saying overused) is Hollywood juniper (*J. chinensis* Kaizuka), with dark green foliage and tall, twisted shape.

Hardy to zone 4 to 6. Make sure the soil mix drains quickly; slow drainage is enemy No. 1, closely followed by spider mites (see Chapter 21). Perhaps because of their wide use, junipers suffer from more pests and diseases than other conifers; check with local nurseries and extension agents for recommendations.

Pine (Pinus)

Of many kinds grown and sold, a few do really well in containers, often for a decade or more.

Japanese black pine (*P. thunbergiana*) can become a big tree in the ground, but behaves itself in pots. Prune to limit size and open up structure (show more of branches and trunk).

Mugho pine (*P. mugo mugo*) is a favorite plant for rock gardens, spreading slowly into a dense, dark green mound. Mugho grows slowly in containers, eventually developing character — you may not see its trunk for years.

Other picturesque pines for containers: bristlecone (*P. aristata*), Scotch (*P. sylvestris*), and tanyosho (*P. densiflora* Umbraculifera) — this last one is rare but well worth a search because of its aged look while young, sometimes even with youthful cones while in a container.

Hardy to zones 3 to 5. To control height of pines, partly cut back or pinch "candles" (bundles of new growth) in the spring while they're still soft, before they fully open. Root-prune and repot pines to keep them in the same containers.

Redwood (Sequoia sempervirens)

We had to include this king-sized forest monarch to illustrate the amazing possibilities of container gardening: You can grow the world's tallest tree (more than 350 feet in the wild on the northern California coast) in a container — at least for a few years. Plant in a large box, 24 inches or wider, for a big screen to block a view or create privacy. Prune to control height and spread; you can cut off the top for bushier but less elegant-looking growth.

Hardy to zone 8. Keep the soil moist. In nature, redwoods thrive in areas of high rain and fog.

Spruce (Picea)

More candidates for the living Christmas tree role, spruces sure have the desired upright conical form. Norway spruce (*P. abies*) and Colorado blue spruce (*P. pungens Glauca*) make good-sized trees in time. Most notable of slow-growing types is dwarf Alberta spruce (*P. glauca* Conica), which takes years to reach 7 feet tall and looks like a perfectly symmetrical miniature Christmas tree when only a foot or so tall; it's a favorite for small containers.

Hardy to zone 3.

Thuja

Never grow a plant that you can't pronounce — a rule to live by. You never know when someone may ask you, what's that plant? Thuja sounds like *thew-ya*; it has a common name of arborvitae that also is a puzzler.

Thuja is prized for its rich green foliage as well as the bright yellows or golds of certain varieties. Look for compact varieties, about 3 or 4 feet tall: *T. occidentalis* Aurea (bright yellow) or Globosa (bright green); and *T. orientalis* Aureus Nana (golden foliage).

T. occidentalis is hardy to zone 3 to 6; *T. orientalis* hardy to zones 6 to 9. Watch for spider mites.

Cotoneaster

Among many kinds of cotoneaster, several are container standouts. Creeping cotoneaster (*C. adpressus*) and bearberry (*C. dammeri*) can spill from pots and hanging baskets, producing bright berries. They're small (less than a foot tall) and easy to grow.

Provide full sun.

Hardy to zone 6.

Crape myrtle (Lagerstroemia indica)

Take your choice — a handsome small tree or hanging basket trailer. Not many plants can fill both those roles. Choose full-size varieties to grow as single-trunk or multitrunk trees, 8 or 10 feet tall, in large containers. Bark develops interesting scaliness and smoothness. Summer flowers come in rich pinks, reds and purples. Foliage is deciduous. A favorite tree for shopping centers and business parks, crape myrtle is always handsome and can be planted at large sizes. Miniature varieties really can go into hanging baskets; they bloom nicely and have trailing branches.

Provide full sun. Watch for mildew — which probably means your climate is too cool.

Hardy to zone 7. Growth can die back to the ground in cold climates; treat the plant like a perennial.

Daphne

Which daphne are we talking about here? One is a garden workhorse, easy to grow and reliable. The other is a thoroughbred, temperamental, unpredictable, but potentially spectacular. *Daphne burkwoodii*, the Clydesdale, is a 3- or 4-foot evergreen shrub with sweet flowers in spring. *D. odora* grows about that same size, if it lives that long, and produces amazingly fragrant blossoms in late winter and early spring in mild climates. Grow both of these in containers that you can place where you can enjoy the fragrance — near a door or walk. Enjoy them while they last.

Provide part shade in most climates, full sun in cool areas. Take care not to disturb roots when planting. This plant can stay in the same container for a long time without repotting. Make sure drainage is perfect — especially with *D. odora*. Let the soil dry out between waterings. Don't feel guilty if a plant just up and dies.

D. burkwoodii is hardy to zones 6 to 8; *D. odora* to zones 8 and 9.

English laurel (Prunus laurocerasus)

Often used in hedges, English laurel in a container makes a dense glossy evergreen screen or backdrop for shady spots. Plants grow up to 6 feet tall. Compact types, such as Zabeliana, stay lower.

Provide sun or shade. This plant is easy to grow. Prune to shape rather than shear like other hedge plants.

Hardy to zone 7. Move into protection in cold areas.

Fatsia, or Japanese aralia (Fatsia japonica)

Bold leaves add drama to shady spots. This evergreen shrub, which can grow to 6 feet tall and more, can make a specimen plant in an entry or dark corner. This is a favorite plant to bring indoors for the winter; it can also serve as a permanent houseplant.

Provide part shade or full shade. Plant in a large container. Don't let soil dry out. And don't be afraid to prune back stems, which otherwise become leggy.

Hardy to zone 8.

Ferns

It's hard to think of ferns as trees! Many kinds do well in containers in shady spots — as striking single plants or combined with shade-loving annuals in mixed plantings. Most are not hardy and must be brought indoors in cold climates. Plant in lightweight soil mix with plenty of organic matter. Keep the soil moist. Give foliage a misting whenever possible — especially when indoors. Here are a few among many great ferns for containers:

Big statuesque ferns

Give these a good-sized container, up to 16 inches wide, and a prominent spot in the garden. When the roots fill the container, transplant the fern into the garden.

Tasmanian tree fern (*Dicksonia antarctica*) produces arching fronds as long as 6 feet. It's the hardiest of the tree ferns (to zone 9).

Australian tree fern (*Cyathea cooperi*) grows even larger but is dramatic in a container while young. Hardy to zones 9 to 11.

Small ferns

These combine nicely with other plants. Some are standouts in hanging baskets — alone or with other plants. All are on the tender side (zones 8 or 9 at best).

Maidenhair ferns (*Adiantum*) are delicate, with wiry little stems and lacy fronds. Tuck maidenhair into a mixed hanging basket.

Squirrel's foot fern (*Davillia*) gracefully fills a hanging basket by itself, creeping and clinging to the moss lining the basket.

Sword ferns and Boston ferns (*Nephrolepis*) are classic outdoor and houseplants — with dark green, feathery fronds.

Flowering fruit trees

Not for beginners, but the beautiful spring blossoms may tempt you to try flowering cherries, crabapples, or plums. Advice in a nutshell: Get a big container (like a half barrel), choose small varieties, and prune after spring bloom to keep trees small.

Fuchsia

The climate-blessed can grow fuchsias as permanent plants — terrific in baskets (trailing types) or pots (upright types up to 6 feet tall). Flowers are spectacular: intricately flared and dangling, richly colored in white, pink, purple, and many other colors.

Provide part shade. Use containers from 6 to 12 inches in diameter. Make sure that soil mix is high in organic matter and drains quickly. Keep the soil moist; increase humidity in dry climates by daily misting. Start pinching new growth early in spring. Fertilize every two weeks during the growing season. Watch for mites. Fuchsias are demanding but worth it.

Hardy to zone 8 — frost does in fuchsias. Grow them as annuals in cold climates.

Gardenia

A prima donna — but at least you stand a better chance of giving gardenia the conditions it needs when you plant it in a container. No other plant can match the romance of its legendary fragrance. While they're alive, the plants are handsome too, with glossy, deep green leaves. Mystery (what a perfect name for a plant you may never figure out!) grows 4 or 5 feet tall. Veitchii is a compact 3 feet.

Provide part shade in hot climates and full sun in cool places. Use a fast-draining, acid-type soil mix. Plant so that the top of the root ball is just above soil level. Make sure the soil stays moist. Fertilize frequently with acid food (azalea fertilizer) during the growing season. Good luck!

Hardy to zone 8.

Harry Lauder's walking stick (Corylus avellana Contorta)

A genuine conversation piece in a container — didn't you suspect as much from the name? Contorted branches and shiny brown bark show off best when the plant is leafless in winter. In a container, expect a height of about 4 to 6 feet. Put it where you can inspect it up close

Provide full sun or part shade. Make sure that the soil mix drains quickly. In spring, prune branches that interfere with the shape you want.

Hardy to zone 4.

Heavenly bamboo (Nandina domestica)

Not a real bamboo, nandina is a graceful, erect-growing evergreen shrub that performs solidly in all seasons. It's easy to grow in a container. Clusters of small white flowers bloom in spring and summer; red berries and crimson foliage follow in fall and winter. Expect mature plants to grow 5 feet tall or more in a container; dwarfs are much more compact (Nana is only about a foot tall, without the grace of the taller types).

Provide sun or part shade. This plant can live in same container for several years without repotting.

Hardy to zone 7. In cold climates, you can move heavenly bamboo indoors for the winter.

Hibiscus

Symbol of Hawaii, of course this shrub is tender. But cold-climate gardeners are tempted every year by nursery plants sporting huge (up to 6-inch) blossoms in bright reds, yellows, and other vivid shades. The decision is easy. Transplant hibiscus into a 12-inch or so container, put it in a warm spot, grow it for the summer, and then get rid of it — treat it like a petunia or other annual, in other words. You can also bring it indoors for the winter in cold regions, but you probably already have gotten your money's worth with summer blooms. In containers, plants grow quickly to as tall as 6 feet; leaves are bright green and glossy.

Provide full sun (reflected light, too, if you have it). Make sure the soil stays damp. Feed at least once a month during warm weather. Pinch young shoots for bushy growth.

Hardy to zones 9 or 10 in protected spots. In colder areas, move hibiscus indoors when temperatures drop in fall.

Holly

Share the fantasy: a pair of glossy, spiny-leafed hollies covered with red berries in matching containers flanking your front door for the Christmas holidays. How possible is it? Well, hollies can grow well in containers — if they're suited to your climate and you satisfy their rather demanding needs and have enough patience to grow the plants for at least several years. Also, for berry development, you have to grow both a male and female plant (they're sold labeled by sex). English holly (*Ilex aquifolium*) is the traditional type; it grows to 6 to 10 feet in a large container. Chinese holly (*I. cornuta*) is easier to grow, especially in hot climates. Yaupon holly is native to the southeast U.S. and is the most reliable choice for that region.

Provide full sun or part shade in hot climates. The soil mix must be high in organic matter and drain quickly. Shear young plants to encourage bushiness.

Hardy to zone 7. In the United States, English holly is really reliable only in the Pacific Northwest and northern California.

Hydrangea

Huge flowers and bold foliage make *Hydrangea macrophylla* a summer show-off in large containers (18 inches and more). Flowers in clusters a foot or more wide come in blue, pink, red, or white. Plants are deciduous and grow 4 feet tall and larger.

Provide sun or part shade; protect from hot summer sun. Use a soil mix with plenty of organic matter. Hydrangeas are water hogs, but they're good about drooping and telling you when they need water. Apply aluminum sulfate to the soil before the bloom season to make pink-flowering varieties turn blue.

Hardy to zone 6. Overwinter plants in cold climates. Stems die back to the ground; the bloom isn't reliable in cold areas.

India hawthorn (Rhaphiolepis)

The dependable, versatile landscape plant also is — surprise — a dependable, versatile container plant. It provides year-round, glossy flowers, with bright pink flowers in spring. Plants form rounded mounds up to 4 feet tall. Nurseries sell India hawthorn trained as small trees (standards) with globelike tops on 3- or 4-foot trunks.

Provide full sun or part shade. You don't need to worry about any special care. Plant in a 12-inch pot, and keep plants small and bushy by regular pinching starting when they're young.

Hardy to zone 7.

Japanese barberry (Berberis thunbergii)

This spiny evergreen with colorful foliage and bright berries usually goes to work as a hedge plant. It's also a handsome container plant, especially the compact more colorful varieties like Atropurpurea Nana and Gold Ring. Plants grow several feet tall in a container — so they make a nice choice for an entry.

Provide full sun, no special treatment.

Hardy to zone 4. Japanese barberry doesn't do well in hot summers.

Japanese maple (Acer palmatum)

If you know what's good for you, you put Japanese maples at the top of your container plantings list (provided you live in an appropriate climate). Why? Japanese maple is just plain beautiful — in form and leaf color, whether spring green or fall red. Some also say that its bare branches in winter are so handsome that they never need leaves to look great. And it's the right scale for a patio container plant. Typical Japanese maple can grow 15 feet or more in the ground, way less than that in containers. More compact varieties work best in containers: Dissectum and Crimson Queen are just two. Look for varieties with bright fall colors or even colorful bark (Sango Kaku has coral bark).

Provide part shade in most climates (afternoon shade, that is). Plant in soil mix with lots of organic matter. Keep the soil most. Japanese maple grows fairly quickly; keep moving it up to a larger container, or repot and root-prune frequently to keep it in the same container. Start with a gallon-can-size plant in a 12-inch pot, 5-gallon-size in a 16-inch pot or tub. In spring, prune lightly to remove dead wood or shape growth.

Hardy to zone 6. Japanese maple doesn't do well in hot dry climates; it's also sensitive to alkaline soil and water — leaves show brown at the tips. Shelter from dry winds.

Lantana

Bright colors suggest sunny tropical places, and this vinelike shrub is tender. Clusters of flowers bloom over a long season in white, gold, pink, orange, red, and white. Use trailing lantana (*L. montevidensis*) in hanging baskets for sunny dry spots; expect it to sprawl gracefully over the sides of the basket. Common lantana is good in a big container, growing to 4 feet tall, spreading about as wide. It's also available trained as a small tree (standard).

Provide full sun. Keep the soil on the dry side. Prune off dead wood in spring.

Hardy to zones 7 or 8.

Lily of the valley shrub (Pieris japonica)

This shrub is so understated that you may not guess that it's a rhododendron relative. Lily of the valley shrubs always looks nice. Foliage is handsome year-round, tinged with red in spring; little bell-shaped white flowers are charming in spring. Expect a height of 8 feet in the ground, lower in a container.

Provide part shade or full sun in cool, overcast climates. Use acid soil mix suggested for azaleas and rhododendrons.

Hardy to zones 6 to 8.

Myrtle

Shear this little evergreen into topiary or other formal shape. For containers, look for dwarf myrtle varieties (Compacta and Microphylla, for example) — they reach 2 or 3 feet.

Provide full sun. Make sure that the soil stays moist.

Hardy to zone 8.

New Zealand flax (Phormium tenax)

Does any plant better illustrate the definition of a spiky accent plant? Sword-like leaves form dramatic fans to 6 feet or more — usually less in containers. Leaves are bronze, red, purple, or green striped with white. Plant this one alone in a large pot (18 inches or wider), or combine it with mounding perennials and annuals.

Provide full sun or part shade. Let the soil dry out between watering. This is not a fussy plant.

Hardy to zone 8.

Norfolk Island pine (Araucaria heterophylla)

You may not know its name, but this is a popular and highly recognizable tree for containers. Unusual growth habit displays feathery foliage in horizontal tiers. Shape is slender and tall, up to 10 or 12 feet. Another outstanding quality: Norfolk Island pine can live indoors for the winter (it has to in cold climates) — or even all the time. Use it as a living Christmas tree.

Provide full sun or part shade. No special care is necessary.

Hardy to zone 9. This is not a true pine — it comes from the South Pacific.

Oleander

Tough and easy to grow — in California, it's a freeway plant — oleander is another one of those basic landscape plants that takes on a whole new personality in a container. Use it as a specimen in a big pot, or create a privacy screen with a row of plants in containers. Or oleander can be trained as a small tree. Summer flowers are white, pink, red, or yellow. Plants grow to 6 feet or more. Best choices for containers are dwarf varieties ("Petite" in the name is a good clue).

Provide full sun. You can keep soil on the dry side, but oleander can also take frequent watering. Give plant big enough container: at least 14 inches for best growth. Prune hard in spring to control size.

All parts of the oleander are poisonous.

Hardy to zone 8. Oleander can move indoors for the winter.

Palms

Indoors and outdoors, palms are proven winners as traditional potted plants. Actually, most kinds benefit from an arrangement that keeps them outdoors for the warm months (see Chapter 13) and indoors when frost threatens. In mildest climates, palms can live outdoors all the time. Palms make striking container plants for decks, patios, and doorways.

- ✔ Parlor palm (*Chamaedorea elegans*) is a classic. It grows just 3 or 4 feet tall, with a single trunk and feathery leaves. Fit three or four plants in one container to create a grove effect.

- ✔ Pygmy date palm (*Phoenix roebelenii*) reaches 6 feet — very slowly. It develops a single trunk and a dense, feathery-leafed top.

- ✔ Kentia palm (*Howea belmoreana*) is a bit taller, up to 7 feet, with a pretty, feathery look. Lady palm (*Rhapis excelsa*), reaches 10 or 12 feet. This is terrific indoor plant, tolerating low light. Slender stems grow in clusters like bamboo.

- ✔ Mediterranean fan palm (*Chamaerops humilis*) is one that takes a few degrees of frost. It's great in containers when young and small. Growth is clumpy, with fan-shaped leaves.

Outdoors, grow palms in part shade or even full shade, protected from wind, which can tatter fronds. Indoors, palms get along on average light conditions. Plant in a container just a bit larger than the nursery container. Keep the soil moist. Fertilize as often as once a month during growing season. Watch for spider mites (see Chapter 21). Hose off palms every few weeks to wash away dust and insects.

Pittosporum

Several kinds used as evergreen landscape plants also excel in containers. Not particularly showy, they're just solid-citizen types: with dense, shiny foliage that can be sheared into formal shapes. Use several to create a portable hedge or privacy screen. *P. tobira* Wheeler's Dwarf is very compact; Variegata has cream and light green foliage that lights up in shade. Cape pittosporum (*P. viridiflorum*) can make a multitrunk small tree in large container.

Provide full sun or part shade. No special care is needed.

Hardy to zone 8.

Pineapple guava (Feijoa)

This subtropical can produce edible green fruit while in a container and makes a handsome specimen plant for a patio or deck. Expect the plant to grow 5 or 6 feet tall; pruning keeps it more compact.

Provide full sun. A large container (14 inches and up) encourages best growth. Don't let the soil dry out.

Hardy to zone 8.

Podocarpus

Dependable and evergreen, podocarpus grows slowly and can live in a container for a long time. It's useful where you want something tall and slender — to block a view or accent a corner. Podocarpus lends itself to growing along an eave or training to grow flat against a support like a wall. Fern pine (*P. gracilior*) has thin gray-green leaves. Yew pine (*P. macrophyllus*) has broader, dark green leaves. Neither is a true pine.

Provide full sun or part shade.

Hardy to zone 8.

Pomegranate

An unlikely choice for a container, but pomegranate has much to offer. The orange-red flowers are pretty and the fruit is fun (and tasty). The full-sized variety can turn into a rambunctious handful (that means a tangled over-sized mess) in a container. Try Nana, a more compact type growing to 3 feet; flowers are abundant but fruit is small and not worth eating. Deciduous foliage has nice fall yellow color.

Provide full sun. Keep the soil on the dry side. Prune in spring by cutting back long shoots and removing tangled branches.

Hardy to zone 8. Pomegranate thrives in hot climates.

Privet (Ligustrum)

Grow this shrub or small tree when you want a dependable evergreen for a privacy screen. Or you can shear it into formal shapes. Flowers are insignificant. Japanese privet (*L. japonicum*) reaches 10 feet or more in the ground but can be kept to half that size in a container.

Provide full sun or part shade. Keep the soil on the moist side.

Hardy to zones 7 or 8.

Pyracantha

A great reason to grow pyracantha is to bring bright red berries into the fall and winter garden. Buy nursery plants with berries showing, and transplant them into containers. Best bets for containers are dwarf varieties like Red Elf or Tiny Tim — they grow to 3 feet. Taller types can be trained on a trellis or flat frame (espalier) in a container.

Provide full sun; plants grow fine in part shade but produce flowers and berries. Keep the soil on the dry side.

Hardy to zone 7.

Rose

There are thousands of roses, and theoretically you can grow all of them in containers. But some varieties are much better suited to container life than others.

If you want to grow a particular rose just because you like the flower (most likely, it's a Hybrid Tea type — that's what florists sell), feel free to go ahead. You can enjoy the nice flowers, but there may not be very many of them, the plant may not look that great, and it may quickly outgrow the container. We suggest the smaller, more compact roses growing from less than 2 to 5 feet — categorized as miniatures, polyanthas, floribundas, and some shrub roses. They have handsome growth habits, and their bloom season is long (spring through early fall) and prolific (especially the floribundas and polyanthas). Here are our favorites for containers:

- **Betty Prior:** pink floribunda
- **Bonica:** pink shrub
- **Brass Band:** apricot-yellow floribunda
- **Carefree Delight:** pink shrub

- **Carefree Wonder:** pink and white shrub
- **China Doll:** pink polyantha
- **Europeana:** red floribunda
- **Flower Carpet:** several colors, shrub
- **Iceberg:** white floribunda
- **Margaret Merrill:** white floribunda
- **Margo Koster:** coral floribunda
- **Regensberg:** white and pink floribunda
- **Sarabande:** orange-red floribunda
- **Sun Flare:** yellow floribunda
- **The Fairy:** pink polyantha
- **Watermelon Ice:** pink shrub

Provide full sun and typical soil mix (nothing special). Make sure that the container is big enough to encourage vigorous root growth. Give miniatures and other small roses at least a 12-inch diameter container. For larger varieties, use a 14-inch pot or a half barrel (especially if you combine a rose with annuals or perennial). Select containers that are at least 16 inches deep to provide room for roots. Make sure that the soil never dries out.

Rose hardiness depends on variety, and we also know that people sometimes go to extreme measures to create special conditions for roses. Best advice: Check locally for climate adaptability.

We all also know that much is involved in growing first-rate roses. That's why there are books on the subject. May we recommend *Roses For Dummies* by Lance Walheim (IDG Books Worldwide, Inc.), for advice on pruning, feeding, pest control, as well as choosing varieties?

Roses are great in containers. They're fun. Try one.

Sago palm (Cycas revoluta)

Botanists tell us that this is not a true palm. It may fool you, too. Whatever, it's a bold container plant, with slow-growing spiky fronds, arising from a central core, that take years to grow taller than 2 or 3 feet.

Provide part or full shade. Water and fertilize lightly.

Hardy to zones 9 or 10. Bring it indoors during cold weather.

Strawberry tree (Arbutus unedo)

This can make a handsome miniature tree or shrub in a container. It's evergreen, with attractive bark, small white flowers, and beautiful red berries (the "strawberry" in the name). Compact varieties like Compacta work best in containers: expect a maximum height of 5 or 6 feet.

Provide full sun or part shade. This plant can stay in a 12-inch container for a number of years.

Hardy to zone 8. This is a favorite West Coast landscape plant.

Sweet bay (Laurus nobilis)

A cook's dream: to have sweet bay in a container right outside the back door. This evergreen is the source of bay leaves used in the kitchen and wreaths for the home and head (in ancient Greece). This plant grows to 6 feet tall but can be sheared to stay smaller and more formal as cones, globes, and other shapes.

Provide full sun or part shade. The container needs to be 12 to 14 inches or larger.

Hardy to zone 8. In cold climates, bring indoors for the winter.

Sweet olive (Osmanthus fragrans)

This nondescript evergreen shrub shows the value of container planting: Keep it in the background most of the year and then move it near the front porch in fall when its barely noticeable flowers produce a truly delicious fragrance. This plant grows 5 or 6 feet tall, eventually much larger.

Provide full sun or part shade. No special care is needed. Prune to shape growth.

Hardy to zone 9.

Six Vines for Containers

Check out the vine section at most nurseries and you won't see many likely candidates for containers. Get those twining, tangled young plants out of your mind and instead picture a grown-up climber gracefully making its way up a trellis or wall. For colorful blooms or year-round greenery, the following vines all are well worth a try.

Bougainvillea

The sight of bougainvillea sprawling along a lush roadside in Hawaii or engulfing a building in Puerto Vallarta hardly suggests that the plant can thrive in a container. Actually, bougainvillea's a great choice — if you select the right variety and put it in the right place. It seems most perfectly at home in a terra-cotta pot near a swimming pool. The papery flowers have a tropical vividness in shades of red, orange, purple, white, and others. Look for dwarf varieties (La Jolla is a good one) for containers — they spill nicely over the sides. Trailing types (Crimson Jewel) are best for hanging baskets. Tall varieties can be tied up as a vine.

Provide full sun except in hottest climates. Keep the soil on the dry side; drainage must be perfect. When planting, take pains not to disturb roots at all. In spring, prune off any cold-damaged wood or crossing branches. During the growing season, prune off branches growing where you don't want them to go.

Hardy to zone 9 (some varieties are hardier than others). Yes, bougainvillea is tender and can be grown outdoors in only the mildest climates. But in cold places, you can grow it as a summer-only container plant, and bring it indoors for the winter; give it your sunniest spot near a window.

Clematis

Fortunately, the most spectacular clematis are also the best suited to containers. These are the deciduous hybrids with the beautiful and huge six-petaled flowers in blue, purple, red, and many other shades. The vines can climb as high as 20 feet. Use one in a container with a trellis or train the vine up and over an entryway. Choose from many varieties at your local nursery or in mail-order catalogs.

Provide full sun or part shade. Conventional wisdom says to put the container in shade and the uppermost growth in sun if you can find such a location; the idea is to keep the roots cool and the flower buds exposed to light. Roots need room; make sure that the container's at least 16 inches deep. The soil mix must drain quickly; don't let it dry out. For top flower production, proper pruning is critical and depends on variety; consult with local experts.

Hardy to zone 5. You need to move clematis into a protected spot for the winter.

English ivy (Hedera helix)

It's easy to train and, in a container, easy to bring indoors. Let English ivy drape from a hanging basket filled with shade-loving annual flowers. Train it into topiary shapes. Use it in a container where it can climb up a trellis or wall, like in an entry or on a patio. Choose from among hundreds of varieties: with different shaped leaves, small leaves, variegated leaves, and so on.

Provide part or full shade, or even full sun in cool climates. Keep the soil moist. Pinch young plants to encourage bushy growth.

Hardy to zone 6. Bring plants indoors during the winter in cold regions.

Mandevilla

You can find this tropical vine sold almost everywhere during the warm months. Buy it in bloom, move it into a 12-inch-wide container or hanging basket, and enjoy it for the summer. Flowers of *Mandevilla amabilis* Alice du Pont are big pink trumpets, up to 4 inches wide.

Provide full sun or part shade. Keep the soil moist. Feed at least monthly.

Hardy to zone 10. Frost kills the plant. Try bringing it indoors and growing it in a sunny window for the winter.

Star jasmine (Trachelospermum jasminoides)

With its glossy evergreen foliage and wonderfully sweet white flowers in summer, star jasmine deserves a spot in any garden where it can grow. One of California's widely used landscape plants, it can be a ground cover or vigorous vine. In a container, train star jasmine up a trellis or espalier and tie it to a nearby wall — wherever you can appreciate the fragrance.

Provide full sun or part shade in hot climates. Keep the soil moist for best growth, although plants can withstand dry conditions. Pinch branch tips of young plants to encourage bushy growth. Shear older plants after bloom to shape growth. This plant is easy to grow.

Hardy to zone 8. Star jasmine can move indoors for the winter in colder climates.

Wisteria

Hard to imagine this awesomely vigorous vine in a container, but try it at least for a few years. Train it on a trellis or frame, or prune it into a small single-trunk tree over a number of years. The main attraction, of course, are the long clusters of blue, pink, purple, or white blossoms.

Provide full sun. Training a wisteria in a container is probably not a candidate for your first gardening project.

Hardy to zones 5 or 6.

Chapter 10
Vegetables and Herbs

In This Chapter

▶ The taste pleasures of vegetables in containers

▶ Vegetable needs

▶ Eligible herbs for container gardening

Deep red, vine-ripened tomatoes marinate in olive oil with garlic and fresh basil, and the lettuce in the salad bowl is practically still growing — all harvests from your patio. You have to be kidding! Achieving this vision isn't as daunting a task as you may expect. Growing vegetables in containers — for a patio, deck, balcony, or even out in the garden — is not that difficult. And the tasty payoff makes mobile vegetable farming even more rewarding.

With some care and a lot of sun, you can be eating your own container-grown produce all summer long. Apartment dwellers and homeowners alike find container vegetables appealing. First, the convenience is tough to match: Just walk out on the deck and snip some lettuce for a salad or swipe a few peas for a stir-fry. And second, the flexibility yields some fresh ideas: Combining ornamentals and edibles in the garden is a popular design concept these days. You can even move containers from deck to garden and back. With vegetables in containers, you truly can have a movable feast.

And don't overlook herbs for containers. Usually less demanding than vegetables, many perennial culinary herbs are of Mediterranean origin and like it on the hot and dry side. Brush by a pot of thyme, rosemary, or sage on the way to the door and you may imagine you're in the south of France.

What Container Vegetables and Herbs Really Need

If you grow vegetables in the ground, you know that the No. 1 rule is to keep them racing along — with plenty of water, fertilizer, sunlight, and whatever else the specific crops require. Vegetables and herbs in containers are no different. In fact, providing the essentials to vegetables and herbs growing in containers can be more challenging because their growing space is limited. To ease the caretaking task, container plants can grow right outside your back door where you can dote on them. When you know what it needs, your portable garden is likely to reward your attention with tasty returns!

The right container

First question: Are you growing vegetables and herbs for show or just production? If all you want is to pick the produce and you don't care what the container looks like, requirements are pretty basic.

The container must be big enough. A minimum size for most vegetables and herbs is a diameter of 8 inches and depth of 12 inches, but a diameter of 12 to 18 inches and a depth of 15 inches is preferable — the larger size can accommodate the necessary volume of soil and water. And the container must have drain holes at the bottom. Vegetables and herbs can be found thriving in all sorts of containers that meet the size and drainage requirements, but that miss the boat in beauty: leaky buckets, garbage cans with holes, large plastic buckets from delicatessens, and even plastic milk jugs.

If the containers are going to be part of your garden scene, you probably want something more presentable (but with the recommended size and drain holes). Remember that terra-cotta, no matter how attractive, tends to dry out quickly — a major problem for vegetables and herbs racing full steam ahead. You may be better off planting in plastic. If you want a big container to hold a number of vegetables and herbs or a whole salad's fixings, an oak half-barrel is hard to beat.

Soil mix

Commercial soil mixes, as described in Chapter 4, can be used straight from the bag. But many vegetables and herbs benefit from additional organic matter like bagged compost or ground bark: Add one part of organic matter to each three parts of soil mix.

Fertilizer

In general, vegetables and herbs are heavy feeders — especially when grown in containers. Nutrient needs vary according to what you're growing. Lettuce and other leafy crops need nitrogen to produce those leaves, whereas tomatoes need some nitrogen to grow, but too much can inhibit flowering — no flowers, no tomatoes.

As a general rule, add an all-purpose dry fertilizer — organic or chemical — according to package directions when you plant. Organic fertilizers release their nutrients slowly; chemical fertilizers release all their nutrients at once, unless you pay a lot more and get the slow-release kind.

As container crops are growing, fertilize regularly, following label directions, and the suggestions for different crops discussed later in this chapter. Most people prefer to use a soluble fertilizer applied as you water. Some gardeners swear by fish emulsion — smelly for a while but not likely to burn or overfeed.

Water, water, water

Watering is always important with container plants, even more so with vegetables and herbs — let them wilt once and they may never really get back on track. Containers can dry out in a day or in a few hours depending on the planter's size and intensity of the summer heat; rewetting a dry pot may seem impossible. To avoid the problem, check pots and planters often and do not allow the soil to dry out more than an inch or two below the surface.

Experienced tomato growers know that if watering is not consistently maintained, tomato plants are unable to take up calcium, a much-needed nutrient. The result is tomatoes with a dark, leathery spot on the blossom end (the bottom). The tell-tale coloration doesn't signal a disease, and there's no magic spray to fix it, so pay attention.

Sunlight

Along with watering, sunshine is the other limiting factor in vegetable and herb gardening anywhere. Most vegetables need an minimum of six hours of direct sunlight — that is, sun on the plant, not somewhere nearby. Exceptions are lettuce and spinach, which actually benefit from some shade in the heat of midsummer to keep them from *bolting* — sending up flower heads that end your salad-picking days.

Favorite Vegetables for Containers

Theoretically, you can grow just about any vegetable in a container. Questions do come up, though, about the appropriate pot for those 600-pound pumpkins — maybe the right container is the back of the pickup that hauls the monster to the county contest weigh-in. We suggest that you grow crops that can provide you with at least a few fresh meals and that don't monopolize your whole patio or life.

Try to choose container-friendly varieties, vegetables that are naturally limited in size or that are the results of breeding specifically for potting (lots of vegetables are bred for small spaces, including containers).When you read seed catalogs, look for varieties described with words like these:

- Compact
- Good for containers
- Bush-type
- Baby vegetable
- Midget
- Dwarf
- Tiny
- Teeny-tiny
- Teeny-weeny-tiny

You want to avoid varieties with names like these:

- Jumbo
- Gargantua
- Mammoth
- The Whopper
- Big Bertha
- Big Bopper
- Shaquille

The following vegetables are great choices for moderate-size containers, from 8 to 18 inches in diameter. Plan to plant when you put out ground-grown vegetables in your area. Start with seeds or nursery transplants, and follow the recommendations for spacing provided on seed packets and in vegetable guides.

Beans

Bush varieties like Kentucky Wonder Bush, Jade, and Royal Burgundy stay compact, have high yields, and mature all at once, usually earlier than pole beans. Despite their leggy style, pole varieties such as the standard Blue Lake can do fine in pots as long as you provide stakes or taut strings for them to run up; the effect can be attractive, especially for a balcony. Pick pole beans continually or they stop blooming. Plant bean seeds in spring when it finally gets really warm in your part of the country — as late May in some areas. After seeds sprout, thin seedlings so that they stand 6 inches apart.

Beets

Beets offer a two-for-one treat: You can eat the tops as well as the roots. Plant seeds in early spring or fall in mild-winter climates. For containers, choose smaller varieties like Action or Kestrel.

Cabbage and kinfolk

The Brassicas include broccoli, cabbage, cauliflower, and kale: All need similar care and cool weather. Plant nursery seedlings in early spring or fall in mild-winter climates. Broccoli and kale require less fertilizer than cauliflower and cabbage. Cabbages can grow 10-pound heads — how much coleslaw can you eat? You may want to try the mini-cabbage Dynamo, an All-America winner.

Carrots

Carrots need a light soil mix (plenty of sand) to form the roots that we all like to munch. But, do you want to grow a 9-inch-long carrot in an 8-inch deep pot? Think about it. With containers only 8 inches deep, the stubby types like Planet make more sense. Thumbelina is the taste-test queen. Also, give Minicor or Partima a chance to prove themselves.

Corn

Surely not! But yes, a few scaled-down varieties of corn can be grown in deep containers — as long as you don't demand something as high as an elephant's eye. Provide soil mix with lots of organic matter and a deep, large container like a half-barrel (up to 20 seeds planted per barrel). Plan on watering abundantly. Sow seeds in spring when weather warms up. Choose from shorter varieties such as Sugar Buns and Quickie (both extra sweet); popcorn Tom Thumb; and ornamental Wampum or Little Jewels.

Cucumbers

If you choose a vining type of cucumber, like Marketmore or Sweet Success, provide space and a trellis for climbing. Or go with a bushy type: Fanfare or Salad Bush, for example. Cucumbers need hot weather. Sow seeds in spring after the weather warms up.

Eggplant

Warm, rich soil mix and hot sun are the ingredients for successful eggplants. Try Bambino or the eloquently named No. 226. Plant nursery seedlings, one to a pot, after weather warms up in spring.

Lettuce

Reward yourself with green salad early in the year. Lettuce grows quickly, can be planted in cool, spring weather, and harvested within four weeks. Plant seeds or seedlings every few weeks for a constant supply; keep summer plantings in a partly shaded spot. Leaf lettuces (Slobolt, Red Sails, Oak Leaf, Salad Bowl, to name a few) can be harvested the earliest by cutting leaves rather than cutting the whole plant. (Crops that are continually harvested need fertilizing every couple of weeks with a weak solution that's heavy on the nitrogen.) Leaf lettuces can also be cut down whole; if watered and fertilized, they resprout from the base.

Buttercrunch and Tom Thumb are butterhead lettuces: They make small, loose heads that stand up well to hot weather. For gourmet gardeners, mesclun is a mix of greens that are sown together and harvested small; the blend contains interesting textures and flavors, including some hot greens.

Onions

Scallions, green onions, bunching onions — call them what you may, but try to plant some every couple of weeks from early spring to fall for a constant kitchen supply. Don't be concerned about what type; buy a bag of onion sets at the garden store and plant 2 to 3 inches deep.

Peas

Pick from peas for shelling — Maestro, Lincoln, and many others; peas for pea pods like Oregon Sugar Pod II; and snap peas such as Sugar Snap and Sugar Ann. Some are climbers and need support; others are bush types and can, thankfully, be left alone. Plan to sow any variety by April 1 in most climates; fall is a good time to plant in mild-winter areas.

Peppers

Nearly all peppers, even the sweet ones, are a hot item in the garden, and just the right size for containers. Set plants out when the weather turns warm for the season. Colorful sweet peppers include Early Cal Wonder, Northstar, and Jingle Bells. The following are a few hot peppers rated for their temperature, from mild to steam-coming-out-your-ears: Anaheim, Surefire, Riota (particularly good choice for a container), and Habanero.

Potatoes

In March, take a big, plastic trash can (really), poke holes in the bottom and sides, put 10 inches of soil mix in the bottom, then plant potato eyes (hunks of potatoes with growth buds) 1 or 2 inches deep. When the plants sprout, layer straw around the stems to cover all but the top leaves. Continue to fill in with straw as leaves grow taller, water well, and you can expect a can-full of spuds by summer harvest. We're not saying that a trash receptacle is the most attractive container around, but it's certainly a conversation piece and fun for kids. Choose from potato varieties offered at your garden center in the spring or order from a catalog.

Radish

Radishes provide an easy salad ingredient that can be ready to eat just three weeks after the seeds sprout. Go with round types like Easter Egg because they're shallow-rooted.

Spinach

Spinach comes in several main types: smooth-leafed varieties like Mazurka, Olympia, and Hector; crinkle-leafed savoy types such as Bloomsdale Savoy; and the semi-savoyed types like Tyee and Italian Summer. Each variety produces delicious greens for salads or light steaming. Many varieties, such as Tyee, overwinter well in milder climates.

Squash

Summer squash plants can be bullies, taking over the garden. Even varieties described as compact, such as Spacemiser or yellow Gold Rush, can fill a half barrel — one plant is enough. Trade your squash plantings with gardener friends. You can wind up with a much more colorful pot of ratatouille. Plant seeds or nursery transplants in spring after the weather has warmed up.

Swiss chard

Easy to grow, but watch the size — no more than three plants, even for a large container. Plant in early spring. Good bets for containers are Fordhook Giant and Rhubarb (with red stems).

Tomatoes

You have to try at least one tomato in a container just for the fun of observing it up close. And even if you get only a few fresh tomatoes fruits, you're assured that they taste better than those pink, mealy objects found in grocery stores most of the year. Tomato plants are classified as either determinate (those that grow to a point and stop) or indeterminate (those that have yearnings to take over your entire living space). Either type needs some sort of support — cage, trellis, or stake and twine.

Delicious and prolific cherry tomatoes include Sweet Million and Yellow Pear (both indeterminate), and Sun Gold (determinate). Some cherries (Patio or Micro-Tom) are small enough for a hanging basket. Determinates that slice up well include Oregon Spring, Celebrity, and Santiam. Indeterminate slicers are Stupice, Big Beef, and Early Cascade.

Tomatoes need a deep container. Plant nursery seedlings in spring after weather has warmed up. Bury the seedlings past the bottom sets of leaves (after removing the leaves); the stem develops roots along the buried part. Plan on conscientious watering and fertilizing.

Herbs in Containers

Herbs make perfect sense for containers. Most of them look good as they grow. And you want them handy to the kitchen or patio. Who's in favor of jogging out past the pumphouse to the back 40 when you desperately need rosemary for the chicken you're barbecuing on your back patio?

Most herbs are easy to grow. Commercial soil mix is fine. Many herbs prefer conditions on the dry side because they are used to spartan conditions in nature. Regular feeding once or twice a month can be a big help.

Planting herbs is pretty simple: Space out seedlings in your container and fill the the gaps with soil, as shown in Figure 10-1.

Figure 10-1:
Planting
herbs
couldn't be
easier.

Here's a selection of herbs to tuck into almost any pot in full sun:

Basil

Basil is an annual that needs hot weather to grow. Plant seed or transplants when you're sure that the overnight temperature is not below 50°F, and expect to be rewarded with fast-growing plants and lots of pesto by summer. Fertilize moderately with nitrogen. Many types are available (cinnamon, Thai, lemon, globe); all do well in pots.

Chives

Growing from bulbs, this onion-family member begins growth in early spring and is hardy to zone 3. Snip and use the leaves. Keep plants outside (dormant) over the winter or bring them inside, place in a sunny window, and continue to snip and use. During the growing season, cut down plant completely once or twice and fertilize with nitrogen. Chive blossoms are edible, and the lavender color gives a nice tint to herb vinegars.

Oregano

This herb is easy to grow in pots, although it still develops long, lanky branches; don't be afraid to cut them back. Use the leaves fresh or dried.

Parsley

Choose between curly-leafed and flat-leafed (sometimes called Italian) — both pretty, bright green plants. Parsley is biennial, growing one year, and then flowering and setting seed the next. Sow seeds every spring (even though sprouting is slow) or start with nursery transplants. Parsley has a long taproot, so be sure to use a container at least 12 inches deep. Part shade is best.

Rosemary

A shrub in its native habitat, rosemary requires a large container with a well-drained soil mix (even a cactus mix) and hot sun. Rosemary is not reliably hardy below zone 8, but small plants may overwinter indoors with bright sunlight.

Sage

More cold-hardy than rosemary, sage can survive outside to zone 4. Sage is available in many varieties: tricolor, purple, golden, and dwarf — a good bet for a container.

Savory

With a strong peppery aroma, winter savory is a wonderful addition to a pot of beans. It's hardy to zone 6. Summer savory is an annual with a more delicate aroma.

Tarragon

An ungainly plant, tarragon belongs in a pot with more orderly herbs (such as sage). It's hardy to zone 4.

Thyme

Varieties abound, but don't pass up common thyme for any kind of cooking. Hardy to zone 5, thyme likes dry conditions and lots of sun. Special culinary thymes include lemon and silver.

Chapter 11

Fruits and Berries

In This Chapter

▶ Fruits and berries: The facts of life

▶ Characteristics of winning candidates for containers

▶ Your fruit-producers' needs

▶ Plants to pick from

*F*ace it, growing fruit-producing plants is one of the trickier forms of gardening — even more so when you want to grow the plants in containers. You need to become conversant about such things as rootstocks, pollination, and climate adaptation. You may need to prune and thin. We're going to get to all those details, but first, the good news:

Growing your own fruit is tremendously rewarding. Nothing, and we mean nothing, tastes better than homegrown fruit harvested at peak ripeness. And fruiting plants can also be quite good-looking — many have colorful fragrant flowers, attractive foliage, and, of course, beautiful fruit.

Many types of fruits and berries adapt nicely to growing in containers. But you must choose varieties wisely and understand some quirks about fruit growing that really don't occur with other types of plants.

There are advantages to growing fruit in containers, as well. Most noteworthy is the mobility that containers provide. If frost threatens, you can move your fruit trees under cover for protection.

Growing fruits and berries in containers may take a little more labor than the attention required by other types of plants, but the payoffs are big.

A Bowl of Fruit Facts

Before you can set off on your growing adventure, you need to pack in a few fruit-gardening terms and concepts that come up again and again in this chapter. You notice that we concentrate on deciduous fruit trees (apples, peaches, and so on). They are the most complex and also the most rewarding.

Pollination

You must remember from Sex Education 101 all about the pollen moving from the male part of the flower to the female part, fertilizing it, and causing a fruit to grow. Do you need a picture? Some fruit trees, like peaches, have flowers that produce both suitable male and female flower parts on the same plant, and pollenize themselves — this kind of plant is called self-fruitful. You can grow one peach tree, or other self-fruitful plant, by itself and it produces fruit. Other fruit trees, including some apples and blueberries, must be cross-pollenized, which means that they need pollen from another variety of the same or closely related species to produce fruit. If you grow one blueberry plant by itself, don't count on getting any fruit. Add another variety nearby, or even in the same pot, and bingo — blueberries galore. To complicate matters even more, you sometimes need a specific variety (usually one that blooms at the same time) to properly cross-pollenize a certain fruit.

So now that you know about pollenizers, what about pollinators? Pollinators carry pollen from flower to flower, or even from one part of a flower to a another part. Pollinators are usually bees, flies, or other insects, and you probably have plenty of those in your garden. We just want to make sure that you can keep all the words straight. By the way, pollen can also sometimes move around in the wind.

Rootstocks and dwarfs

Most fruit trees have two parts, the *rootstock* and the *scion*. The rootstock is the rooting, mostly below-ground portion of the plant. The scion is the above-ground, fruiting part of the plant. Why are there two parts? We figured you'd ask. In simple terms, when nurseries grow fruit trees, they bud or graft (methods of fusing or joining two closely related plants) the scion variety onto the rootstock to take advantage of the best attributes of each plant. Obviously, the scion produces great tasting fruit — that's a considerable attribute. But a good rootstock, and there are many, can contribute qualities like adaptation to specific soil types, hardiness, or size control. Size control? Yes, size control. And that's why we brought up this whole rootstock-scion business in the first place.

If grown on their own roots, most fruit trees get huge — way too big to grow in containers. But if grown on rootstocks that keep them smaller, called *dwarfing rootstocks,* these same fruit trees become ideal for containers. Apples perfectly demonstrate the value of dwarfing rootstocks. A normal apple tree can grow up to 40 feet high. But the same variety grown on one of several dwarf apple rootstocks can be reduced in size by over 75 percent. (Some nurseries sell fruit trees as semidwarfs, which are usually on rootstocks that dwarf the trees about 25 to 50 percent, but eventual size can vary by the type of tree.)

Every type of fruit is not available as a dwarfing rootstock. But luckily, another type of elfish fruit tree exists — a genetic dwarf. The genetic dwarf fruit tree's scion or fruiting part is naturally smaller. For example, a standard (normal size) peach tree may reach 25 feet high. A genetic dwarf peach rarely gets over 6 feet high — perfect for containers. The number of genetic dwarf fruit trees is limited, and their fruit is not always as good as standard varieties', but they're still a great choice for containers. One advantage of using dwarf rootstocks rather than genetic dwarfs scions is that you can put any tree variety on a dwarf rootstock. Genetic dwarfs are restricted to only those varieties that come that way.

One more point before we leave rootstocks and dwarfs: The point at which a scion joins the rootstock is called the *graft union* or *bud union.* The graft union (that's what we call it) is usually the swollen or curved part of the trunk a few inches above the soil level. Below the graft union is the root-stock; above is the scion.

Fruit thinning

Some fruit trees (but not berries) produce so much fruit that, if you don't remove some, you end up with nothing but small fruit at harvest time. Removing fruit before they reach maturity is called thinning. Apples, peaches, nectarines, and plums all have to be thinned by hand or fruit turns out small. The best time to thin is in early spring when the fruit is about the size of a dime to a quarter. Simply pinch off the small fruit so that you have one per cluster and about 6 to 8 inches between fruit. Thinning can be a bit painful, especially with genetic dwarf trees where you may have to remove more than 75 percent of the young fruit to achieve the proper spacing. But if you don't do it, you later regret your restraint.

What to Grow in Containers?

What are the characteristics that make one fruit better than another for growing in containers?

Small size

Beyond the characteristics of drawf fruit trees, some fruiting plants are just smaller than others and, consequently, make better container subjects. Strawberries, for example, grow on little tiny, clumpy plants that are perfect for pots. Even within fruit types, some varieties can be better for containers than others. Meyer lemons, for instance, are compact plants that easily stay below 6 feet in a large container. Eureka lemons, on the other hand, get huge — upward of 20 feet — not a good container choice. You can keep some fruit trees smaller with vigorous pruning, but the roots still eventually outgrow the container — in which case, you may want to try root pruning.

Climate adaptation

Not all fruits can be grown everywhere. Fruit trees have varying degrees of hardiness to winter cold temperatures. Many also need a certain amount of winter cold (called chilling hours) before they bloom and set fruit; types that set fruit in mild winters are called low-chill. Some, like peaches, grow best where summers are hot and dry. Other, like raspberries, prefer cool summers. Remarkable differences in adaptation even exist between different varieties of the same fruit type. The point is, if you want to grow quality fruit, select types and varieties that are well-adapted to your area. To find out for sure, ask your local nursery person or cooperative extension agent.

Easy maintenance

We won't lie to you about this. Many fruit trees take more work than other types of plants, fruiting or not. Some have serious pest problems that require frequent control measures, many need annual pruning to remain productive, and some fruits must be hand-thinned or else they won't reach acceptable size. So ease of care is an important consideration when deciding which fruit to grow. If you really want to be a good fruit grower, you probably need more information than we provide here. Again, we suggest that you get well-acquainted with your local extension agent or nursery.

Soil, Pot Size, Planting, and All That

Most good potting soils work fine for growing fruit and berries. Blueberries are an exception; they require a very acidic soil, which can be created by mixing any good potting mix with 50 percent peat moss.

In general, the bigger the container the better, as demonstrated in Figure 11-1. For most fruit you need at least a 15-gallon size container. Half barrels work well. Strawberries and some dwarf blueberries can be grown in smaller pots.

Figure 11-1:
When it comes to fruit, the bigger the pot, the better.

Fruit and berries can be purchased bare-root (without any soil around their roots) during the dormant season or already growing in containers at other times of year. Planting techniques are covered in Chapter 5.

Fruits and berries need full sun and regular water and fertilizer. Skimp on any of that, and you have reduced yields and fruit quality. Any specific cultural requirements are included in the fruit descriptions that follow.

Pruning techniques vary for each type of fruit. And to get the full scoop, you have to get a good book on growing fruit. However, there are some basic techniques that apply to most types:

- ✔ Remove criss-crossing, diseased, or dead branches.
- ✔ Keep the center of the plant open for light penetration and air circulation.
- ✔ Keep branches evenly spaced throughout the plant.
- ✔ Remove old or unproductive branches. Replace them with new ones.
- ✔ In general, prune peaches and nectarines more severely than other fruit trees.

Fruit and Berries for Containers

With persistence and constant care almost any fruit or berry can be grown in a container, but some are much easier than others. We describe the less-demanding possibilities here.

Apples

Most apple varieties are available grown on a nice selection of dwarfing rootstocks that allow you to choose almost any size tree. The rootstocks are usually labeled Mark, EMLA, or MM plus a number. One of many good rootstocks for containers is EMLA 27, which usually gives you a 5- to 7-foot-high tree. Your best selection of apples varieties grown on dwarfing rootstocks come from one of the mail-order catalogs listed in the appendix. Some genetic dwarfs are also available (sometimes called spur varieties, like spur Gold Delicious) which are smaller than standard varieties. Colonnade apples, sold by Stark Bros. Nursery (see the Appendix for an address), grow just 8 feet high and 2 feet wide, perfect for containers.

Growing tips

Most apples need cross-pollination to produce a good crop, so you may need to plant more than one variety. Trees need regular pruning to remain productive. Fruit must be thinned if you want large apples.

Adaptation

If you choose the right varieties, apples can be grown almost anywhere temperatures don't fall below –20°F. Varieties like Red Astrachan, Haralson, and Honeycrisp are particularly hardy. In mild-winter areas, choose low-chill varieties like Anna and Dorsett Golden.

Apricots

Apricot trees generally get too big (about 15 feet) to grow in containers for any prolonged period. Some catalogs sell varieties on dwarfing rootstocks, which may reduce their size by 25 to 50 percent. The smaller trees are the best choice for containers.

Growing tips

Some varieties need cross-pollination to produce fruit, others are self-fruitful. Trees require annual pruning to remain healthy and fruitful. Fruit must be thinned to reach full size.

Adaptation

Apricots have a rather limited range of adaptation, preferring areas with long, dry summers. In other areas, they're prone to disease. Trees also bloom very early, making the blossom subject to frost damage. In areas where apricots don't grow well, try Flavor Delight aprium, a plum-apricot hybrid with wider adaptation and apricot-like flavor. For pollination, plant nearby a Flavor Supreme pluot, a similar hybrid with fruit more like a plum — say it *plew-ott.*

Blackberries

Most blackberries are too vigorous, thorny, and rangy to grow in containers easily. They really need more room and a trellis to do the job right. But there are a few varieties of thornless blackberries, like Arapaho and Navaho, that are easier to handle and can be grown without a trellis in a large container.

Growing tips

Plant three to five plants in a half barrel or similar size container. Let the canes grow about 4 feet tall during the first summer; then pinch the tips to force lateral branches. The following spring, pinch the laterals back to 2 feet long; fruit appears soon after. The following winter remove the canes that have borne fruit and repeat the process with the new canes that grow from the base of the old ones.

Adaptation

Blackberries are one of the more widely adapted berries, growing well almost anywhere they're planted.

Blueberries

Blueberries adapt well to growing in containers as long as you give them the acidic soil they require. The plants are very attractive with pretty spring flowers and handsome foliage that turns bright red before dropping in fall.

Growing tips

Create an acid soil by mixing any standard potting soil with at least 50 percent by volume peat moss. Plant at least two different varieties to ensure cross-pollination (you can plant three in one large container). Mix early-, mid-, and late-season varieties for a long harvest season. Prune regularly to renew fruiting wood. In hot summer areas, grow in part shade. Don't let plants dry out. Fertilize with an acidic plant food like those formulated for azaleas and rhododendrons.

Adaptation

Most blueberries prefer cool-summer areas with cold winters, but different types demonstrate varying adaptation. Lowbush blueberries reach about 2 feet high and are grown mostly in northern climates. Hybrid blueberries like North Country and Northsky are very hardy and grow only 18 to 24 inches high. They can be grown in smaller pots. Highbush blueberries are the familiar supermarket type. They reach up to 6 feet high and only develop high quality berries in cool-summer areas. Rabbiteye blueberries grow better in hot summer climates, like the southeastern United States.

Citrus

Where winter temperatures don't fall much below 26°F, many varieties of citrus make excellent container plants year-round. In other areas, trees can be brought indoors (only a well-lit, cool spot with ample light and humidity can keep the tree healthy) or into greenhouses for protection during winter. Plants have deep green, evergreen foliage, fragrant spring flowers and very colorful fruit — all in all, combining to make very handsome container subjects.

Some of the naturally smaller citrus that can thrive in containers for years include Meyer lemon, Bearss lime, and the hardier Nagami kumquat and Satsuma mandarin. Otherwise, grow just about any variety grafted on Flying Dragon dwarf rootstock for the perfect 6- to 8-foot-high container tree.

Growing tips

Most varieties are self-fruitful and do not need to be pruned to remain productive. Feed with fertilizers that contain zinc, iron, and manganese to avoid micronutrient deficiencies (see Chapter 19 for more information).

Adaptation

Varieties vary by cold hardiness and the amount of summer heat that they need to ripen fruit. In very cool summer areas, grow acidic fruit like lemons and limes.

Cherries

Normally quite large trees (upwards of 35 feet), most sweet cherries are not well-adapted to growing in containers. Dwarfing rootstocks, like Giessen, result in a tree half the size — still pretty large to stay in a container for very long.

Growing tips

Most varieties must be matched carefully with another to ensure cross-pollination. Some, like Stella, are self-fruitful. Prune annually to keep trees healthy and productive.

Adaptation

Local variety adaptation is very important. Cherries are best grown in areas with mild, dry summers. In other areas diseases can run rampant.

Figs

With beautiful, large, lobed, tropical-looking leaves, figs are really eye-catching in containers. Although they're normally quite large trees (up to 40 feet high), severe pruning can keep them more pot-size — and they still bear fruit. Figs are only hardy to about 15°F, but they can be brought into a cool garage to get them through cold winters.

Growing tips

Figs are pretty much carefree — just keep plants watered, fertilized, and if necessary, protected in winter.

Adaptation

Other than sensitivity to cold temperatures, figs are widely adapted.

Peaches and nectarines

Peaches and nectarines are closely related plants. In fact, a nectarine is just a fuzzless peach.

Both types of fruit are available in genetic dwarf varieties like Honey Babe and Eldorado peaches, and the nectarine, Nectar Babe. All are perfectly suited to container growing. They're attractive trees with a compact, muscular-looking habit that reaches about 4 to 6 feet high in a container.

Growing tips

Prune the trees annually to keep the center open. Thin heavily to ensure large fruit at harvest time. Genetic dwarf peaches and nectarines are self-fruitful.

Adaptation

Peaches and nectarines are best adapted to areas with hot dry summers. They can be grown in other areas, but diseases are more troublesome.

Pears

Pears are available on dwarfing rootstocks, but the result is still a tree that can reach 10 to 15 feet high, pretty big for all but the biggest container. However, pears are quite attractive trees with glossy foliage, nice fall color, and white spring flowers — they may be worth a try.

Growing tips

Fruit thinning is usually not necessary. Some varieties need cross-pollination. Otherwise, pears are pretty easy to care for.

Adaptation

European varieties like Bartlett, Bosc, and Comice are best adapted to dry summer areas that have fairly cold winters. Hybrid pears, like Kieffer often have lower chilling requirements. Asian pears, which are hard like an apple (they're often called pear apples), are widely adapted.

Plums

Plums are generally too large to remain healthy in anything but the largest container for more than a few years. There are some varieties available on dwarfing rootstocks, but even these can get over 10 feet high.

Growing tips

Prune regularly to keep healthy and productive. Thin to maintain fruit size. Japanese plums, the supermarket types, require another variety nearby for cross-pollination. European plums, or prunes, are self-fruitful.

Adaptation

Widely adapted but subject to diseases in areas with warm, wet summers. Japanese plums bloom early and are subject to frost damage.

Raspberries

Unlike their close cousins the blackberries, raspberries can be grown relatively easily in containers if you choose the right varieties and handle them properly — if you live in the right area. Start by planting everbearing varieties like Heritage, September, or Indian Summer, all of which normally produce two crops when grown in the ground (one in early summer and one in fall). Let them produce a crop in summer; then cut them all the way to the ground in late fall or winter (if they're growing in the ground, you only need to cut them halfway back). The new growth that emerges the following spring produces again in summer. Then you whack it back again. Growing raspberries like this sacrifices one crop, but it keeps the plants within bounds without a trellis and prolongs a summer harvest.

Growing tips

Raspberries are self-fruitful and do not require fruit thinning. Plant three to five plants per half barrel or similar size container.

Adaptation

Raspberries grow best where summers are relatively cool and winters are cold. Bababerry is one variety that grows better in mild winter, hot summer areas.

Strawberries

Few edible plants are as well-adapted to container life as strawberries. Their neat, compact habit fits perfectly even into small containers. They can also be grown in hanging baskets and even have a pot named after them — see Chapter 17 for information about planting a strawberry jar. In larger containers, like a half barrel, you can put in enough strawberry plants to provide a pretty substantial harvest — a large raised bed of strawberries can feed the neighborhood. And the plants are really attractive — dark green, lobed leaves, lovely white flowers, and pure poetry in the way the fruit dangles over the edge of a pot.

Growing tips

You can start with bare-root plants in winter or plant from six-packs any time. Strawberries are self-fruitful and the fruit does not need to be thinned. However, if you pinch off the first flowers that form on newly planted strawberries, the plants have a better chance to get established and give you more fruit later. Strawberry plants reproduce themselves by sending out new plants (babies) at the end of runners (stringlike arms); wherever the runners land, they set roots and grow. If you let all the babies take hold, your container becomes overcrowded and starts to decline in production. So thin out the plants occasionally, removing the oldest ones. Strawberry plants begin producing poorly when they're about 3 years old; plan to get rid of the plant then. You can clip off the runners and replant the babies, or purchase new plants and start over.

There are two types of strawberries. June-bearing varieties produce one big crop in late spring or early summer. Everbearing varieties produce a more prolonged harvest over the entire summer — you don't get as much fruit all at once, but you get fruit for a longer period. Either works in containers.

Adaptation

Strawberries can be grown almost anywhere as long as you choose locally adapted varieties, and there are many of those. Check with your local nursery for the best varieties of your area. Everbearing varieties can be grown as annuals; plant in early spring for a late summer harvest.

And just a few more

Many other, less common fruiting plants can be grown in containers. In mild winter areas, you may want to try tropical plants, bananas, guavas, or slightly hardier plants like pomegranate, loquat, and pineapple guava (Feijoa). In colder areas, experiment with currants and gooseberries.

Chapter 12
Cactus and Succulents

· ·

In This Chapter

▶ Sizing up the succulent family

▶ Finding your plant's place in the sun

▶ Picking a suitable container home

▶ Tending to long-term needs

▶ Picking your prickly friends wisely

· ·

*T*here's nothing more pleasing than a pot full of cactus to remind us of dry, warm places where we want to be — unless it's a margarita, but see how long that lasts on a sunny patio. Cactus and succulents (we're lumping them together here) have many other virtues when grown in containers. Here are a few:

✔ Cactus and succulents offer advantages to gardeners who may not have all the time in the world. They usually require far less maintenance than, say, a pot of pansies.

✔ They offer surprising contrasts in the garden or on the patio — instead of flower color, we're talking about shapes that range from bulbous to stringy, and textures from smooth to spiny to hairy.

✔ Most cactus and succulents grow slowly, and that means less time repotting plants that outgrow their containers. Of course, slow growth may also mean waiting a few years (how about 30?) before you're bowled over by the extraordinary blooms some cactus produce.

✔ Most important for gardeners north of zone 9: Containers offer the chance to move those precious plants indoors when the temperature starts to drop. Actually quite a few spiny and not-so-spiny plants can be grown outdoors, far from the desert — hens and chicks, a prickly pear or two — and there are many others that can live through the winter with the benefit of a sunny indoor window seat. Some gardeners may want to build one of those huge Victorian conservatories to house their succulent collections.

Rules of the Game

A succulent is a plant that has adapted to arid conditions by creating water storage units in leaves, stems, and roots. Succulents are native to many different environments: deserts that may suffer slightly cool temperatures at night (50s); high deserts that may get snow or frost; seaside areas where water-holding capacity has more to do with protection from high salinity than the dryness of the surroundings; dry, cold mountainside crevices; and many temperate areas.

Most succulents have evolved to store water during the rainy season, and then use it during the dry season. Some succulents rely on summer rains, but for many, the wet season arrives in winter, and that's when growth occurs. The rest of the year, lying dormant, the plants hunker down and wait. As you may know from visits or pictures, the Southwest desert in spring is a sight to behold: Winter rains come and suddenly cactus everywhere are adorned in bright bursts of flowers.

Cactus are a type of succulent, set apart from other of the fleshy-tissued plants by two features. One is that cactus have a structure called an *areole* at the plant's growing point, sometimes visible as small pads. This is the opening where new leaves, stems, and flowers spring up. The more significant difference between cactus and other succulents is that most cactus have spines, which makes them interesting to look at, and especially amusing to handle. In this chapter when we refer to succulents, we mean to include cactus as well, unless we say otherwise. And while we're discussing really important matters, we better get this right out in the open: We use *cactus,* not cacti or cactuses, as the plural of cactus. *Webster's Dictionary* blesses cactus as the third-choice plural, and we think it sounds better.

Growing Cactus/Succulents in Containers

Light and temperature are the defining needs of many succulents. In general, most need a great deal of bright light, although some take part shade. Most cannot survive for more than a night with temperatures below 40°F, but some are hardy in all climates. Looking on the bright side (so to speak), the range of preferences means that there are succulents for every garden taste and climate.

The basic rules for growing succulents in containers are pretty simple:

✔ Provide as much light as possible during the summer — although full sun in really warm places, including their desert homelands, can be too hot for many succulents in the confines of a container. Some types prefer part shade — see the list at the end of this chapter.

✔ Protect succulents from cold weather in the winter. Move them indoors to a sunny window where temperatures do not drop below 40°F.

If you have large heavy containers, plan to put them on wheels — or start pumping iron.

Choosing containers

Succulents lend themselves to terra-cotta pots — the attraction's probably the desert look about both plants and the containers. Terra-cotta also is porous, which keeps roots from sitting in water; stone and concrete pots also work well for the same reason.

Making sure that the container has drainage holes is another important rule — sometimes so obvious it may be missed. Feel free to use a shallow container (just 4 to 6 inches deep) if it looks best for your plants — succulent roots don't go very deep. For a plant with a rounded shape, choose a container that's 2 inches wider than the plant. For an upright plant, choose a pot that's half the diameter of the plant's height.

When we select containers, cactus and succulents sometimes bring out the eccentric in us. We've seen small hens and chicks or other rosette-forming succulents planted in strawberry jars, old boots, or even worn-out tennis shoes. Could be worse. For suggestions on dealing with unusual containers, see Chapter 17.

Another popular choice is *hypertufa* — a do-it-yourself project made with concrete, peat moss, and the mold of your choice. Hypertufa's rugged beauty provides an appropriate setting for ornamental succulents like sedum, echeveria, and sempervivum.

Selecting soil mix

Quick drainage is the most important quality of a soil mix designed for succulents. The standard mix consists of one-half organic matter (peat moss, leaf mold, or something like that) and one-half grit (crushed rock or sand). You can find many cactus and succulent mixes already bagged.

Planting

Design your succulent containers following the same principles that you apply for other plants: combining something tall and spiky, something mounded, something trailing. A well-balanced landscape can be accomplished by using one large container with several plants. Or put each plant in its own container and then group the pots — this mix-and-match method gives you freedom to rearrange on a whim.

When planting cactus, care is the key word — for yourself and the plant Wear thick gloves and/or wrap the cactus in a sleeve of thickly layered paper and use the ends as a handle. (If you get stuck with a few spines, use a piece of cellophane tape to remove them.)

1. **First cover the drain hole, as described in Chapter 5.**

2. **Fill the container part way with soil mix and ease the plant into the container, as shown in Figure 12-1.**

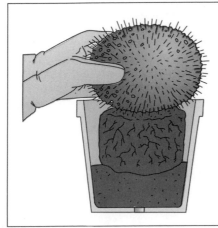

Figure 12-1:
With some
soil already
in the
container,
carefully
set the
cactus in.

3. **Use a narrow trowel or spoon to fill around the cactus with soil mix (see Figure 12-2).**

Most cactus and many other succulents have shallow roots, so do not plant too deeply. Burying part of the stem invites rot to set in. Make sure that the soil level in the pot is no higher than the level of the soil in the plant's nursery container.

4. **After planting, add a top layer of gravel or crushed stone, as shown in Figure 12-3, to provide a finished, desert-like look that also helps keep the base of the plant dry.**

Buy any bag of gravel you like or choose crushed rock that enhances the look of the plant and the container — something with a pinkish tone, for example, may look nice with terra-cotta. Feel free to add any decorative details at this point — miniature dry steer heads, thirst-craved miners, and so on.

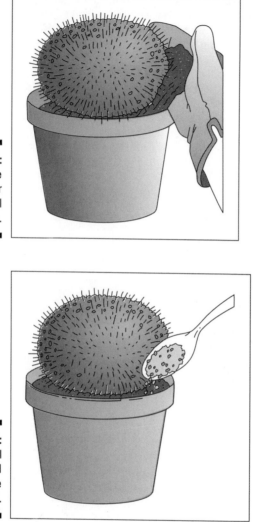

Figure 12-2:
Fill the
container
with soil
mix.

Figure 12-3:
For a final
touch, add
some
gravel.

Maintenance

First of all, forget some of the myths that you may have heard or imagined about cactus and succulents. You do need to water them and feed them.

Water regularly during the growing season — remember that this can be winter for some species. Thorough watering is better than a sprinkle every day or two. When the soil is completely dry, it's time to water again. One effective way to water smaller pots is to sit them in a tub of water nearly up to their rims, leaving them there until the top layer of soil is moist.

During their dormant season and in cool temperatures (50°F), most cactus and succulents can go without water for weeks at a time. Don't become complacent and forget that the poor things are even alive. Resume regular watering just before the growing season begins.

When plants are in a growing stage, fertilize about once a month — or every other time you water, if you water every two weeks. Succulents need all the nutrients that other plants do — nitrogen, phosphorus, and potassium — plus trace elements. You can use just about any complete liquid fertilizer or a special fertilizer designed for cactus and succulents; or try a tomato fertilizer at half-strength. For more on fertilizing, check Chapter 19.

If you need to repot a cactus, use a piece of rolled-up cloth or paper to remove the plant from its original container, as shown in Figure 12-4.

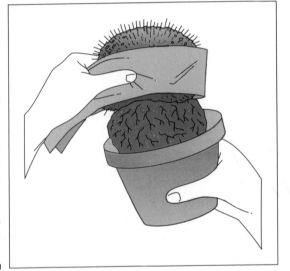

Figure 12-4:
To avoid getting pricked, use a rolled-up cloth to remove a cactus from its container.

Which Cactus and Succulents?

Mail-order sources (see the Appendix) offer tantalizing pictures and descriptions of what's available. As with any plant purchase, read carefully and plan ahead. If you live in a cold-winter area, remember to keep in mind what happens to those beauties in January. Buying cactus and succulents locally is always possible — check out nearby nurseries to get a feel for what different plants look like and which are adapted to your climate.

As you shop, look for plants that aren't wrinkled or shrunken at the base near the soil. Avoid cactus with broken spines. Buying a plant with good color you see in the descriptions that follow — and certainly not always the best choice.

Because succulents come from many different parts of the world with different altitudes, temperature ranges, and rainfall patterns, it's impossible to make blanket statements about which plants to choose and how to care for them. Pay attention to the cultural information for each species, then group the plants in containers accordingly.

Here are just a few of the hundreds of cactus and succulents to look for and try in containers. The plants are listed alphabetically by common name, with the botanical name given to avoid possible confusion. Most are hardy outdoors in zones 9 and 10; in other climates, plan to move the pots indoors for winter. Remember that hardiness zones, when listed, are for plants growing in the ground, and container plants are not that tolerant of cold.

Cactus for containers

You may enjoy growing any of these cactus:

- ✔ *Acanthocalycium glaucum:* Moderate-growing, small grayish mound with brown to black spines has showy yellow or orange flowers. Give it part shade in really hot areas; water in spring and summer.

- ✔ **Beehive cactus *(Coryphantha missouriensis):*** Native to Canada and the United States, this is a true cold-hardy species, able to grow as far north as zone 3. Only 3 inches tall, the beehive forms clusters with gray spines. Flowers are fragrant and green, followed by red fruit in summer. During the dormant season, beehive cactus may actually shrink so much that it retreats underground. *C. vivipara* is a cold-hardy relative with magenta flowers.

- ✔ **Bishop's cap or bishop's miter *(Astrophytum myriostigma):*** Short and rotund, its white speckles (rudimentary spines) give the plant a silvery look. Expect it to grow to the size of a large grapefruit by ten years of age.

- ✔ **Golden barrel cactus *(Echinocactus grusonii):*** A globe with golden-yellow spines, it grows slowly to 6 inches, sometimes larger. Don't wait around for flowers — they appear only after 30 or 40 years. Provide full sun.

- ✔ **Hedgehog cactus *(Echinocereus viridiflorus):*** Stems form clusters to 6 inches. Flowers are fragrant and lime-green. *E. triglochiodiatus*, a hardier species (to zone 5), has stem clusters to 1 foot, 1-inch pale gray spines, and deep pink flowers.

- ✔ **Old-man-of-the-mountains (*Borzicactus celsianus*, also listed as *Oreocereus celsianus*):** White hairs create a shaggy beard look. The plant forms a medium-size column eventually reaching a foot tall, with magenta flowers popping out here and there.

- ✔ **Orchid cactus (*Epiphyllum*):** Excellent hanging basket plant, orchid cactus resembles a wad of stems, but in bloom can be spectacular — fragrant flowers in neon colors. Provide part to full shade.

- ✔ ***Parodia:*** Globular plants to 1 foot tall grow by forming offsets. Flowers look like daisies. Don't water in winter. Try *P.magnifica* (*P. notocactus*), with white-spined ribs.

- ✔ **Pincushion cactus (*Mammillaria bombycina*):** Short cylinders up to a foot tall produce offsets covered in soft, white down and yellow spines. Pink flowers are big — at least 3 inches wide.

- ✔ **Prickly pear or cholla (*Opuntia*):** Prickly pear has flattened, oval stems, and cholla has cylindrical stems. Some are spinier than others. They tolerate more rainfall than other cactus. Try *O. compressa, O. fragilis,* or *O. vivipara.*

- ✔ **Sea urchin (*Echinopsis*):** This is a big group of globular or columnar, medium-to-fast growing plants. Expect a wide choice of flower colors.

Succulents for containers

These are our favorite succulents. By the way, if you're looking for the aloe plant, it's covered in Chapter 13.

- ✔ **Cub's paws (*Cotyledon tomentosa*):** This is a shrubby, spreading, little plant, about a foot high. Deciduous green leaves are toothed at the top and have a reddish margin. Provide part shade.

- ✔ ***Crassula pubescens:*** Tuck this small, creeping ground cover into a container. Give it plenty of sun to bring out the leaves' bright red tones.

- ✔ ***Echeveria:*** Choose from several species of rosette-forming plants with colorful foliage.

- ✔ **Houseleeks or hens and chicks (*Sempervivum*):** These rosette-forming plants are probably the best known succulents. They're available with leaves in shades of green and red — cobweb-looking hairs circle some of the leaves. Plants spread by offsets; if one breaks off, tuck it into another pot, and it roots easily.

- ✔ **Jade plant (*Crassula*):** In mild climates, this shiny-leafed favorite can grow up to 6 feet tall, and produce little pink flowers in midwinter.

- ✔ ***Jovibarba heuffelii:*** Tuck these rosettes into fast-draining pots. Choose from many varieties with leaves of different colors — bronze, chocolate, violet. Hardy to zone 6.

- ✔ ***Lewisia redidiva:*** Native to the Rocky Mountains (and hardy to zone 4), this is a colorfully blooming plant that demands very fast drainage. *L. tweedyi*, native to the Cascade Mountains, is hardy to zone 5.

- ✔ **Queen Victoria century plant** *(Agave victoria-reginae):* Spiky short-green leaves edged in white form a dramatic 1-foot rosette. Plant is slow growing, and 13-foot (!) flower stalks take 30 years to bloom — not a century. *A. utahensis* is a cold-hardy relative.

- ✔ **Sedum:** Many species are among the more versatile container plants. Check on their hardiness — certain varieties can grow in climates as cold as zone 3. Some form very showy flower heads; a popular choice is *S. spectabile* Autumn Joy.

Chapter 13

Indoor Container Gardening

. . . .

▶ Finding the right fit with indoor plants

▶ Selecting containers and soil

▶ Taking care of your plants

. . . .

Do you live in a high-rise, 10 stories up, with no garden or even a balcony? Maybe you need a philodendron. Does your apartment seem sterile despite all that artwork? A terrarium may be just the right touch. How about those empty corners in the dining room? And why waste all that humidity in the bathroom? Living room feel stuffy? Umbrella plants, Dallas ferns, and spider plants to the rescue.

Okay, we're biased, but an apartment or house without plants lacks a sense of life, and can almost always use a infusion of nature. We're not all up to owning a conservatory filled with exotic trees, vines, and shrubs, but we can grow at least a few indoor plants — without having to worry about hardiness zones.

Looks aren't everything. Indoor gardening offers benefits beyond decor — many plants are known to improve air quality. Spider plant, ivy, mother-in-law's tongue, and bamboo plant are among those found to absorb toxins from the air. In addition, plants use up carbon dioxide while releasing oxygen during photosynthesis.

Determining Your Plant Preferences

From begonias to lemons, the indoor plant possibilities are as limitless as your budget, patience, and imagination. Whether you're wintering over a geranium on the windowsill or raising orchids in the bathroom, you can grow plants indoors that are native to the tropics or to the desert. Some plants reputedly thrive on neglect and others require great care. Still others expect entirely too much nurturing, as anyone with experience in keeping a gardenia alive and blooming under normal living conditions can attest.

What we focus on here are plants that are reasonably easy to grow indoors, along with a few special plants that require a bit of extra care but are worth it.

Choose plants to suit your tastes and the amount of light and attention you have to offer:

✔ Foliage plants alone can provide a variety of looks. You get bright color from crotons with their glossy, stiff leaves veined with yellow, orange, and red. You find texture in the delicate and symmetrical Norfolk Island pine or the imposing, sort of somber cast-iron plant. You have available a huge range of sizes, from the diminutive African violet to the towering umbrella plant.

✔ For frequent travelers, choose indoor plants that do not need constant attention. You can go away without worrying.

✔ For a really self-sufficient indoor garden, try a terrarium, such as the one shown in Figure 13-1. Closed up in a large jar or aquarium, this kind of garden creates its own atmosphere and moisture. A terrarium needs only a good start in life, an occasional breath of fresh air, and, if necessary, the removal or addition of a plant here and there.

✔ Some plants have special needs that allow them to fit neat into our homes. Native to the shady understory of the tropics, pothos grows happily in low light, vining its way up a bookcase (or pinched back in a hanging basket). Bird's nest ferns thrive in the bathroom, steamy from showers. And for that sunshine streaming in the dining room window all day, try a real lemon tree — Meyer's lemon. A caution: A location too close to a sunny window in summer can burn leaves; or too close in winter (depending on how energy-efficient your windows are) can send a chill through a heat-lover. Be sure to match the right plant with the right environment — as with any gardening, proper placement yields healthier plants that are less susceptible to pests and diseases.

✔ Just as families once escaped summer in the city by traveling to the seaside, many houseplants can leave their indoor environments for summer lounging on a patio or deck. Be sure that the season is really summer when you put your houseplants out. Before you bring plants back indoors in the fall, be sure to check for any hitchhiking pests on the undersides of leaves, on the stems, or on the soil surface.

Choosing Containers

Considering the wide array of available container styles, you can safely let interior design or personal taste guide your selection. The only requirement, as always, is to make sure that there's a drainage hole in the bottom of the container. Don't despair if your choice is a gorgeous copper pot: Just plant

in a plastic pot, set the pot in a drainage dish, and put both in the copper pot; or grow the plant in a plastic pot with a built-in tray that can fit into the pot.

For a terrarium, use a clear glass or plastic bottle, dish, or aquarium with or without a cover. If the glass becomes foggy, all you do is uncover the aquarium; if the terrarium is without a cover, you need to water it occasionally.

Getting the Right Soil Mix

A general indoor potting mix is adequate for most plants. Exceptions are orchids and cactus, and you can find commercial specialty mixes clearly labeled for both types. Most indoor plants need generally well-draining soil, but there are always exceptions. Cactus require drainage that is faster than fast. The orchids that we discuss later in the chapter are epiphytes, accustomed to growing on the trunks of trees; when grown indoors, they need to grow in a medium containing little soil and a lot of bark.

To build a terrarium, start with a layer of aquarium gravel (up to 2 inches), cover with a thin layer of charcoal, and top with material to serve as a screen (plastic or a layer of sheet moss or landscape cloth). Then add the soil and start planting. Create your own little world by incorporating rocks, driftwood, tiny dinosaurs, or whatever accessories appeal to your imagination.

Keeping Your Plants Alive

Providing the right conditions and maintenance is the secret to success with indoor plants. Here are some key things to keep in mind:

Watering

Some of us are overzealous and drown the poor things, while others let a plant dry up past redemption before noticing that it may be time to water. Check the requirements of the plants, and, if you have a difficult time remembering who needs what, use refrigerator notes, a calendar, or whatever works to jog your memory.

Don't just water once a week year-round. Winter is a slow season for many indoor plants and they don't know what to do with a deluge. Pay attention to phrases like "evenly moist," "allow to dry out between waterings," and "undemanding of water" in plant descriptions.

For many indoor plants, providing humidity is just as important as watering. Some require high humidity through proper placement (the bathroom's always a good candidate). You can also increase humidity by misting (check mail-order catalogs for mister-gadgets); or set the pot in a water dish filled with gravel — so that the pot doesn't actually sit in the water, but above it. Remember that turning on the heat in winter can dry the air out; compensate accordingly.

Temperature

In order to form flowers, plants may have strict requirements for day and/or night temperatures. Orchids, in particular, are fussy about temperatures, but they're fussy about everything. If you are growing plants for foliage only, the requirements ease up. For most plants, ideal temperatures range between 55°F and 75°F — descriptions such as "cool," "average," or "high" fit into that range. Just like in their native habitats, plants indoors generally prefer cooler temperatures at night and in the winter.

Light

Another limiting factor to an indoor plant's well-being is light level. For example, a polka-dot plant requires high light levels. With less light, the plant may not die, but stems become elongated (with wider spaces between leaves), the leaves are stunted, and the pink-polka-dot effect fades — in general, the plant starts to look ratty.

POT
FEET

Photo 1

Photos 2–4:
Hanging baskets can provide a solo focal point (Photo 2), enhance a collection of container plants (Photo 3), or serve as the central element in your decorating scheme (Photo 4).

Photo 2: Trailing verbena quickly fills and then spills out of a hanging basket.

Photo 3: A colorful medley is achieved with English ivy and tuberous begonias in the hanging basket, gardenia in the clay pot, and at lower left, angel-wing begonia.

Photo 4: Fibrous begonias make colorful hanging baskets.

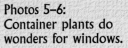

Photos 5–6:
Container plants do
wonders for windows.

Photo 5: Classic container plants work well together,
like these two kinds of English ivy (one "needlepoint"
and one with white-variegated leaves) and geraniums
(*Pelargonium*).

Photo 6: Six dwarf yellow marigold plants, two
red geraniums, sweet alyssum, and lobelia provide
a welcome view from outside and in the home.

Photos 7–8:
You can't go wrong
with a few containers
at the base of walls.

Photo 7: English ivy trails from an array of interesting pots. Creeping fig covers the wall behind the containers.

Photo 8: Dwarf periwinkle *(Vinca minor)* streams from pots that are nearly covered by English ivy and creeping fig.

Photos 9–11:
Container plants can
enhance walls and windows
in many ways.

Photo 9: Use wrought iron plant shelves to raise plants. These hold pots of geraniums and ferns.

Photo 10: A favorite flower of butterflies and moths, arching lantana is tied to supports.

Photo 11: A shady northside wall is home to rows of impatiens.

Photo 12: Purple tinged common sage is accented by bromeliads.

Photos 12–17: Mixed plantings can produce some interesting effects.

Photo 13: A mound of boxwood is surrounded by swags of English ivy.

Photo 14: Elegant pots host multilevel splendor.

Photo 15: Oregon grape *(Mahonia)* enjoys the reputation of being a long-lived container plant.

Photo 16: Trailing rosemary spills from the right toward purple-tinged common sage.

Photo 17: Golden Japanese forest grass complements annuals and perennials.

Photo 18: Fragrant lemon grass (*Cymbopogon citratus*) adapts readily to life in a pot.

Photos 18–23: Distinctive containers can enhance the decorative effect of your plantings. In Photo 18, the container itself isn't all that special, but the pedestal it sits on provides some decorative flair; a more elaborate container would compete with the overall look.

Photo 19: Plants grow anywhere their roots can gain a foothold. Here, dwarf shrubs live comfortably in irregular stones.

Photo 20: Swiss chard combined with primroses and other annuals.

Photo 21: An otherwise abandoned corner of the house is a good place for container plants, such as these impatiens, pansies, and daises.

Photo 22: Japanese forest grass (*Hakonechloa macra*) and verbena make a nice match.

Photo 23: A variety of sedums show off well in containers.

Photos 24–29:
Enhancing the appear-
ance of a patio is easy
with a few well-placed
container plants.

Photo 24: In a mild winter area, permanent shrubs, such as sasanqua camellia and mother fern, survive year to year. Trailing over the sides is sweet alyssum.

Photo 25: A potted dwarf orange tree thrives in a wind-protected corner of this garden.

Photo 26: Small patios are eligible for container gardens.

Photo 27: Mandevilla Red Riding Hood appears near peak bloom atop the corner post of a wall.

Photo 28: A plant collector's garden in containers is staged for height on stone blocks.

Photo 29: Evergreens can produce a formal look.

Photos 30–34:
You can decorate a deck with a few containers, as in Photo 30, or you can go all out and cover a deck with a variety of plants and containers, as in Photo 31. Photo 32 shows the middle ground.

Photo 30: Containers you can easily move from storage to sun are ideal for handling temperamental plants like these Rhodohypoxis.

Photo 31: No room for a garden? Growing on this deck is a green menagerie of exotic plants.

Photo 32: Bonsai plants appear center stage.

Photo 33: Good garden scents are provided by rosemary (left) and lemon verbena (right).

Photo 34: Use container plants to segue from patio to garden. These are pots of jewel-like dianthus and nasturtium.

Photo 35: Variety is the spice of this garden.

Photos 35–37:
Container plants can
even decorate outdoor
paths and gardens.

Photo 36: These Meyer lemons fill an otherwise empty spot.

Photo 37: A pot of papyrus (*Cyperus papyrus*) thrives in two inches of water in a large, drainless pot.

Photo 38: Make islands of container plants by arranging pots in clusters.

Photo 33: Good garden scents are provided by rosemary (left) and lemon verbena (right).

Photo 34: Use container plants to segue from patio to garden. These are pots of jewel-like dianthus and nasturtium.

Photo 35: Variety is the spice of this garden.

Photos 35–37: Container plants can even decorate outdoor paths and gardens.

Photo 36: These Meyer lemons fill an otherwise empty spot.

Photo 37: A pot of papyrus (*Cyperus papyrus*) thrives in two inches of water in a large, drainless pot.

Photo 38: Make islands of container plants by arranging pots in clusters.

Photos 39–41:
You can grow great
vegetables year-round
in containers.

Photo 39: Ornamental cabbages attract attention in
bowl-shaped containers.

Photo 40: Choose a patio-type tomato variety
and you can grow and harvest fresh tomatoes
in minimal space.

Photo 41: Grow perfect bell peppers in a simple pot.

Photos 42–33:
Cactus and succulents
are quite comfortable
in containers.

Photo 42: A garden of specimen cactus is safely exhibited in some interesting pots.

Photo 43: A heat- and sun-hardy bowl garden features agaves, an upright cactus, draping elephant's food *(Portulacaria afra)*, and sedums.

In contrast, plants that prefer low light levels may show browned, burned leaf edges and splotches when placed in direct sunlight.

That wonderful group of plants in the middle — those that prefer medium light levels — can put up with the widest range of light. Later in this chapter, we provide description of plants that are grouped according to their light needs.

Since leaves turn toward light — trying to make the most of photosynthesis — you may eventually find many of your plants leaning toward the windows. To prevent that, turn pots every week or so if you want a more symmetrical look. You may not want to bother with that 8-foot rubber tree in the corner, since no one sees the other side anyway.

Fertilizer

Just how big do you want that philodendron to be? Overfertilization can result in lush growth, requiring more frequent repotting and offering a dinner invitation to any stray pest that prefers soft new growth. On the other hand, underfertilizing gives you plants that just look wan and worse.

A happy medium for most indoor plants is to use a soluble fertilizer three times during the growing season (spring and summer). Exceptions to this are noted in the plant descriptions — some plants, as always, are more demanding than others.

Pests and diseases

Unfortunately, pest and disease problems do make their way indoors. As with outdoor plants, the cause is often cultural. In other words, if you put the right plant in the right place (meeting its requirements for light, water, humidity, and temperature), you're much less likely to have a problem. See Chapter 21 for more on pest and disease control.

Pruning

Regularly try to snip off spent flowers, dead leaves, or stems. Individual plants may have some specific needs:

If you have a spider plant, prune off *spiderlets* (miniature plants or offsets at the branch tips), place them in water until they show roots, and then transplant.

Occasionally, take a deep breath and cut the tallest, leggiest dumb cane stem down to 3 inches so that shorter stems may take over.

Knowing Your Plants' Needs

Before selecting indoor plants, try to become familiar with the available light in your home. Here we group plants according to the amount of light that they need for optimum growth, and we provide information on required watering, humidity, or other special care.

Plants that get along in low light

Place these plants in east or north windows, foyers, stair landings, anywhere that does not receive direct sun. But remember, if it's too dark for you to read a book, it's too dark for a plant to grow there.

- **Cast-iron plant (Aspidistra elatior):** Dark green leaves up to 3 feet long give a lush look. Provide cool to average temperature. Plant is slow growing. Let soil dry out between waterings; fertilize infrequently.

- **Chinese evergreen (Aglaonema):** Grow it for the 2-foot-long dark green leaves marked across with white (Maria); or yellow-green leaves with darker splotches (Silver Queen). Provide average temperature — no cold drafts. Let soil dry out between waterings. Cut back older canes to promote new growth from the base.

- **Dracaena:** Choose from many species, mostly slow growing. Most familiar is Madagascar dragon tree (*D. marginata*), with long, thin leaves coming out like a fountain. Give average temperature, medium humidity. Let soil dry out between waterings; fertilize infrequently.

- **Mother-in-law's tongue (Sansevieria trifasciata):** This has been a houseplant since Neanderthal times, which explains the politically incorrect name. Familiar vertical blades grow slowly to 18 inches. Provide cool to hot temperature; fertilize infrequently. Hahnii is shorter, more horizontal, yellow-variegated.

- **Peace lily (Spathiphyllum):** Here's the ubiquitous mall plant and for good reason — dark, glossy foliage, on 1- to 4-foot plants, looks sharp without too much attention. Plants also tolerate low humidity. Let soil dry out between waterings.

Plants that grow in medium light

Some direct light is fine for these plants, but for the most part, they need bright but indirect light. Place them near a west or southeast window.

- **African violet (Saintpaulia):** A classic indoor plant — one of those that seems to bloom like crazy for a few owners and hardly at all for others. See what you can do. Fuzzy leaves form a rosette; flowers come in white, pink, lavender, and purple. Provide average to warm temperature, medium to high humidity. Keep the soil evenly moist (don't get water on the leaves). One good way to feed: Use a diluted fertilizer every watering — choose from many special African violet foods.

✔ **Begonia:** Colorful and varied foliage, plus showy flowers — begonias have it all. The begonias with large, gorgeous flowers (called tuberous or Rieger begonias) are considered disposable. Longer-lasting begonias include angel wing (spotted leaves, insignificant flowers); Rex begonias (foliage variegated with gray, purple, magenta); and *B. schmidtiana* (dark green crinkled leaves with reddish undersides). Provide average temperature, evenly moist soil. Fertilize lightly and regularly during the growing season. Repot annually.

If you grow bedding begonias outdoors during the summer, bring them in their containers indoors for winter. Move them inside before the first frost, cut back leggy stems, and keep the plants in a sunny window.

✔ **Bird's nest fern *(Asplenium nidus):*** Apple-green fronds unfurl to 3 feet — a great plant for close proximity to the shower. Provide high humidity, average temperature, evenly moist soil. Growth is slow.

✔ **Boston fern *(Nephrolepis bostoniensis):*** Don't overlook this fern just because it's so popular. The look is tropical, full and lush when well kept — scraggly when not. Dallas fern (*N. exaltata* Dallasi) is short and dense; Fluffy Ruffles has frilly fronds. Provide average temperature, evenly moist soil.

✔ **Christmas cactus *(Schlumbergera):*** Name comes from the bloom time — abundant flowers are pink, salmon, or red with bent-back petals. Plant is also known as Thanksgiving or even Halloween cactus, depending on when it blooms. Flowers and buds knock off easily, so keep plants away from traffic. Provide average to warm temperature. Let soil dry out between waterings; give less water in winter.

✔ **Croton *(Codiaeum variegatum):*** A striking plant — colorful orange, yellow, or red midribs make shiny leaves look as if they were dipped in paint. Provide medium to warm temperature, high humidity.

✔ **Dumb cane *(Dieffenbachia):*** This is another easygoing indoor favorite, with white and green variegated leaves on 3-foot tall canes. Provide average temperature, medium to high humidity. Let soil dry out between waterings. When older canes become bare except for top leaves, you can cut them back to 3 inches (take care — the sap is irritating and dangerous to pets).

✔ **Moon Valley pilea:** Leaves have dark veins and look finely quilted. Plant grows fast. Provide cool to warm temperature, high humidity. Let soil dry out between waterings. Pinch back to keep bushy.

✔ **Moth orchid *(Phaleanopsis):*** This is the easiest orchid, which isn't saying much. Many varieties come in flower shades of pink and white; one blooming stem can last 18 months, which makes all the effort worthwhile. Provide warm days, cool nights. Do not overwater; fertilize once a month all year with orchid formula.

✔ **Norfolk Island pine** *(Araucaria heterophylla):* This is a charming small tree (indoors at least), 4 to 6 feet, with branches in tiers — a good candidate for an indoor Christmas tree. Provide cool to warm temperature. Keep soil evenly moist.

✔ **Peperomia:** Widely available plant forms a dense mound of pleated leaves. Red Ripple has deep red stems. Provide average temperature. Water when soil is dry.

✔ **Philodendron:** Choose from wide variety of plants to suit any taste — cutleaf, purplestem, elephant ear. Plants become vines unless pinched back. Pothos *(Epipremnum)* looks almost the same. Provide average temperature. Let soil dry out between waterings.

✔ **Spider plant** *(Chlorophytum comosum):* Here's a fine choice for a hanging basket; Vittatum, with variegated foliage, is most common. Provide cool to average temperature. Let soil dry out between waterings. Repot when roots fill pot. Grow more plants by rooting spiderlets (the mother plant's extensions) in soil or water. Fluoride in tap water can cause brown leaf tips.

✔ **Umbrella plant** *(Schefflera actinophylla):* An imposing 6 to 8 feet at maturity, this is a good choice for a big empty corner. Provide average temperature, evenly moist soil (drier in winter). Repot every two years.

Plants that need lots of light

To stay in top condition, these plants — sun-lovers that they are — need a south or west window exposure and direct light much of the day.

✔ **Aloe vera** *(Aloe barbadensis):* Long succulent spikes grow from the center of the plant. The gel inside the leaves is used to relieve minor skin irritations. Plant is slow growing, undemanding of temperature and water. Divide offsets and pot them up for new plants.

✔ **Coleus:** Traditionally used outdoors in shady summer beds, colorful foliage in reds, yellows, and oranges can brighten up indoors as well. Provide high humidity; keep soil evenly moist during the growing season, barely moist in winter. In spring, cut well back and repot plants. Pinch tips to keep growth bushy.

✔ **Meyer's lemon:** In addition to fruit (which is far from a sure thing indoors), this small tree produces glossy leaves and fragrant flowers. Put the plant outside in summer. Indoors, provide average to cool temperature. Keep soil evenly moist. Growth is slow; don't repot too often.

✔ **Polka-dot plant** *(Hypoestes phyllostachya):* Plant must be described as perky, with dark green leaves speckled with pink. Growth is fast. Provide average temperature. Keep soil evenly moist. Cut back to keep plants small and bushy.

Part IV
Designing and Decorating

In this part . . .

Plants and containers, containers and plants. Which came first — the color, the whimsy, the beauty, the surprise, the pride? Who cares? Probably not the pot. The plant — perhaps. Meanwhile back at your grand designs and exquisite taste, you're ready to dress up all those lackluster nooks and crannies. But when you think living splashes, you need to consider caretaking duties — sort of form follows function. In this case, you peform the function that keeps your wonderful plants in good form. The payoff: You notice how knicknacks never get bigger, no matter how much dust they collect? Get ready to glimpse into what you can do with a little dirt and a lot of polish for picking the right touches in your personal environment.

Chapter 14

Matchmaking, Container-Style

In This Chapter

▶ Discovering the what and why of mixed plantings

▶ Considering design elements

▶ Choosing the container

▶ Keeping the show going

*E*ver notice how well some things go together? Like peanuts and baseball, canoes and lakes, stripes and plaids (just wanted to see if you're paying attention). The good news is that we can find some pretty awesome pairings in the container plant world, too. A pot full of purple pansies may dazzle the eye, but watch what happens when you add a splash of spring bulbs like fragrant white hyacinths or classic yellow daffodils.

Imagine the results when you combine more than just a couple of plants? Like adding a beer to the peanuts-baseball combo, the outcome can be sublime. A hanging basket becomes a rainbow of color with a mix of cascading red petunias, dazzling pink and white snapdragons, dainty deep blue lobelias, and perfectly formed Transvaal daisies in vibrant orange.

Mixed plantings go from modest to majestic when you fill a stately urn with combinations like this: classic evergreen Alberta spruce accented with pale pink trailing ivy geraniums and brimming with multicolored annuals — from white, rose, purple, and peach phlox to tufts of two-toned, fragrant sweet William.

The key to success in all these examples is the same: a well-designed mix of different plants. We're talking about plants that look terrific together. In other words, the plants bloom at the same time, their colors contrast or complement each other beautifully, and they're in scale with one another.

So the goal in this chapter, beyond introducing you to the wonderful world of mixed plantings, is to give you a detailed road map of how to produce your own outstanding displays. We cover design ideas and acquaint you with the color wheel and how to effectively combine colors in a variety of ways. We look at other design basics, too — form, texture, and proportion — and show you how to incorporate these ideas into just about any decorative scheme. We help you choose the right container by evaluating material, style, and size. Finally, we leave you with some tips to help you keep the show going with ideas about continuing care and long-term maintenance.

And in the next chapter, we put all these ideas together as we profile a variety of winning combinations — over a dozen in all — in all sorts of cool containers.

Why Mixed?

A mixed planting featuring two or more types of plants can be as simple as a tabletop decoration for a festive holiday or as grand as a classic urn standing out as an impressively colorful focal point on your patio or porch — or, for that matter, on your piazza. Your containers may feature flowering trees, brilliant annuals, cascading ground covers and vines, or an array of long-blooming perennials. With nearly endless possibilities, you're really limited only by imagination — and, of course, climate and, even possibly, budget. Here's a sampling of what mixed plantings can offer you:

✔ Color and interest in every season

✔ Long bloom periods in a single container

✔ Wonderful options for creating specific color combinations

✔ Excellent extras, including fragrance, texture, and interesting foliage

✔ A wide range of plant sizes and forms, from upright to cascading

✔ Plenty of specialty plants to fit a theme or specific location

Plants as a Palette

Many people consider the No. 1 design element to be color, which also happens to the most fun to play with. Look at a color wheel and examine how it works. You see that the wheel is broken down into the same colors in the same order as a rainbow. Primary colors — red, blue, and yellow — are *equidistant* on the wheel, and all colors result from mixing these three. Next, you find complementary colors *opposite* each other — yellow and blue or red and green, for example. Finally, you see harmonious colors blending gradually *between* two primary colors like red to orange to yellow. *Shades* refer to lighter and darker variations of the same color. Now that you know the basics, here's a quick primer on what happens when you experiment with various combinations:

- ✔ For bold, vibrant looks, choose contrasting colors (on opposite sides of the color wheel), such as yellow and violet.

- ✔ For pleasing, compatible combinations, choose harmonious blends of related colors like blue, violet, and purple.

- ✔ Create a soothing style with variations or shades of the same color — from pale pink to rose.

- ✔ Add plenty of pizzazz with energizing warm color combinations using red, orange, or yellow.

- ✔ Or cool things down with refreshing blues, greens, and violets.

- ✔ Don't forget white. It adds welcome dimension, lightens dark areas, and works with all other colors.

- ✔ Consider foliage, too. There's much more than green. You can find stunning results with silver and gray foliage, and variegated (two-toned) leaves are sure to add interest.

Breaking the rules

Classic color schemes are one thing, but personal taste is your ultimate authority. The bottom line: Pick colors that you like. If you like it, it can't be wrong whether you're going for a rainbow effect, planting orange marigolds and pink petunias, or simply arranging a single-color display. And, of course, you're never really locked in. If that "can't live without it" dusty red daylily turns out to be a dud, you can always replant.

Fun with Form, Texture, Proportion

Yes, you can have fun with the basic elements of design, and at the same time use them to add great depth and interest to your mixed planting.

Form refers to, well, basic plant shape. Upright, spiky iris, for example, clearly has a different form than round-leafed, cascading ivy geranium.

Texture is determined by the look and feel of the foliage and flowers and runs the gamut from harsh and hard cactus to light and lacy ferns. Both form and texture are most effective when the elements balance each other without competing for attention. Your design may run into trouble if you go off the deep end with lots wildly different-looking plants — although such diversity does create a certain look all its own: chaotic. And, hey, there may come a time when that's the effect you want.

No design discussion is complete without a word on *proportion* or scale. The important principle is to put plants and containers where they can look their best. Making sure that everything fits together is usually a matter of balance. A tiny trailer in a huge tub or a wide shrub in a narrow box simply doesn't work — just as a big-flowered, big-leafed perennial looks odd on a small table or combined with dainty, delicate annuals. Disparity is okay, but just make sure that the leap isn't too great. If you're uncertain, test out potential combinations when you're shopping at the nursery. Put plants and pots together and see what you come up with. You know that the design works when the plants fit the pot and the containers fit the location.

These tips on form, texture, and proportion apply to your mixed plantings:

- Make sure that the plant fits the pot. Your design looks best if small plants are used for small pots in small spaces, and larger plants are reserved for tubs, barrels, or big pots.

- Catch the eye and add balance with contrasting forms (spiky iris with rounded geraniums, for example) but be careful not to overdo it.

- Create both a soft and pleasing feel with finely textured, lacy plants like lobelia, small ferns, or baby's breath. Delicate-looking plants soften hard container edges and blend well with other textures.

- For a bold focus, try big flowers (zinnia or dahlia) or large, dramatic leaves (hosta, hydrangea, or sunflower). These are particularly effective in large pots alongside smaller plants.

- Group similarly sized plants, but feel free to vary height. Avoid extremes like tall shrubs and trees paired only with ground-hugging creepers.

- A natural, gradual flow results from tall plants placed toward the back of the container with middle-sized plants in the center, and low or trailing ones along the edges.

- Use balance and scale for container placement, too. A huge barrel on a tiny patio looks as out of place as a tiny dish garden lost on an expansive deck.

Container Compatibility: Picking the Right Pot

We suspect that you have some thrilling ideas for your mixed container plantings. That's great. But you're not done yet, because you still have an important matter to consider: the container. Picking the right transportable home for your garden — one that enhances the plants and the location in which they're displayed — can guarantee you a place in the gardeners' hall of fame.

Choosing the container involves a number of decisions. You need to determine what type to use: wood, terra-cotta, ceramic, clay, metal, or a whimsical, recycled container like an old pot, wheelbarrow, or milk can (for discussions of possibilities, see Chapters 3 and 17). You also want to select a material that fits your style and the location where you plan to display the plant and its container. A formal brick patio, for example, is ideal for glazed or terra-cotta pots; a rustic woodland deck is just the place for a planter box of recycled barn wood.

Size is key, especially with a mixed planting, because some of your choices may be plants that last longer than a single season and eventually reach substantial size. Consider the time factor as well as the mature size and spread of the plants. Your sweet little rosemary in a 2-inch pot may eventually grow 2 feet tall, so make allowances unless you plan to repot often. Keep in mind that annuals can give you colorful and interesting options for filling spaces on a temporary basis.

Here's a quick and handy checklist of elements to consider when choosing your container:

- ✔ Make sure to match your container with chosen plants and location. Test the fit at the nursery by trying out various plants in different pots.

- ✔ Be sure that the container size can accommodate all the plants when they have fully developed root systems. However, don't rule out small containers; they're ideal for compact plants but need frequent watering.

- ✔ If you display multiple containers, keep to one material or style but perhaps vary sizes or styles. A collection of terra-cotta containers — from bowls to herb pots with openings in the sides to tall pots — makes an impressive arrangement.

- ✔ Consider, especially with large containers, using a dolly or rolling tray so that you can move the pots later on. Be sure that the dolly or tray is designed to support the weight of the plant and its container when wet.

- ✔ Wood containers are a good value and have excellent insulating properties. Plastic pots, while inexpensive, may not hold up year after year. Clay pots tend to dry out quickly and may break under frosty conditions.

- ✔ Use cedar and redwood or softwood containers treated with preservative for long use under damp conditions.

- ✔ For that special look, consider unusual containers, including those that have been used for other things. With drainage provided, a hollowed-out tree stump, galvanized tub, or even an old pair of work boots can host a small collection of plants.

The Show Can Go On

So now you're sitting back with your feet up, admiring your work as you gaze at the stunning mixed planting on your patio. Relax and enjoy, but keep in mind that your job isn't exactly over. Don't worry excessively, though. You're expected to continue down the path you're already familiar with: watering, fertilizing, grooming, staking, and protecting from weather extremes. Mixed plantings require only slight variations from regular container care.

Watering, of course, is the biggie. The rules apply to just about all combinations you're apt to try (not counting water lilies and cactus). Your goal is even moisture — not too soggy, not too dry — with a short period of drying out to allow air in the soil. This drying-out can extend only to the first inch or so of soil. Of course, you need water before plants begin to droop or wilt. And when you water, do it thoroughly, until you see water drain away. Overhead watering on cloudy days washes dust off the leaves. With permanent plants, it's a good idea to occasionally do a deep, long, gentle soaking to wash away any accumulated salts in the soil.

Fertilizing follows the same basic guidelines as described in Chapter 19. Be consistent with your supply of nutrients, and you can reap the rewards of beautiful flowers and healthy foliage. Permanent plants — shrubs, trees, and perennials — need some form of long-lasting fertilizer; granular, slow-release, or stick varieties work well. Just be sure to get nutrients down into the soil where the roots can benefit. For a quick boost for all plants, especially annuals, feed with a liquid fertilizer. Start this process early when new leaves, stems, and flowers are forming. Continue feeding as your commercial product recommends throughout the growing season.

Good grooming is just good practice, and your containers really shine if you regularly remove spent flowers, dry leaves, and general debris on the soil. By snipping off flowers before they dry and go to seed, you can stimulate the plant to produce more rounds of blooms. Caretaking extends the show on annuals, perennials, roses, and other blooming plants. Keeping debris cleaned up also helps plants avoid pest and disease problems.

The permanent plants in your mixed design may require pruning to keep them in shape and stop them from overrunning neighbors. Pinch the tip growth on annuals (salvia and snapdragons, for example) when the plants are young so that they can get bushy instead of growing too tall. After plants flower, cut back straggly stems on plants like petunias and Shasta daisies. Shrubs and trees in containers need some foliage removed from time to time. Cut away dead, diseased, or weak branches and those growing into other plants. But be careful with flowering shrubs and trees because you may cut off next year's blooms. For guidance, consult a pruning manual for your type of plant.

Staking is key for plants with weak stems or large flowers and for tall plants in windy sites. For best results, put your stake, support hoop, or frame in place when the plant is small. Tie stems with soft twine, plastic ties, or feltlike strips sold for this purpose. Climbers, too, need support; a trellis attached to the container works well. Sometimes a plant surprises you by becoming taller or bushier than you expect. No reason for panic. Simply insert a thin bamboo stake and tie up the offender before it falls on its neighbors.

Your last maintenance task may involve rotating new annuals into your mixed planting. Because annuals offer only a seasonal show, you can easily remove finished plants and drop in current bloomers to keep your display colorful and interesting. As permanent plants mature, though, you may find less room for annuals.

Overall, try to follow these six simple tips for maintaining mixed container plantings:

- ✔ Water consistently, adjusting to hot, dry, or cool spells, to achieve even moisture.

- ✔ Fertilize regularly and be sure to jot down when and what you fertilize so that you can make later applications as necessary. Your flowering plants can benefit dramatically from consistent feeding.

- ✔ Prolong the show of flowers by snipping or pinching off faded blooms, taking flower and stem together.

✔ Don't be afraid to prune back permanent plants, or even take them out and trim the roots back by 20 percent or so when plants are not in active growth or flowering. Snipping may sound harsh, but the plants really respond well, especially if you use a bit of extra care in watching and watering following the pruning.

✔ Plan ahead for staking to avoid bent or broken stems and damaged flowers.

✔ Be ruthless with removal. Annuals can become close buddies, but it's important to pull those old friends out when the season ends (tugging carefully to avoid harming roots of long-term plants). Use this chance to drop in fresh-blooming annuals or perhaps a new trailing plant.

One Final Note

Many of the photos in the color section of this book show some interesting mixed plantings. Sometimes it's easier to come up with your own design ideas when you see how others have successfully experimented.

Chapter 15
12 Tested Recipes for Mixed Plantings

· ·

In This Chapter

▶ A dozen great designs for mixed plantings

▶ A recommended container for each idea

▶ Top plant choices for the 12 designs

▶ Planting instructions for your picks

▶ Special tips to grow on

· ·

*E*ffective container designs offer more than the spectacle of a bunch of plants in pots. Your winning combinations can not only look terrific but also inspire pride in your handiwork! How so?

Try a simple blending of three annuals and two perennials in shades of pink. Or a pairing of two-toned petunias set off by trailing ivy. Or you may go for variety and decide to feature three to five different plants with a contrasting color scheme, two main textures, and three heights. You get the idea. You can venture into just about anything — from window boxes to wheelbarrows, from baskets, bowls, and barrels to trays and troughs.

A Dozen Designs

Take a look at these colorful, interesting and, we hope, inviting mixed container gardens. We outline what you need for each. For more information, don't forget to check the chapters on individual plants (annuals, perennials, and so on). These mixed containers are all provided courtesy of their developer, talented writer-designer Peggy Henry of Sonoma, California.

Early spring bouquet

Celebrate the season with blooming bulbs and attractive annuals in this colorful little mix perfect for an outdoor table or front doorstep. The design features a repeating theme from three types of narcissus, and accents from a rainbow of annuals and perennials. As shown in Figure 15-1, anchoring the bowl in the center are stunning, tall, two-toned daffodils, set off by bright yellow mini-daffodils; a third type of bulb — fragrant paper-white narcissus — adds height and continuity. Effortless violas offer compact color, and the cheery and reliable primroses provide contrasting bright colors and richly textured leaves.

- **Container:** Try a clay bowl or dish at least 18 inches across and 9 to12 inches deep. Classic terra-cotta always looks good, but you may want a glazed ceramic bowl to match other decor or to add color.

- **Plants:** Five paper-white narcissus, six daffodils, six miniature daffodils, six yellow or blue violas, and six yellow or blue primroses.

- **How to plant:** Buy and plant the daffodils in fall, as described in Chapter 8. Then, when the bulbs pop up in spring, buy six-packs of violas and primroses. Space individual seedlings alternately around the rim. *Note:* If you missed the early bulb planting in fall, you can cheat and wait to find sprouted and budded bulbs for sale and plant everything all at once later in spring.

Figure 15-1:
Early
spring
bouquet.

✔ **Special tips:** The daffodils may need a bit of help to keep them from flopping over. Use slender stakes to tie them as soon as you detect trouble. Feed plants with liquid fertilizer monthly throughout the blooming season. Dig up and store bulbs when foliage dies back if you plan to reuse them.

Nature's bounty

This tub offers a profusion of sensory delights — including tasty fruits. The star of the show — a dwarf peach — combines with luscious strawberries spilling over the rim (see Figure 15-2). Golden hues of tall marigolds and trailing gazanias contrast nicely with masses of rich purple petunias. The dwarf tree performs well for years in the generous tub, offering the double bonus of pink spring blossoms and summer fruit. The strawberries add wonderful texture and an interesting cascading form, and the annuals fill the gaps with bright, bold color.

✔ **Container:** A sturdy oak half-barrel is ideal for long-term enjoyment of this collection. Be sure to drill several drain holes. The barrel lasts longer if you coat the interior with nontoxic preservative. If the staves start to slide, use nails to hold them in place.

✔ **Plants:** One dwarf peach tree, three strawberry plants, three marigolds, two petunias, and two gazanias.

Figure 15-2:
Nature's
bounty.

✔ **How to plant:** First, plant the tree in the center just slightly higher than the surrounding soil level. Then add the marigolds along the back, dropping the petunias next to them toward the front. Alternate strawberries and gazanias along the front rim of the barrel where they can cascade over the rim.

✔ **Special tips:** As the tree bears fruit over the years, the peaches may become too heavy for the small branches (look forward to this problem!), so either remove part of the crop or support the branches with small stakes. Cut off faded blooms (deadhead) from the petunias, marigolds, and gazanias to encourage more flowers. Strawberries may die back in winter, but the plants usually come back, producing well for two or three years.

Autumn romance

Borrow from yesterday with a rustic wooden wheelbarrow overflowing with blooming flowers — ideal for a cool, crisp autumn days. Two varieties of chrysanthemums in rich rust, gold, and maroon offer classic good looks, anchoring the planting with height in the center and spots of color throughout, as shown in Figure 15-3. Bright and easy-to-grow calendulas in dazzling yellow and orange complement the chrysanthemums, while the paludosum daisies are neat little fillers with eye-catching white blossoms. Using a harmonious color scheme of red, orange, yellow, and colors in between creates continuity. The repeating flower form from daisy-like blossoms further ties the design together, and varying flower size adds contrast and balance.

✔ **Container:** The rustic charm of an old wooden wheelbarrow adds appeal even before you put in attractive plants. Look for these unique gems in antique stores, barn sales, and flea markets. Age may provide your container with natural drain holes, but be sure to drill holes if the wheelbarrow's still watertight. Older metal versions make suitable substitutes.

✔ **Plants:** Three upright florist's chrysanthemums, six Cushion florist's chrysanthemums, eight paludosum daisies, and nine calendulas.

✔ **How to plant:** Cluster the tall chrysanthemums in the center of the wheelbarrow and then add the cushion mums evenly spaced around the central plants. Continuing outward, plant a ring of calendulas and then add two paludosum daisies in each corner. Allow several inches between plants. Keep the soil level 1 to 2 inches below the rim.

✔ **Special tips:** Give this container lots of sun. Pinch large-flower chrysanthemums to keep them bushy. Stake tall stalks. Cut back both types of mums after flowering, or treat them as annuals and remove entire plants after they stop blooming.

Figure 15-3:
Autumn
romance.

Suspended animation

Full foliage and flowers take over here, completely hiding the moss-lined basket as this collection of annuals, perennials, and vines cascades from the sides and top (see Figure 15-4). Variegated ground ivy spills like a living waterfall with its two-toned leaves and exceptionally long stems. Clusters of bright pansies and deep violet lobelias fill the sides and top; a handful of ivy geraniums adds rich pink tones and ever-reliable sweet alyssum weaves through with a fragrant white touch. The result is a blending of colors and textures — plants naturally growing together — blurring the lines that separate them.

- ✔ **Container:** Expect wonderful results from a galvanized wire basket that you can plant both from the top and *through* the sides. Openings allow you to insert plants just about anywhere to achieve a full, finished look. Use a 20-inch-diameter or larger basket for the best display.

- ✔ **Plants:** Three variegated ground ivies, six lobelias, nine pansies, three ivy geraniums, and six sweet alyssums.

- ✔ **How to plant:** Start by thoroughly soaking sphagnum moss in a bucket of water and then lining the bottom and sides with large, flat sections of dripping moss. Gradually add soil to keep moss in place, filling to the rim with both materials. Plant the ground ivies along the basket rim.

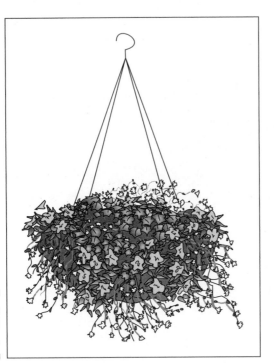

Figure 15-4:
Suspended
animation.

Next gently plant through the sides, using a mix of lobelias and pansies with few sweet alyssums sprinkled in, allowing space for the ground ivies to cascade. Pull plants through the sides and tuck extra moss around the roots so they are secure. Finish by adding ivy geraniums and remaining pansies and sweet alyssum in the top.

✔ **Special tips:** Let the wire framework support your efforts. When you plant, gently separate the wire sections to create larger openings. Then, with the plants in place, push the wires back together to hold everything in place. Water your basket immediately after planting, and replace any moss that washes away. Spray the basket often, hitting both the top and sides — the container dries out quickly. Fertilize regularly with a liquid product.

A new outlook

Life on the outside may just look a little brighter when the view from your window includes an arresting array of plants chosen for outstanding color. Figure 15-5 illustrates an ordinary wooden box coming alive with annuals and trailers that combine good looks with a delicious scent. Upright stock, set along the back of the box, offers a wonderful back-drop of fragrant flowers with a slightly spicy scent in double clusters of purple, pink, rose, and white. Sweet Williams add harmony with a touch of fragrance from flowers ranging from ruby red to a dazzling two-toned pink. Old-fashioned sweet peas link all the plants beautifully, climbing and trailing among the other performers. Needlepoint ivy, with its delicately shaped leaves and arching stems, spills gracefully from the front of the box.

✔ **Container:** We're suggesting a window box about 3 feet long by 9 inches wide by 10 inches deep — big enough to hold an impressive array of plants. Use rot-resistant cedar or redwood or treated planter boxes sized to fit right under your windows.

✔ **Plants:** Five stocks, five sweet Williams, five sweet peas, and two Needlepoint ivies.

✔ **How to plant:** Space the tall stocks along the back of the box, reserving a spot in each corner for a sweet pea. Add one more sweet pea in the center of the box and plant ivies equidistant from the center along the front rim. Fill in the additional spaces with sweet Williams, leaving at least a couple of inches between all plants. Water thoroughly and add soil to low spots.

✔ **Special tips:** For safety and success, be sure that your box is mounted securely. L-shaped galvanized steel brackets work best and can be anchored in wood or masonry; they provide the most stability if the box sits inside the "L". If you plant this box in spring, you may find that the annuals are finished by the middle of summer. Replace stock, sweet peas, and sweet Williams with sweet alyssum, carnations, or scented geraniums.

Terra-cotta collection

Classic terra-cotta pots are hard to beat for their value and eternal good looks, especially when you consider how easy they are to work with. Their versatile styles and sizes offer many possibilities for fabulous groupings, as with this trio of square pots. As you can see in Figure 15-6, perennials star in the summer show, with golden coreopsis leading the way in the center of each pot, flanked by cheerful blue marguerites. Annuals fill the gaps admirably, and a variety of marigolds and sweet alyssums give a final blast of color. The brimming pots are ideal for display anywhere — on a deck, patio, or porch. Their size even allows them to help define and divide seating or dining areas.

✔ **Container:** Good looks come in threes here with this collection of unusual but attractive, square terra cotta pots. The larger middle pot is 18 inches square, while the two smaller pots measure 14 inches. Take some time to find the right location for these guys before you plant, since they will be difficult, if not impossible, to lug around once planted.

✔ **Plants:** Three coreopsis, four blue marguerite daisies, five sweet alyssums and seven marigolds.

✔ **How to plant:** Start with the coreopsis, placing one in the center of each pot, slightly toward the back. Next add two daisies in the large pot on either side of the coreopsis, and plant one in the front corner of each small pot. Plant sweet alyssums in the side corners of the small pots and in the front corner of the large pot. Finish by dropping in the marigolds, three per large pot, two per small pot, mixing the colors as you go.

✔ **Special tips:** Consider dressing up the pots by adding pot feet — small terra cotta pieces that lift the pots off the ground. Place one foot along each side to securely support the containers. These also help improve drainage. Keep these plants deadheaded and you'll have a long summer show of flowers.

Figure 15-5:
A new
outlook.

Figure 15-6:
Terra-cotta
collection.

Timeless beauty, old world charm

Stone sink or cement trough, call it what you will, this kind of container evokes a world of cobblestone streets and horse-drawn carriages. In today's world, it's the perfect place to showcase alpine gems, compact shrubs or perennials, or ground covers. In our spring display, shown in Figure 15-7, a dainty heath with needle-like leaves and wands of white bell-shaped flowers matches up beautifully with a lovely dwarf juniper. The spreading wall rockcresses offer a tide of color, while the bold leaves and distinctive primrose flowers supply interesting and varied texture. Spilling gracefully from the corner, creeping phlox is virtually a mass of spring color, and the saxifrage forms an appealing cushion of foliage topped with star-shaped crimson flowers.

✔ **Container:** If you're lucky, you may find an old stone or ceramic sink or trough, perfect for your alpine or rock garden plants. If your search comes up empty, you have alternatives. First, you can actually make your own hypertufa trough from a combination of peat moss, sand, and cement mixed with water; this forms a stiff doughlike material that you can mold into various shapes. Or you can buy preformed, decorative terra-cotta, concrete, or cement troughs that offer a similar look.

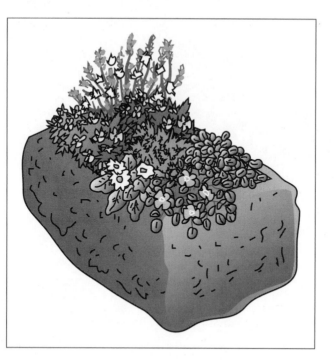

Figure 15-7:
Timeless
beauty, old
world
charm.

- ✔ **Plants:** One heath, two wall rockcresses, one dwarf juniper, one primrose, one saxifrage, and one creeping phlox.

- ✔ **How to plant:** Position the heath in the back corner of the trough and
add the two rockcresses in front of the heath, planted side by side. Set
the primrose in the center along the front rim and place the juniper
next to it. In the back corner, plant the saxifrage and finish with the
creeping phlox in the front corner of the container.

- ✔ **Special tips:** Use a soil mix of crushed rock or grit, topsoil, and high
grade, soil-based potting soil so that you have both good drainage and
high moisture retention. Cover the soil surface with small gravel or
stone chips to keep plants clean and to discourage rot. Attend consci-
entiously to grooming tasks.

Scented sensations

The wonderful fragrances that drift on the breeze add the final exclamation
point in this colorful, highly textured ceramic bowl. As shown in Figure 15-8,
Chocolate cosmos heads the list of unusual flowers displayed here, and its
mahogany blossoms really, truly smell like chocolate. Scented geraniums
spill from the bowl with delicate dark pink flowers and richly textured
foliage that releases a fruity fragrance. Dianthus is the ideal filler with

masses of spicy, two-toned flowers. A handful of dazzling white nicotianas, standing tall in the background, complete the picture. Reserve a spot for this display near your outdoor seating area so that you can enjoy the subtle scents and captivating colors.

- ✔ **Container:** You have a range of colors to choose from when you select a heavy-duty ceramic bowl with a glazed finish. This one — a full 18 inches across — is big enough for a generous collection of plants. Inspect the inside of the pot because you may need to punch out or drill a drainage hole before you plant.

- ✔ **Plants:** One chocolate cosmos, one scented geranium, two dianthus, and three nicotianas.

- ✔ **How to plant:** Starting in the back, center the nicotianas along the rim. Next plant the chocolate cosmos in the middle of the bowl, and add a dianthus on either side. Plant the scented geranium along the front rim, giving it plenty of room to spread.

- ✔ **Special tips:** Don't worry if it seems like the plants don't quite fill up the bowl — give them time. In fact, plan to trim back wayward stems on the geranium and snip off spent stems on the dianthus. Expect everything but the nicotiana to come back in subsequent years, despite looking a bit sparse in winter. Enjoy the scented blossoms and leaves in the house by snipping stems and leaves at their summer peak. This also helps keep plants within your container's boundaries.

Figure 15-8:
Scented
sensations.

Shade-lover's delight

Dappled light, refreshing shade, and cool breezes paint the backdrop for this winning combination featuring a flower-filled rustic planter box. And with scenery defined by lush plants blooming in cool, regal colors, you have a garden retreat that's hard to resist. A combination of trailing and upright fuchsias with striking two-toned flowers anchors the box with long-lasting color (see Figure 15-9). Lacy, light green fronds of maidenhair fern add balance and texture, while the impatiens provide almost constant color. The color combination of lavender, purple, lilac, rose, and pink shades harmonizes well. A classic touch of white brings life and contrast to the collection.

- ✔ **Container:** We suggest a container made of old lumber. You may find rustic, recycled garden containers ready-made at nurseries and garden centers. Or, with a hammer and a few nails, you can put one together yourself using planks or boards. Stick to redwood or cedar for the longest-lasting results. Ours is 4 feet long, 11 inches deep, and 10 inches wide.

- ✔ **Plants:** Three upright fuchsias, one trailing fuchsia, two maidenhair ferns, and nine impatiens in mixed colors.

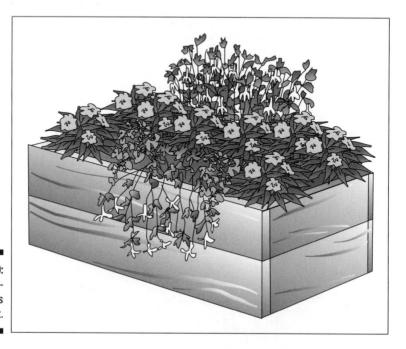

Figure 15-9:
Shade-
lover's
delight.

✔ **How to plant:** Set the tall fuchsias along the back, leaving a few inches in between plants and at the corners. Next plant the trailing fuchsia in the center along the front rim. Now plant the two ferns on either side of the trailing fuchsia. Fill in the remaining spaces with the impatiens, varying the colors as you go.

✔ **Special tips:** It's important to keep your planter from staying overly wet, even though the shade-lovers like plenty of water. Allow the bottom to dry by raising the box a couple of inches; set it on bricks or planks. Since you need to water often, make sure that you maintain a regular fertilizing schedule.

Next on the menu

You can go straight from patio to kitchen with savory vegetables and herbs just waiting to prove their worth in favorite recipes. Showing that tomatoes do well even in captivity, a caged patio variety can offer you scores of fruit (see Figure 15-10). Add to the bounty with plenty of sweet, green (or choose red or yellow) bell peppers. Blending beautifully with tomatoes, sweet basil adds lush and tasty leaves that are a joy to harvest. Rounding out the menu are an attractive little clump of garlic chives and the versatile, super-quick, super-pungent cilantro.

Figure 15-10:
Next on the
menu.

✔ **Container:** Go grand here, if you can, to get the most from your mini-veggie garden. Terra-cotta pots 18 inches or more in diameter can give you good space for all the edibles. And, if you choose a pot with straight rather than tapered sides, you have even more room for roots. As always, terra-cotta is easy to find and relatively inexpensive, and it displays well just about anywhere.

✔ **Plants:** One Patio tomato, one green bell pepper, one sweet basil, one garlic chives, and one cilantro.

✔ **How to plant:** Start with the tomato toward the back, planting it a bit deep by burying a few sets of leaves. Add a wire cage over the tomato to support and train it. Then plant the pepper next to the tomato, and drop the basil in the center of the pot. On one side of the basil along the front, plant the chives, and on the other side, add the cilantro. Leave a few inches between all the plants.

✔ **Special tips:** Save on labor later on by mixing timed-release fertilizer granules in with your potting soil to give plants a good start. A key to success with a container of edibles is early harvest. Take ripe fruit as soon as you can, and regularly clip foliage on the basil, chives, and cilantro to keep plants under control and to ensure continuous fresh foliage.

Reflective beauty

Enjoy the wonderful textures and brilliant flowers of aquatic plants in this easy-to-assemble tub water garden, which is shown in Figurre 15-11. A watertight half-barrel can host a collection of floating and submerged plants. Japanese iris provides dramatic flair with spectacular spring blooms and deep green foliage. Parrot's feather fills the gaps with fine, delicate foliage, and shellflower adds distinctive form from undulating petals in a rosette arrangement. Purple-leaf cardinal flower lends a contrasting note with brilliant red summer flowers on long stems. Water hyacinths finish the scene, with their unique shape and lavender summer flowers.

✔ **Container:** Recycled wine or whiskey barrels are ideal for an impromptu water garden that you can set up on your patio or deck. The watertight barrels are long-lasting and decorative, giving you ample space for plenty of plants.

✔ **Plants:** One Japanese iris, one cardinal flower, one clump of parrot's feather, one shellflower, and three water hyacinths. (These are all special aquatic plants.)

✔ **How to plant:** Use plastic or terra-cotta pots and heavy garden soil for the cardinal flower, iris, and parrot's feather. Plant them in individual pots, and cover the soil surface with rocks. Rinse away loose dirt and debris; submerge the pots in the barrel filled with water. Simply float the surface plants — shellflower and water hyacinth — on the water toward the front of the tub.

✔ **Special tips:** Don't be alarmed if the water turns pea green at first. Discoloration occurs when the dissolved nutrients in the water fuel small algae. The murkiness is only temporary, and the water quickly clears. Add a special touch to your garden with a small submersible pump to give the engaging sounds of splashing water. And don't forget the fish. Goldfish (yes, the kind that you win at the county fair) are a perfect addition and give the water ecological balance — better check locally for cold-weather care of fish in your climate.

Entryway elegance

Greet your visitors in style with this glorious combination of flowers in a classic container perfect for a sunny front porch (see Figure 15-12). You can enjoy years of midsummer color from the dwarf crape myrtle shrub. Ever-reliable petunias match the deep pink of the crape myrtle. Variegated ivy cascades with wonderful grace. Daisies add bright cheer, and the contrasting deep tones of spilling lobelia complete the collection. You can keep this floral display going season after season by simply replacing the annuals as needed with fresh plants.

Figure 15-11:
Reflective
beauty.

✔ **Container:** Sometimes the container is as much of the show as the flowers — the case here with an impressive cement urn. You can discover all kinds of styles, colors, and sizes in nurseries and garden centers and although they may be more costly than traditional clay pots, urns return dividends as garden accents.

✔ **Plants:** One dwarf crape myrtle, two English ivies, one marguerite daisy, five petunias, and four lobelias.

✔ **How to plant:** Start with the dwarf crape myrtle toward the center of the urn, and surround this with the petunias. Drop the ivies along the front rim and plant the daisy in the center. Fill in the gaps along the rim with lobelias.

✔ **Special tips:** Urns that overflow with flowers look best, so make sure that all the annuals fill in evenly. Frequent applications of liquid fertilizer certainly help. Keep faded flowers groomed, and pinch back the petunias if they get leggy.

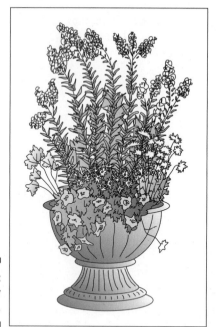

Figure 15-12:
Entryway
elegance.

Part V
Special Effects

The 5th Wave®   By Rich Tennant

"Personally, I think they're beautiful. But I'm not sure a climbing rose bush goes hand in hand with a football team known as The Mad Dogs."

In this part . . .

An eye for the dramatic? Looking for a special lead to make sense of a simple cast? The search may be way above your head — as in hanging from a thread to show the sewmanship in a clever basket of pins-and-needleslike cactus. If you're scouting for original designs, look no further than your own imagination. Container plants appreciate their roles as healthy alternatives to in-ground gardens, and you can help these boundary-resourceful characters take center stage in an interplay of art and science.

Chapter 16

Hanging Baskets

. . . .

In This Chapter

▶ Designing and displaying hanging baskets

▶ Choosing the plants

▶ Caring for your creations

▶ Planting six different kinds of baskets

. . . .

Considering how spectacular hanging baskets can be, we know what you're wondering: Aren't baskets 1) hard to plant and 2) a pain to maintain? Happily, the answers are as follows: a qualified "no" and a bit more qualified "not really."

Planting a hanging basket calls for steps beyond what's necessary for ordinary containers but requires no special skills, tools, or dexterity. Taking care of baskets mainly demands a good memory and a strong sense of duty. Baskets can need regular (read that as daily) care at certain times of year — you can't forget to water during hot weather!

The rewards of growing hanging baskets are pretty obvious — beautiful flowers or greenery at eye level or overhead where you can really appreciate the spectacular view.

Before getting into the nuts and bolts of planting and maintenance, you may want to explore how you can use hanging baskets to decorate.

How and Where to Display Baskets

Thinking about where to display baskets can come before or after you have the plants. We like to bring it up early because location can help determine your choice of container and plants.

Bottom line for displaying hanging baskets: A good-looking basket deserves center stage. Keep in mind that baskets look great in areas where you otherwise have no color. And remember that they can be viewed from indoors as well.

Before deciding on a location, make sure that you figure out how to water the basket. With daily watering in warm weather a must, place the basket where you can reach it with a hose, watering can, or irrigation system. Hanging baskets drain freely, important to keep in mind if you plan to display the suspended containers near seating areas — unless, of course, you have garden guests that you *want* to surprise. Protect winter and spring baskets in a sheltered spot out of strong winds and rain.

Here's a rundown of potential display ideas:

- Add a spark of grace and color to entryways, and let your baskets extend a classy welcome to visitors. Be sure to hang the baskets where they can drain freely and not interfere with walkways or steps. Good spots: under eaves or on brackets on posts or walls near the front door.

- Dress up your porches. Here baskets offer welcome color and greenery for close-up enjoyment.

- Covered patios, arbors, and overhead structures simply cry for hanging baskets — especially if you don't have vines growing on the structures. Different areas may give you different exposures, enabling you to use baskets for both sun and shade.

- Bring life to bare walls or fences with flat-backed baskets or hanging baskets on brackets. Drab areas dress up well with a little added interest. Plain surfaces offer a perfect backdrop or framing element to set the baskets off.

- Pop a bracket on a post and expect to be amazed at how easily a hanging basket can turn ordinary into eye-appealing. Try mounting baskets on two sides at two or three different levels for an impressive show.

- Use natural support and suspend a shady basket from a tree limb. Just be sure the basket hangs high enough so that no one walks into it. Protect the tree by using soft plastic or rubber covers over the mounting cable or chain.

- Position baskets outside a prominent window where you can view them from indoors and outdoors.

What You Need to Plan Your Planting

Basic materials for planting hanging baskets include the basket, liner material (optional), soil mix, and a way to hang the basket.

Start by selecting the basket itself. You have lots of options for either open-sided or closed (solid) baskets. Choose a basket that fits with other nearby containers or that stands out well on its own. Here are the common basket types.

Traditional wire

Typically made of galvanized or plastic-coated metal, these baskets are available in shapes that include round, oval, flat-bottomed, and flat-backed (see Figure 16-1). Typical sizes range from 8 to 18 inches in diameter. Open-frame style enables you to plant through the sides so that plants can cover the entire basket. Typically lined with sphagnum moss, these baskets dry out quickly.

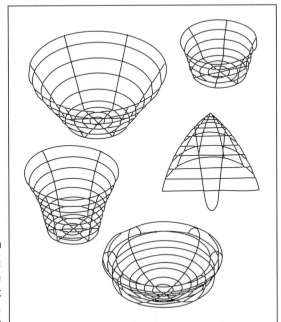

Figure 16-1: Some wire basket variations.

Wooden box

For wooden boxes, your choices include solid wood sides (see Figure 16-2) and slatted sides that allow for planting through the openings. Use liners with open-sided boxes. Wet boxes can be heavy, so use very secure hooks. Solid boxes retain water well.

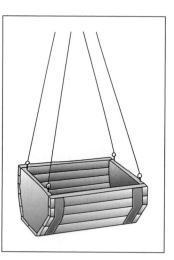

Figure 16-2:
A wooden box hanging basket.

Solid and open-sided plastic

These types of baskets are inexpensive and lightweight. Use lots of trailing plants along the rim of solid baskets and expect them to grow down and cover the sides. Open-sided baskets offer the convenience of built-in planting holes — no liners required. Both solid and open types hold moisture fairly well.

Plastic towers

These are special cylindrical, soft-plastic containers with sides that you can slit open to plant through. As plants fill in, the container seems to disappear. A hard plastic top and bottom give added stability. Some towers have reservoirs in the bottom to keep soil moist.

Self-watering basket

This is usually a plastic pot with a built-in reservoir. Water drains into the reservoir and is drawn up into the soil as it dries out — great for baskets that you can't water daily.

Pre-formed fiber or peat pots

These are rigid and hold water well but often don't have openings in the sides. They only last for about a year.

Looking at liners

For open baskets, liners are essential to keep the soil mix in place. You discover more about how to use liners in the planting step-by steps later in the chapter. The following list offers the common types, along with advantages and drawbacks of each:

- ✔ **Sphagnum moss** is attractive, natural looking, and easy to work with, but it does dry out quickly.

- ✔ **Plastic liners** are easy to cut to shape, and allow you to make openings to plant through the sides. However, they're unattractive until plants fill in and they don't last longer than a season or two.

- ✔ **Coco-fiber liners** offer a neat look and can be cut to fit most baskets. They often accompany baskets that you buy. If you overlap side pieces or cut notches in panels, you can plant through the sides.

Selecting a soil mix

A successful soil mix for hanging baskets relies on two key considerations. First, the mix needs to be light. Second, the soil must stay as moist as possible. Where do you get such a concoction? Easy.

Start with a bag of high-quality potting mix and add perlite or vermiculite at the ratio of three parts soil mix to one part additive. Perlite and vermiculite help absorb and retain water, plus lighten the mix; both are available at garden supplies. You can also mix in timed-release fertilizer granules.

Another option is to combine commercial soil mix with water-storing crystals that absorb water and turn gel-like, releasing moisture slowly as the soil dries. Soak crystals in water and add to the soil mix according to package directions.

Hanging the basket

Despite good intentions and light soil mix, baskets can be heavy. Make sure that you use the type of sturdy wires or chains sold with hanging baskets. (Various hanging devices are shown in Figure 16-3.) Swivels in the hangers allow you to rotate the plant for even sunlight and watering.

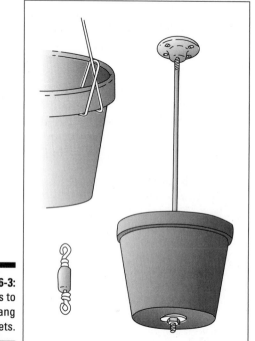

Figure 16-3:
Ways to
hang
baskets.

The Business of Basket Design

There's nothing at all wrong with simply stuffing one glorious fuchsia or begonia in a basket — in fact, the result can be stunning. But for some really special effects, you can combine a variety of plants in the same basket. Here are seven key questions that can help you choose the right basket and select plants that work well together:

- ✔ What do you want the focus to be — flowers, foliage, fragrance, edibles, or perhaps a combination of all these elements?

- ✔ What type of basket do you want? You have lots of options. Consider material, shape, and where and how you plan to mount or hang it.

✔ Do you want plants to grow through the sides as well as fill and spill from the top? Remember your options include trailers, fillers, and upright plants.

✔ What color scheme do you have in mind and how do you expect texture and form of the foliage to fit in? Basket plants can weave together beautifully — make sure that your plants match up well, offering either similarities or interesting contrasts.

✔ How do you foresee the basket being viewed: straight on, from above, or from below? Thinking about perspective helps you decide where to position colorful and trailing plants for the most impact.

✔ What's the exposure likely to be? Sun, shade, wind, and water requirements can guide you to the right plants.

✔ When do you want the peak bloom or how long do you need the display to last? You may choose short-season stars like annuals that provide a colorful show over several weeks. Or you can go for longer-lasting perennials or even evergreen plants such as ivy or periwinkle that offer long-lasting good looks.

A lot to consider? Maybe, but as you gather plants and materials you begin to see the basket taking shape. Don't be afraid to experiment with plant combinations — especially with colors and textures — at the nursery when you buy plants. You can come close to your final look simply by placing young nursery plants side-by-side as you evaluate your choices.

Shoot for the Stars — Selecting Plants

Now comes the fun part — choosing the plants. At this point, we assume that you have your basket and some idea where you to display the finished product. You also put some thought into the effect that you want: color, foliage, fragrance, long-term good looks, whatever.

To finish the puzzle, we must plug in the final and most important pieces — the plants. In general, your selections need to be on the compact side (sorry, no shrubs or trees) because of the relatively small soil area. Even with this one small caution, you still have hundreds of wonderful plants that can give your basket color, class, and character. We list 30 good candidates in just a bit, but for now, here are some general tips to help you with basic plant selection:

✔ Upright or filler plants can anchor the center of the basket. Many plants fit this category. Taller blooming plants work great, as do uprights with interesting foliage or unusual texture. Keep in mind, though, that "tall" as defined here is going to be 18 inches or less in most cases.

✔ Trailing plants cover the basket rim and are usually the show-stoppers of the combination. Baskets can beautifully display trailers of all kinds — from dazzling annuals to classic ivy to luscious strawberries. Trailers can cascade way beyond the basket (ground ivy, for example) or simply spill softly over the rim with lots of color (lobelia).

✔ Mixing plants is one way to dramatize a basket. Variety is especially effective because plants grown so closely together can weave and blend to create striking combinations. Combine ivy geraniums, pansies, and fuchsias; geraniums and fuchsias can send up graceful arching stems that crisscross over masses of bold and bright petunias.

✔ Go wild with plants. Some of the more interesting and arresting baskets combine many kinds and colors of plants. Throw in petunia, lobelia, dwarf marigold, geranium, ivy geranium, verbena, and — for a bold variegated foliage accent — Glacier Ice ivy.

✔ Or calm things down — and still create a striking display — with a single type in a single color. Ivy geraniums, impatiens, begonias, petunias, and pansies are perfect for a solid mass of color.

Meet the cast

Here's a list of the best of the best: ten top trailers, ten outstanding fillers, and ten excellent upright plants for you to consider. You can find more information on some of these plants in the chapters on annuals (Chapter 6) and perennials (Chapter 7).

Trailing plants

Use the following plants along the rims of the baskets where they can spill over the sides. Or plant in the sides and let them dangle gracefully.

✔ Cascading petunia

✔ Ivy geranium

✔ Helichrysum

✔ Kingfisher daisy

✔ Lantana

✔ Lobelia

✔ Nasturtium

✔ Trailing fuchsia

✔ Verbena

Upright plants

These tall types work best when planted in the center of the hanging basket:

- ✔ Calendula
- ✔ Coleus
- ✔ Coreopsis
- ✔ English primrose
- ✔ Geranium
- ✔ Impatiens
- ✔ Marigold
- ✔ Mimulus
- ✔ Transvaal daisy
- ✔ Zinnia

Fillers

These choices are considered versatile performers in baskets. Plant them in the center, or near taller plants, or between trailers. Or plant them in the side holes.

- ✔ Bedding begonias
- ✔ Butterfly flower
- ✔ Calceolaria
- ✔ Dianthus
- ✔ Malacoides primrose
- ✔ Pansy
- ✔ Phlox
- ✔ Salvia
- ✔ Sweet alyssum
- ✔ Vinca

Steps for Sure-Fire Success

Finally, we graduate to actually creating our baskets. Try these steps for planting three different kinds: open wire, wire with flexible liner, and closed (wood or plastic). Planting is really a lot simpler than it may seem at first glance. Even the most involved — the moss-lined wire basket — only takes six steps to put together. Start by gathering all your materials together in a comfortable place to work. You need the basket, liner material, soil mix, plants, bucket, and a watering can.

Planting an open wire basket

1. **Start by soaking sphagnum moss in water for at least 10 minutes.**

   If necessary, support the basket in a large pot or bucket to keep it upright.

2. **Begin to line your basket by laying sheets of dampened moss — about 1 inch thick — along the bottom and halfway up the sides.**

3. **Fill basket with soil loosely to just below the moss level and then continue lining the sides with moss, right up to the top until moss covers the rim area, as shown in Figure 16-4.**

   Use plenty of moss so that you have no gaps, and fill loosely with more soil until you reach the top.

4. **Begin planting the sides by starting near the bottom, as shown in Figure 16-5.**

   Carefully open a space between the wires and through the moss. Loosen any tangled roots, and insert the roots through the hole and into the moist soil. Use more wads of moss to tuck the plant in securely, and gently bend the wires together above and below the plant.

5. **Continue planting the sides.**

   Allow at least 3 inches between plants as you stagger them evenly around the sides. The more plants you place here, the quicker things can grow together and the less basket you see later on.

6. **Plant in the top of the basket, as shown in Figure 16-6.**

   Again, the fuller you plant the top, the quicker your basket can become a mass of color and texture. Space plants evenly with the tallest in the center. Set them so that the soil level is slightly below the rim. Be careful not to plant right over the roots of side plants near the rim. Firm the top plants in, adding more soil as needed but keeping the level below the top of the moss.

Figure 16-4:
Lining the
basket.

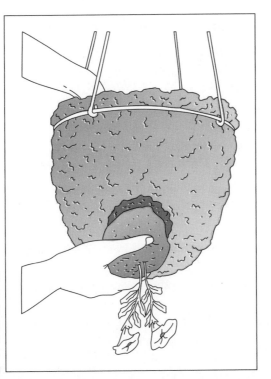

Figure 16-5:
Begin
planting
from the
bottom.

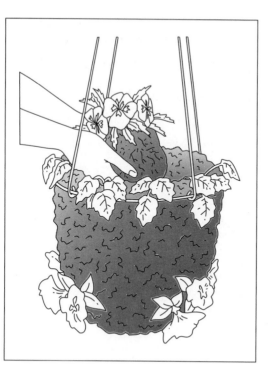

Figure 16-6:
After you've
planted
along the
sides, you
can plant
on top.

7. **Attach the supports and hang the basket.**

8. **Water gently and thoroughly until water drains freely.**

9. **Then replace any moss that may have fallen out, tucking new moss securely around the plants.**

10. **Water daily as plants become established.**

Planting a wire basket with a flexible liner

1. **Set the liner in the basket, seating it firmly against the frame. Side panels overlap slightly.**

2. **Add a small amount of soil mix in the bottom.**

3. **Gently insert plants through the slits in the sides where pieces overlap. Loosen any tangled roots.**

4. **Tuck the liner edges back together around the plant to keep soil from spilling out.**

5. **Add more soil around the roots, and fill to just below the rim.**

   Firm the soil in with your fingers and double-check to see that the liner is securely in place.

6. Plant the tall selections in the center of the basket and drop in any fillers between the central plants and the rim.

7. Plant trailers along the rim, positioning them so that the longest stems spill over the sides.

8. Firm all the plants in and add soil to any low spots.

9. Attach the chain or wire hanger and put the basket in place.

10. Water thoroughly and often for a week or two.

Planting a solid basket

1. Add a few crockery pieces or stones over the drain holes in the bottom of the basket.

2. Fill the container with a lightweight potting mixture containing granular or timed-release fertilizers (either as part of the mix or added by you).

3. Plant the upright plants toward the center, firming the soil around them.

4. Add the fillers, if you have room for them, near the plants in the center, and finish with the trailers along the rim.

5. Hang and water the basket immediately.

6. Water daily for the first few days and then ease off if the soil is staying moist. Step up watering if the weather turns hot.

Tricks for Trouble-Free Maintenance

Sorry. There really aren't any tricks here. No magic either. What you need is just a bit of consistent care to keep your baskets in top form. The basics of routine care — watering, fertilizing, and grooming — lead the list of caretaking tips, followed by a few other maintenance mainstays:

✔ **Watering:** The key here is do it. And do it and do it again. Watering regularly is especially important if you have moss-lined baskets because they dry out quite quickly. Water once or twice daily in warm weather using a thorough, gentle overhead soaking. Hit the top and sides. Watering wands or fan nozzles are an ideal way to disperse a gentle shower. Make life easy for yourself by setting up a drip system with a mister attachment to spray each basket. If you go away for a few days, rather than entrust a neighborhood water-person, move the basket into a shady spot on the ground where sprinklers can hit it.

✔ **Fertilizing:** If you didn't add timed-release or granular products to your potting mix, give plants a boost every two weeks with liquid fertilizer. Package directions tell you how much to mix with water. Wet the soil and the foliage. A monthly liquid boost is a wise move even if you have nutrients in the soil mix.

✔ **Grooming:** This is probably old news to you — remove faded flowers and stems, pick off dried or yellowing leaves, and cut back nonblooming stems or flower stalks. You're really forcing plants to make more buds. As you groom, check liners to be sure that no soil is spilling out. Tuck in extra moss or reposition liners to cover any gaps.

✔ **Replant:** Remove dead or fading plants as soon as you find them and fill in any bare areas with fresh plants; a little pampering can help keep your basket balanced and full. Check trailers to see that they are not all leaning in one direction and add new plants or reposition stems for better balance.

✔ **Rotate:** If plants are all leaning toward the light, spin your basket. Rotating gives everything even exposure for a full, lush look and overall color.

Six Hanging Basket Designs

These designs can get you started. Feel free to substitute local favorites for varieties suggested here. Thank writer/designer Peggy Henry for all six of the following designs.

Color connection

The goal for this wire basket is a mad mix of multi-colored flowers. Trailing lantana sets the stage with arching stems and spectacular flower clusters in yellow, pink, peach, and orange. Another awesome trailer, ivy geranium, adds arresting red as it weaves through marigolds and lavender and purple petunias. Completing the picture, lobelias in shades from white to deep blue grow through the sides, as shown in Figure 16-7.

Expect this basket to stay thirsty. You need to water it regularly. Check to be sure that the moss stays in place.

1 Confetti trailing lantana

2 Mini Cascade ivy geraniums

6 Boy o' Boy mix marigolds

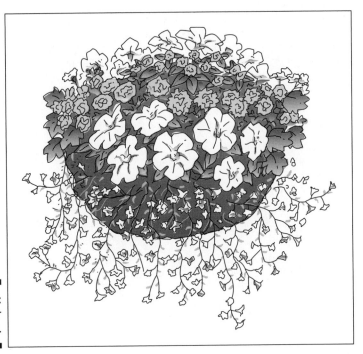

Figure 16-7:
Color
connection.

12 Cascade Mix lobelias

3 Cascade Purple petunias

3 Cascade Lavender petunias

Scented sensations

Fragrant flowers and foliage offer sensory delights in this unforgettable basket. Sweet alyssum spills from the sides as twining stems of sweet peas and scented geranium blend beautifully. Dianthus adds dramatic color and light fragrance, and catmint contributes attractive gray-green foliage and purple flowers. Hang this basket near windows or seating areas to enjoy its charms (see Figure 16-8).

Trim the foliage if it gets out of hand. Dry the geranium and catmint leaves and all the flowers for use in potpourris.

1 Catmint

1 Lemon-scented geranium

6 Knee-high Mix sweet peas

Figure 16-8:
Scented
sensation.

4 Purple sweet alyssum

4 White sweet alyssum

5 Telstar Mix dianthus

Edible aerials

Adaptable herbs and a tiny tomato give this basket tremendous appeal, with both a visual and a culinary payoff. Enjoy sprigs of rosemary and compact spicy globe basil in your favorite dishes, and top off salads and main dishes with a garnish featuring bright, bold nasturtium blossoms. Rounding out our collection is elegant, variegated garden sage with striking gold-edged leaves, as shown in Figure 16-9.

Trim plants as you harvest leaves to keep the basket under control. Consider cutting back leaves and flowers for drying or freezing if plants become too crowded.

Figure 16-9:
Edible
aerials.

1 Tumbler Hybrid tomato

1 "Spicy Globe" basil

1 trailing rosemary

1 Aurea's garden sage

6 Jewel Mix nasturtiums

Shady delight

This combination of flowers in rich colors and textures is sure to light up a shady spot on your deck or patio — lavenders, purples, blues, and pinks are set off by bright white. Featured are the arching stems and abundant fuchsia flowers, followed by big, bold begonias. Impatiens beautifully fill the gaps, and ivy winds its way throughout, lending texture and style (shown in Figure 16-10).

Watch for powdery mildew: leaves covered with a grayish dusting. Remove damaged leaves and water early in the day to prevent mildew.

Figure 16-10:
Shady
delight.

1 Cascade fuchsia

3 'White Nonstop' begonias

9 Impatiens — mixed colors

12 Cascade Mix lobelias

3 Variegated English ivies

Textured treasures

Splendid textures, outstanding shapes, and wonderful colors give this collection of succulents special status. Succulents are easy plants to grow in baskets, filling gaps and spaces ideally. Here the rosettes of hen and chicks play off the smooth texture of the jade plant. And you have the interesting colors of various upright and trailing sedums, as shown in Figure 16-11.

Use a special soil mix for cactus and succulents, and don't overwater them. Take care handling delicate trailers such as the donkey tails. Simply tuck in extra stems in bare spots, holding plants through the wire with extra moss.

Figure 16-11:
Textured
treasures.

1 Jade plant

1 Hen and chicks

1 Sedum spectabile (upright)

3 Donkey tails

1 Sedum cauticolum

6 Cape Blanco sedum

6 Pink Blush sedum

6 Pork and Beans sedum

Wall basket collection

Symmetry and style are the hallmarks of this trio of flat-backed wire baskets featuring outstanding annuals. Multicolored sweet William grows through and covers the sides. Pansies, in a pretty pastel mix, and Malacoides primroses, with lacy and delicate tiny flowers, spill from the top (see Figure 16-12).

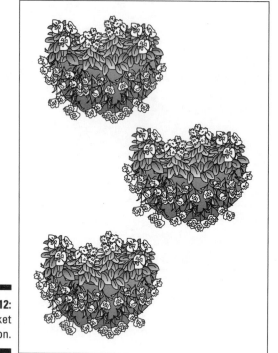

Figure 16-12:
Wall basket
collection.

We're suggesting that you use three small baskets for looks. They'll have a tendency to dry out quickly, so water them often in dry, warm, or windy weather. These baskets are easy to mount and add interest and color to fences, walls, posts, or arbors.

9 Wee Willie sweet Williams

6 Imperial Shades pansies

6 Prima Mix Malacoides primroses

Chapter 17

Containers with Extra Character

· ·

In This Chapter

▶ Why use special containers?

▶ Window boxes, water gardens, strawberry jars

▶ The lowdown on troughs and stone sinks

▶ Urns for elegance

▶ Whimsical containers

· ·

*W*hy ride a roller coaster, have parties, or plant petunias in an old wheelbarrow? Because it's fun — unless you get motion sickness, are allergic to onion dip and small talk, or desperately need something to haul a load of bricks.

We better stick to the safety of the garden, where we suggest you break away from standard terra-cotta pots and take your container gardening to a different level.

We're talking about using containers that get noticed, that bring an amusing touch to the landscape, that really show off your prize pansies. You can put plants in dramatic places or add a touch of nostalgia. You can create charm or even tackiness in the good sense of the word (didn't know there was a good sense to that word, did you?).

This chapter introduces you to a wide range of unusual containers and how to use them — including window boxes, water gardens, urns, troughs, strawberry jars, and even wheelbarrows and old buckets. We look at each suggestion in detail and check out which plants work best with these slightly offbeat options.

You're already familiar with many of the containers described in this chapter. Strawberry jars and urns are available at nurseries and garden centers all over. Expect to do a little more searching for the wacky and whimsical: the wheelbarrow, the antique milk can, the pair of leather boots, the slightly rusted coal scuttle. More on the adventure later.

Now for the specifics in each category. Besides being unusual, all these containers share two essentials: They must offer room for root growth and provide drainage in some way.

Window Box Basics

Window boxes need no introduction. We show one anyway in Figure 17-1. Picture the classic eye-catcher: a narrow box painted perfectly to match the house trim, abundantly spilling forth ivy geraniums, pansies, and petunias. You can come across plenty of these old-fashioned favorites embellishing gingerbread houses or jazzing up everything from a ranch-style home to a city flat.

Figure 17-1:
Window
boxes can
dress up
the exterior
of any
home.

Window boxes, of course, are just containers attached to the house. They're easy to plant. Here are some key points to keep in mind to help you choose, plant, and care for a window box:

✔ Start by selecting a style that matches your house. Treated softwood or hardwood boxes are easy to paint or stain to blend in beautifully with their surroundings. Plastic, metal, terra-cotta, or concrete boxes can work too, but are harder work with.

✔ Pay attention to size, too. A window box looks best if its length is within a couple of inches of the size of the window, although slight differences — long or short — won't hurt. Plants need room to grow and soil that doesn't dry out too fast — boxes should be at least 8 inches wide to provide room for top growth and 8 inches deep for the roots.

✔ Make your own box if your window is oddly sized. Use 1-inch boards and simple joinery with waterproof glue and galvanized or brass screws to secure the pieces. Drill several drain holes along the bottom.

✔ Go for a sunny exposure to please the most plants. This, though, increases your watering chores. Remember that some window boxes are protected from rains, so you need to check regularly for dryness. Don't worry if there's shade. Many excellent shade plants thrive in partial or full shade.

Position the box below the window by a few inches. If you happen to have a window that opens outward, you have to lower the box. Use steel brackets every 18 inches or so and fasten them into the siding or masonry with the proper screws. Rest the box on the supports and screw the bottom to the brackets. Always mount the box before you plant.

Planting and caring for your window box

You have three options for planting your window box:

✔ You can plant directly in the container.

✔ You can drop in potted plants and fill around them with moss, bark, or another lightweight material.

✔ You can put plants in a plastic or metal liner that fits inside the box. With this method, you can rotate liners and add fresh plants when current plantings pass their prime.

Basically, you plant the same way you do in any container. Cover the drain holes, fill with soil mixture, and firm soil around plants, leaving at least 1 inch at the top for watering. Use routine good care on the window box, starting with regular watering, feeding with a liquid fertilizer, and grooming to remove faded flowers and leaves.

Picking the (plant) winners

Picking a container and a location is a fine start for window box gardening, but picking the right plants really makes the difference in your growing success. Generally, select a mixture of *trailers,* compact *upright* plants that grow tall enough to be seen without blocking the window, *filler* plants, and *bulbs.*

For a dramatic display, choose plants that contrast with the background — bright plants against light siding or wood, pale flowers against dark brick walls. Here's a brief rundown of the top 12 plants — both annuals and permanent ones — for window box culture. But remember that our list is intended only to get you started; your plant choices are many and varied for dynamic window boxes.

Annuals

- **Sweet alyssum:** Stalwart, reliable, fragrant trailer in white, cream, pink, and purple. Alyssum is exceptionally easy to grow and fills in beautifully, often reseeding itself.

- **Lobelia:** Sound familiar? Yes, we often call on this little annual with clouds of cascading color in white, sky blue, dark blue, rose, lavender, and cobalt. Simply great in window boxes.

- **Pansies:** Perfect in any box, pansies offer prolific color in many hues and quickly fill gaps between permanent plants or other annuals, offering long-lasting color.

- **Petunias:** Choose these when you want a stunning summer box that shines in the sun. Try cascading varieties, as well as multifloras, for an abundance of blooms in a wide range of colors.

- **Impatiens:** *The* plant for shade, and awesome in window boxes — especially valuable for continuous color in a range of hues. Use low-growing, dwarf varieties. New Guinea hybrids also offer excellent foliage.

- **Dianthus:** You get the bonus of fragrance with the gift of color. Plants are well-behaved. If all goes well, a breeze blows, sending sweet scents through your open windows.

Permanent plants

- **Ivy geranium:** Yep. The selfsame winner in hanging baskets, this one also works really well in window boxes, gracing us with wonderful trailing stems covered with bright flowers. In cold climates, grow it as an annual.

- ✔ **Geraniums:** Bedding geraniums are the classic window box plant — grown for clusters of brilliant flowers in colors ranging from white to crimson to apple blossom pink. Plants are easy to grow. Consider geraniums an annual in cold climates.

- ✔ **Dwarf bulbs:** Forgive us for lumping so many bulbs together, but the miniature nature of many flowering bulbs — daffodils, crocus, grape hyacinth, cyclamen — makes them ideal players in the window box.

- ✔ **Ground ivy:** Impressive long stems spill from your window box in shimmering green or variegated tones. Ground ivy can survive through winter in milder climates.

- ✔ **English ivy:** Hardy, versatile, attractive, and useful for any box where you want trailing plants, ivy handles in sun or shade. For extra color, choose varieties with cream or yellow accents on the leaves.

- ✔ **Miniature roses:** You have dozens to choose from, and each one can be trusted to perform elegantly and effectively in combinations with annuals or other permanent plants. Some varieties also offer fragrance.

Water Garden Wisdom

Whether you pick barrels or ceramic bowls or galvanized tubs, all you really need for a water garden is something that holds water. By including water plants and special features like fish, stones, a small submersible pump, and maybe a fountain nozzle, you can create a container garden with tremendous appeal.

The process for planting your water garden is a simple one — after you select a vessel that holds water, you're halfway there. Find a permanent location for the container (especially if it's large) and level it. Then fill it with water within 4 to 6 inches of the top, and add a few bricks to set potted plants on.

Now you're ready to plant in containers that go underwater. Choose special bog or water plants that prefer a rather wet existence. You can find these plants in nurseries and some garden centers. They range in size from tiny 3-inch guys to larger 1-gallon plants. Look for plants with outstanding flowers (Japanese iris, water lily, cardinal flower, marsh marigold) or attractive foliage (water clover, houttuynia) Some give you interesting form (horsetail, fiber-optic grass, sweet flag) or wonderful texture (shellflower, parrot's feather, waterpoppy).

For underwater containers, use terra-cotta pots or special plastic baskets designed for water plants. Here's how you plant them:

1. **Fill the containers with heavy garden soil (lightweight potting mixes dissolve or float up) and pot them just like any container plant.**

2. **Leave room, though, for a layer of gravel or small rocks on the soil surface to keep the soil from washing away, as shown in Figure 17-2.**

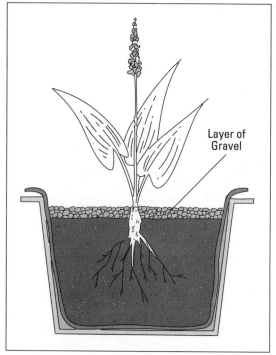

Layer of Gravel

Figure 17-2: Potting your soon-to-be-underwater plant.

3. **Rinse the container to remove any loose soil or debris before you drop it in the water.**

4. **Place your potted plant underwater.**

   Place most plants so that the rims are at water level. Allow others to float, and set water lilies a bit deeper, lowering them as new growth appears, as shown in Figure 17-3.

Figure 17-3:
You can place your containers at different depths.

Here are some quick tips for success with water gardens:

- ✔ Combine plants with different forms and textures for maximum interest. In deep pots and barrels, elevate containers on bricks so that they don't sit too deeply in the water.

- ✔ The easiest plants to use are floating ones and as a bonus, they help keep the water clear by using up nutrients in the water.

- ✔ Use waterproof sealant to seal cracks in barrels or holes in ceramic pots.

- ✔ Choose your location carefully: This is one container that you won't be moving, even if you want to. Look for a spot with sun to partial shade.

- ✔ Select compact plants, because even with barrels, there's little space. Many water plants become invasive; stick with smaller varieties or young plants and divide them if they grow too large.

- ✔ Add a goldfish or three if your container is at least 15 inches deep. Be careful with ceramic bowls or metal tubs in the summer sun — they can get hot, raising the water temperature dangerously high for fish.

Check with a garden center that handles water garden supplies for information on pumps, fish, maintenance, local factors, and other planting steps.

Pocket Planting in Strawberry Jars

Strawberry jars can be spotted at many nurseries and garden centers. Originally designed to hold strawberry plants (good guess!), they're tall terra-cotta pots with "pockets" scooped out of the sides all the way around at different levels. The cool part is that you get to plant both the top and sides for a mass of flowers or foliage when growth fills in. Sizes range, but most jars have between 8 to 15 pockets that are ideal for small plants like herbs or annuals.

Easy to plant and easy to care for, this type of container is a great choice for an unusual look if you have a small space such as a balcony or patio. Follow these easy steps for designing and planting an impressive strawberry jar:

1. **Decide what you want in the jar: herbs, mints, strawberries, or small flowers.**

   Or you can mix in sunny annuals with tasty herbs and have the best of both worlds.

2. **Buy enough plants for all the pockets, including one to four plants for the mouth at the top.**

   Six-pack plants are the ideal size for the side openings.

3. **Add a layer of rocks or pot shards over the bottom drain hole, and add potting mix to the level of the lowest openings (see Figure 17-4).**

Figure 17-4:
Start with rocks or pot shards and then add soil to the level of the lowest pocket.

4. **Decide where each plant goes.**

   Alternating themes or repeating patterns work well if you don't want a different plant in each slot.

5. **Gently break apart the root ball and carefully slip the roots through the opening, pulling from inside the jar.**

6. **Fill in soil up to the level of each pocket as you plant, as shown in Figure 17-5.**

Figure 17-5:
Add soil to each pocket.

Firm soil around the roots and pack it down around the plant in the mouth of each pocket. Repeat for all pockets.

7. **Plant the top of the jar with the remaining plants.**

8. **Immediately water the top and each pocket and replace any soil that washes away (see Figure 17-6).**

Keep the pot moist. Cut off flowers as they fade. Pinch tips for bushy growth. Harvest herbs often.

Troughs and Stone Sinks

Long and shallow is what these containers are all about.

Rectangular terra-cotta or ceramic troughs come in various sizes and you find them at nurseries or home centers. Troughs and sinks are perfect for a mini-alpine garden, or a collection of succulents, or awesome trailers, or

Figure 17-6:
Water the
top and
each
pocket.

compact perennials. Outstanding trough and sink plants include thrift, rock cress, bellflower, pinks, gentian, rock rose, dwarf phlox, primrose, stonecrop, or saxifrage.

Antique stone sinks can be found if you're lucky and not afraid to spend money; there's also a version to make at home called hypertufa, as we describe in the following directions for making a charming faux stone planter that can resemble an aged stone sink or trough. Here's what you need and how you construct this easy-to-make, lightweight hypertufa container:

1 bag of Portland cement

1 bag of coarse sand

1 bale of peat moss or large bag of vermiculite

Chicken wire

2 rectangular cardboard boxes (for the mold, one fits inside the other with a 2-inch or larger gap in dimension)

1. **Mix together equal parts of cement and sand and two parts of peat moss or vermiculite in a wheelbarrow. Then add water until you get a stiff "dough."**

2. **Cut chicken wire to fit around the outside of the smaller box (to reinforce the inside of the form).**

3. **Place 2 to 3 inches of the mix in the bottom of the larger box, set the smaller box inside, and fill with the mix all around the sides between the larger and smaller boxes, packing firmly.**

   Keep the container in a dry spot.

4. **After two weeks, pull a corner of the inner box away to determine whether the trough is hard and dry. If so, fold in the box and pull it out.**

5. **Cut or peel away the outer box carefully, avoiding damage to the walls. Wet stubborn pieces and then remove them. Texture the sides with a light brushing.**

Timeless Classics: Urns

Urns are impressive. Typically, they're made of solid, one-piece construction with a base, pedestal, and decorated bowl. Urns are available with lots of decorative touches and finishes in all kinds of styles. Sizes range from table-top miniatures to massive jobs suitable for estates. They make fine focal points and work well in entryways, near double doors, on patios, freestanding in the garden, and in matched pairs to frame walkways, doorways, or seating areas.

Commonly, urns are made of concrete, which makes them nearly indestructible, but also quite heavy and fairly expensive. Cast-aluminum urns are lightweight, durable, and attractive, but expensive. Plastic urns are available, but unless you're using them to accent some beautiful and lifelike garden flamingos, you're better off with the earthier materials.

For the best results, choose a deep urn that offers ample space for roots. Containers that can accommodate a heavy root mass effectively hold bold specimen plants with dramatic foliage, such as a New Zealand flax or cabbage palm. Deep urns also are impressive with dwarf varieties of evergreen trees such as false cypress (*Chamaecypris*) or Japanese maples.

Achieve classic looks by combining an impressive upright plant with a few bright annuals (impatiens or begonias) and a trailer or two (ivy or ivy geraniums). Just be careful that the plants don't obscure the container. You want the attractive nature of the urn to show off, too.

To get started, check out this brief list and description of seasonal selections and permanent plants that can work wonders in urns — either as a medley or a solo act:

✔ **Spring specials.** Try a collection of classic bulbs — tulips, hyacinths, ranunculus, and daffodils — or go with a colorful patchwork of annuals like pansies, primroses, stock, and snapdragons. Mix and match the bulbs and annuals, and soften the edges of the urn with trailers — ivy, vinca, or ground ivy. For drama, add an unusual upright like flax or a dwarf evergreen.

✔ **Summer splendor.** This means mountains of color. Go with excellent annual flowers — petunia, phlox, marigold, nicotiana, Transvaal daisy — and add in some spilling color from lobelia, trailing geranium, and Dahlberg daisy.

✔ **Fall favorites.** You can go for a simple but elegant look by filling an urn with chrysanthemums in many colors and forms. Or, in milder climates, choose permanent plants that offer excellent fall foliage, such as a dwarf crepe myrtle, Japanese maple, or heavenly bamboo. Accent with other fall flowers — calendula, pansy, dianthus, or ageratum — and trailing plants.

✔ **Winter wonders.** A deep urn gives you the stage to showcase hardy evergreens. Try dwarf Alberta spruce, holly, false cypress, mugho pine, or small spruces. Another excellent choice is camellia, with attractive, shiny foliage and winter flowers. Sasanqua camellias, small-leafed and small-flowered, work very well in containers.

Saucers — Not So Shallow After All

Yes, these are the flat little dishes designed for a dull life under a pot. But, if you give them drainage, they can make ideal homes for small bulbs, succulents, or miniature plants like bonsai. Saucers also make ideal tabletop displays. Larger saucers work well on steps, patios, or decks.

Look for ceramic or terra-cotta saucers between 1 to 3 inches deep; they come in a variety of sizes. Use a high-speed electric drill and a masonry bit to drill drainage holes. Be patient and don't exert too much pressure on the drill bit, and you can expect good results. Try three to five small holes around the bottom of the saucer.

Planting a saucer is a snap. The key is finding plants that don't mind the shallow conditions. In the short run, you can try small bulbs like crocus, grape hyacinth, dwarf daffodils, or reticulata iris. The easy and portable nature of the saucers allows you to bring them indoors for bloom time.

Succulents are another great choice; their shallow roots enjoy plenty of space. Look, too, for rock garden plants and miniatures like tiny primroses, lobelia, violas, mosses, or bonsai plants.

Check saucers often to be sure that they don't dry out, and water the shallow-rooted plants as needed.

Whimsical One-of-a-Kinds

We're not even going to attempt to make aesthetic judgments here. All kinds of things can be and have been made into containers for plants: retired wooden and metal wheelbarrows, old cans and canisters, well-loved but retired garden boots. Do they look good? Beauty's in the eye . . . We just say, make sure that the improvised container has proper drain holes and room for roots to grow.

Where to find potential containers? Try thrift stores, farm supply stores, barn sales, garage sales, antique shops, your grandmother's toolshed, or estate sales. The key is to keep your eyes open and get the word out among friends and fellow gardeners who may run into exactly what you're looking for.

Because these are not run-of-the-mill containers, your prize picks deserve special consideration so that can show them off properly. Consider these tips for putting your more unusual plantings in the proper locations:

- ✔ Avoid clustering too many different kinds of containers together. This keeps you away from the garage-sale look, which also takes away from the uniqueness of each individual container.

- ✔ Go for a prominent place for a single outstanding container. Put it where it can't be missed — on the front porch, atop a table (if it's small), near a window where you can see it from indoors too, or even indoors, if the container's not too big.

- ✔ Groupings can be effective if you have, say, a collection of antique cans or buckets. Use pairs, as with urns, to frame a doorway or window. Dress up stairs, a corner of the deck, or a spot on the patio with groupings of the same type of container.

- ✔ Consider how the container drains, and plan to drill drainage holes if necessary. Keep in mind that small containers need water often.

- ✔ Expect long-term service outside to take its toll on some materials, including wooden buckets or wheelbarrows. Apply a preservative to keep wood from rotting.

- ✔ Give your whimsical container a home that suits it. A hollowed-out piece of tree trunk is perfect brimming with colorful impatiens in a shady glade near a deck. And that old pair of leather boots filled with succulents or compact annuals and ivy may fit perfectly on the steps near the garage or workshop.

Overall, you may find that unusual containers provide welcome exclamation points in the garden. They open avenues of creativity and attract sometimes surprising, always interesting, comments and conversation.

Part VI
Maintenance

The 5th Wave®   By Rich Tennant

"Before I show you the rest of 'Castle Dracula', let me show you my garden. It's a hobby with me. I do most of the work myself; however, Renfield helps keep the garden free of bugs."

In this part . . .

Sing it, if you know the first two words: "Staying alive, staying alive." Now that we know the goal, maybe we can agree how to make it happen. Without water, plant nutrients, periodic transport to a bigger place of residence, maybe a haircut now and then, and, okay — an occasional debugging — the green stuff that you love so much can show you shades of brown that don't match anything in your decor. This part can inspire you to reach new heights in tender care, starting from the ground up.

Chapter 18

Thirst Quenching

. . . .

In This Chapter

▶ What affects container water use

▶ Different ways to water

▶ How often to water

▶ How much water to apply

▶ Ways to conserve water

. . . .

You have to admit that our advice so far has been pretty laid-back: Choose terra-cotta or plastic pots, try impatiens or delphiniums, whatever. But when it comes to watering container plants, we are hard-liners. Do it the right way or get out of the game.

Unlike plants growing in the ground that can rely on deep roots to get them through dry spells, container-grown plants have limited soil from which to draw. When they dry out, they really dry out. And the repercussions of becoming parched are usually more severe and permanent than if the plants were in the ground.

What it comes down to is this: If you want to be successful growing plants in containers, that is, if you want your flowers to bloom well and your fruit, herbs, and vegetables to produce a bountiful harvest, you're going to have to become an attentive and efficient waterer. And in this chapter, we show you how.

Why and When Containers Need Water

How often container plants need water and how much they need when they need it depends on several factors, which the next sections cover.

Climate

If you live in an area like Seattle, Washington, or Biloxi, Mississippi, where rainfall is regular and reliable, watering isn't a constant chore, except in prolonged dry spells or periods of drought. In drier, hotter areas like Los Angeles, California, and Phoenix, Arizona, watering container plants is something that has to be in squeezed into your schedule almost on a daily basis.

Weather

Climate is determined by the average weather where you live on a season-to-season, year-to-year basis. Weather is what's happening outside right now. Out-of-the-ordinary weather can wreak havoc on your plants. Hot, dry winds can dry out a plant growing in a hanging basket or a clay pot, literally, in a matter of minutes.

Table 18-1, in a nutshell, tells you how to adjust watering according to weather conditions. Forgive us if our little chart is too common-sensical:

Table 18-1	Watering According to Weather
Water Less	*Water More*
Cooler temperatures	Warmer temperatures
Cloudy or overcast	Bright sunshine
Low wind	High wind
High humidity	Low humidity
Rain	No rain

Pot type

The porosity of a container influences how much water evaporates through its sides. And that can be a lot. At one extreme are hanging baskets lined with sphagnum moss, which seem to dry out as soon as you turn your back on them in hot weather. At the other end of the spectrum are plastic pots, metal, or thick concrete containers that hardly lose any moisture through their sides. In the middle are unglazed clay pots, which are pretty porous and dry out quickly, and wooden containers, which dry out slower but, depending on their thickness, tend to lose water through their sides.

Pot color

Lighter-colored containers reflect more sunlight and dry out more slowly than darker-colored ones that absorb heat.

Rootboundedness

Is that a word? Even if it isn't, the term means a lot to anyone who grows plants in pots. As a plant grows in a container, the roots become more and more crowded. At first, the roots of a recent transplant may not even fill the pot, so the plant's drinking system may not be able get to all the water in the soil. Over time, the roots fill the container and the rootball (roots and soil) becomes a tight mass of roots, especially on larger plants. The rootball then becomes hard to wet, making more frequent waterings necessary.

So, in summary, here are the high points of Watering 101: Just after planting a new container, you have to water it carefully until the roots start to fill the pot. Then you go through a period when you can back off a bit because the roots have a larger soil reservoir to drawn from. But then (all good things must come to an end), as roots start to fill the pot and become rootbound, you have to start watering more often again. Or you could transplant into a large pot. For help doing that, see Chapter 21.

Soil variations

Most potting soils used for containers are lightweight and dry out fairly quickly. But some dry out faster than others. For example, potting soils that are higher in organic materials like peat moss or compost can hold more water than those that contain a higher percentage of mineral components like sand or perlite. You can find out more about potting soils in Chapter 4.

Location, location, location

Containers placed in full sun almost always need more frequent watering than those in shady areas. That's pretty obvious, but things can be more subtle. For example, containers situated on a hot surface like a concrete patio are likely to dry out faster than those on a wood deck, which tends to stay cooler.

Genetic disposition

Most plants grown in containers need consistent soil moisture to grow well. But some plants can go drier than others. For example, let a pot full of lettuce go dry and the leaves lose moisture and probably never completely recover — you may as well replant. Cactus and succulents, on the other hand, are a lot more forgiving and can go through dry spells quite well; in fact, most prefer to be on the dry side. If they stay too wet, many cactus and succulents rot. Lavender is another plant that does best if soil goes a bit dry between waterings.

You have to remember that some things are beyond your control, but these contributing factors still affect your watering practices. Just go with the flow and make adjustments when and where you can.

Ways to Water Container Plants

Some methods for watering container plants are better than others, but making choices often depends on how many containers you have.

In some areas, certain watering techniques become a matter of necessity rather than practicality. Where droughts are common or water supplies are unpredictable, conservation is the order of the day. You need to water in ways that respects every precious drop. Where foliage diseases like powdery mildew are common, you want to keep water off the plant leaves and apply it to just the roots.

The next few pages describe several fundamental ways to water containers.

Hand watering

Probably the most commonly used method, hand watering allows you to easily make adjustments in how much water each pot gets according to its size and specific needs. Indoors, it's generally easiest to use one of many handheld watering cans, but there are also little hose setups that can be hooked to the sink faucet. Outdoors, most gardeners find it convenient to drag a hose around to water their pots. Many excellent types of hose-end attachments let you turn the water on and off without going all the way back to the faucet. Bubbler attachments soften the output of the water, which can prevent washing soil mix out of the container. There are even extensions that make it easier to water hanging pots (see Figure 18-1). Whatever you do, don't let the hose run so forcefully into the container that it washes out soil; soften the water stream with your hand, at least.

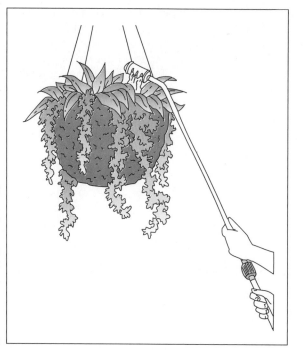

Figure 18-1:
A bubbler
on a hose
extender is
a neat tool
for watering
plants in
hanging
baskets.

Sprinklers

Although hose-end sprinklers are available in a variety of styles, they're not very efficient for watering containers — just too much water wasted. In a pinch, you may set up a sprinkler to water a raised bed or a grouping of containers, but if that becomes a habit, you're better off putting in a drip system, as described in the next section.

There is one possible problem with overhead watering, whether from a hose, watering can, or sprinkler. In humid climates, overhead watering can spread disease and turn your flowers into a moldy mess. In such areas, either install a drip system or hold the hose or watering can spout right above the rim of the pot so that the water doesn't get on the foliage or flowers.

Drip irrigation

Drip irrigation is a very effective and efficient way to water containers. A drip system provides water slowly through holes or emitters in black plastic pipe. Connect the pipe to a water supply, filter, and often a pressure regulator, and then weave it out (in constantly smaller pipes) to your containers. Water is slowly applied (or dripped) directly to the plants, as shown in Figure 18-2. Emitters differ by how much water they put out per minute: one-half gallon an hour, 1 gallon per hour, and so on. Drip systems usually have to run at least several hours to wet a large area, such as a raised bed. Smaller pots may only need to be run for an hour, depending on the output of the emitter. Larger pots may need more than one emitter. Watch your system carefully the first few times that you water. Poke around in the soil to see how long you need to water to wet a container, or how long it takes before water runs out the drainage holes. Then make adjustments.

Figure 18-2:
A drip
irrigation
system.

Drip irrigation systems are sold in most nurseries. You can also purchase them through the mail (see the Appendix). Pressure-compensating emitters apply water consistently from one end of the line to the other regardless of pressure changes due to uneven ground. Leaky pipe hoses (sometimes called soaker hoses, which are made of recycled tires) release water along their entire length. If the ground goes up and down at all, they apply water unevenly, but can still be useful in a level raised bed.

Drip irrigation systems hooked to automatic timers can really relieve the chore of watering a lot of containers. And although you may be hard-pressed to imagine weaving plastic pipe all over your porch or patio without creating a messy nightmare, rest assured that all it takes is a little creative thinking, burying some pipe, or running pipe above your plants, along eaves.

If you live in an area where the soil freezes, don't leave your drip system outside in winter. Your pipes may burst. Instead, drain out the water, roll up the pipe, and store it in the garage.

Self-watering pots

Best suited for smaller house plants, self-watering pots are also available in larger versions. Basically, they include a water reservoir, usually in the walls of the container, which is connected to the rootball of the plant through a small wick (like they use in Tiki torches). As the rootball dries out, the wick sucks up water from the reservoir and supplies it to the rootball, keeping it nice and wet (see Figure 18-3).

Figure 18-3:
A self-watering pot.

Be careful with self-watering pots. You don't want to forget about them and not fill the reservoir on time. They can also keep some plants too wet, causing them to rot and die. And because there's no way to leach the salts from a self-watering pot, salt burn can develop. For information on curing salt burn, which is not easy, see Chapter 21.

How Often to Water?

You know that a plant's water needs vary with the weather and the seasons — less in cool weather, more in warm weather, and so on. Even an automated system requires adjustment so that it waters less in spring and more in summer. Plan to practice your powers of observation and make watering adjustments accordingly.

However, there are other ways to tell when your plants need water or when containers are getting dry:

- ✔ **Your plants can send you a message.** That's right. When plants start to dry out, the leaves droop and wilt. The plant may also lose its bright green color and start to look a little drab. Make your goal to water before a plant reaches that point (consider it a cry for help).

- ✔ **Dig in the ground.** Stick your finger an inch or two into the soil in the top of a pot. If the soil feels dry, it's close to watering time.

- ✔ **Lift the pot.** As a pot dries out, it gets lighter. Compare how heavy a pot is right after watering thoroughly with how it feels a few days later. By simply tilting a pot on its edge and judging its weight, you eventually figure out how to tell when it's dry or getting close to it.

- ✔ **Use a moisture sensor.** Your nursery sells various devices for reading soil moisture. Most have a long, needlelike rod connected to a meter. You push the rod into the soil, and the meter tells you how wet the soil is. These sensors can be pretty handy, but don't trust them too much right off the bat. Some can be thrown off by salts in the soil. To start, see how their readings compare to what you discover by feeling the soil and lifting the pot. Then make adjustments.

Eventually, through observation, digging and lifting, you start to develop a watering schedule and a lot of the guesswork disappears.

How Much Water to Apply

When you water a container plant, the goal is to wet the entire rootball and apply just enough water so that some drains out the bottom. Now, if the container is properly planted, there's space between the top of the soil and container rim that you can fill with water. It may be anywhere from 1 inch in small containers to 4 or 5 inches in larger ones. But whatever the case, you have to fill it more than once to get enough water to wet the rootball. That means, you fill the pot once, let the water soak in, then fill it again, and, if necessary, fill it with water again until the whole rootball is wet and heavy.

This whole soaking thing is a bit tricky for one reason. As the rootball in a container dries, it shrinks, usually pulling away from the edges of the pot. So when you water that first time, the water drains down the edges without wetting the rootball hardly at all. This phenomenon explains why you need to make several passes with the hose or watering can — so that the rootball swells up a bit and seals the edges of the container, at which point the water can soak in. This is also why you can never judge how wet a rootball is by the amount of water that comes out the drainage hole. You can get fooled every time. Check water penetration by lifting the edge of the pot, as described earlier.

You can wet shrunken rootballs or plants that are really rootbound in a few other ways:

- ✔ **Water from the bottom.** If you place small trays or saucers underneath your pots to catch excess water, that water is gradually reabsorbed by a dry rootball. You're basically watering from the bottom and at a pace dictated by the plant.

  Its not a good idea to have a container sitting in water for a long time. The rootball becomes too wet and eventually the plant drowns. But submerging a pot partially, or even completely, for just a little while won't hurt and is a great way to wet a really dry rootball. In fact, if your houseplants get too dry, just fill up the kitchen sink with water and let the pots bathe for an hour or so, then drain the water. You see that the rootballs are wet.

- ✔ **Use drip irrigation.** Drip emitters apply water at a slow, steady rate and do a great job of thoroughly wetting the rootball.

Water-Saving Ways

Water shortages are a reality in almost any climate or region. And container plants use a lot of water, more than the same plants in the ground. Here are a few things that you can do when water is scarce or limited, when you just want to conserve the precious resource of fresh water, or if you just want to ease your watering chores:

- ✔ **Install drip irrigation.** It applies water slowly without runoff. Drip is definitely the most frugal watering system that you can use.

- ✔ **Double pot.** If you take a small pot and put it in a bigger pot, you reduce the amount of sunlight that hits the sides of the smaller pot, which helps cool the soil. Cooler soil means less water used.

- ✔ **Use soil polymers.** Soil polymers are weird Jell-O-like materials that hold hundreds of times their weight in water. If you mix them dry with your soil before you plant, you can stretch the time between waterings.

- ✔ **Transplant.** Moving a rootbound plant into a bigger container, where it has more soil to draw water from, can greatly reduce your watering chores. Better yet, if a container plant is really too much trouble to water, maybe you're better off planting it in the ground.

- ✔ **Move pots into the shade.** If the weather really gets hot, move your pots into the shade to cool them down and reduce water use. A few days of less sun won't hurt them.

- ✔ **Group pots.** If you put pots close together, they can shade each other and reduce the amount of sun that hits their sides.

- ✔ **Bury the pots.** Huh? That's right, just dig a hole and bury the pots just deep enough so that the rims are covered. Or you can build a wooden box, put the pots in, and fill around the edges with potting soil or organic material like peat moss or ground bark. You still have to water, but you use a lot less, especially if you also wet the soil around the pots. This method is drastic, but if water is really tight, or if you're going out of town for a while, it works.

- ✔ **Mulch.** A mulch is a layer of organic matter that's spread over the root zone beneath a plant. Several inches of heavy mulch, like large pieces of bark (so that they don't float away when you water) or other material, can cool the soil and reduce evaporation, thus saving water.

- ✔ **Pull weeds.** Weeds steal water meant for container plants. So keep them pulled.

✔ **Water efficiently.** Do as we suggested earlier in this chapter, and wet the entire rootball. You can have happier and healthier plants, and use less water in the long run.

✔ **Use rainwater.** Put a barrel or other collector where the drain pipes from your roof empty. Then use that water on your flowers.

✔ **Measure rainfall.** Keep track of how much rain you get. An inch is usually enough to let you skip a watering.

✔ **Plant unthirsty plants.** Some cactus and succulents can get by on little water, even when grown in containers.

Who Waters When You're out of Town?

So you're going on vacation and can't find anyone to water your plants. What are you going to do? Start by considering some of the water-saving methods described in the previous section, especially burying the pots or setting up a drip system with an automatic timer. But there are a couple other things you can do.

Wick water

Choosing to wick water is kind of like building your own self-watering pot and works best on smaller containers, especially houseplants. Go to a hardware store and buy some long wicks used for Tiki torches (for really small pots, you can use thick cotton string). Wet the wick and use a pencil to push it a few inches into the wet rootball of the plant. Stick the other end in a bowl or glass of water. As the rootball dries, it sucks water from the bowl through the wick, keeping it wet.

Don't try this the day you're getting ready to leave. Set it up a week in advance, to make sure it works, and to see how much of a water reservoir you need. If you use a big bucket to hold the water, you can water several plants at once.

Use soil polymers

Buy some soil polymers (we told you about those a few paragraphs back) at your local nursery, put some in a small plastic cup, and add water to turn them to Jell-O. Turn the cup upside down on top of the soil in your pot. Over time, the polymers slowly release their moisture to water the plant.

Again, don't wait to try this on the day you decide to leave. Test it a week or so before you go away to see how fast the water is released and how much polymer you need to use.

You may be able to buy a product that already has ready-to-use, hydrated polymers in a cup. You just flip it over on top of the soil in your pot. See if your nursery has it in stock.

Other Container Watering Tips

To sum up this whole watering business, here are some things not to forget:

- ✔ **Make sure that your pots have drainage holes.** Without them, the plant drowns.

- ✔ **Check drainage.** Even if your containers have holes in the bottom, they may fill up with roots, preventing proper drainage. Check the holes occasionally, and cut them open with a knife if necessary.

- ✔ **Use catch trays or saucers.** They help prevent water from getting all over the place when you water houseplants and give any plant a chance to suck up water from below. Remember, though, that the pot isn't happy sitting in water for more than a day or so — the roots drown. If necessary, raise the bottom of the pot out of the tray by placing it on small pieces of wood or bricks.

Chapter 19

Feeding

. . . .

In This Chapter

▶ Nourishing your plants for healthy growth

▶ Scoring comprehension in chemistry

▶ Shopping smart with fertilizer lingo

▶ Growing with organic fertilizers

. . . .

*T*hinking of your container plants as pets is understandable — after all, plants and pets are living things that provide you with amusement, companionship, and even an occasional gift of shedding (fortunately, hair balls aren't important to this discussion). In return for what your pets/ plants do for you, you have certain obligations, with feeding right near the top. Your plants depend on you in much the same way that your Border collie Max does. Generations ago, Max lost the ability to go out and forage for himself. Likewise, container plants can't send roots down deep and wide in the ground as do garden plants. Plants grown in the cushy but confined environment that you create for them search for nutrients within their own boundaries.

We promise to drop the pet metaphor before you start barking back, but not before we stress the importance of properly feeding container plants. You're the caretaker who provides your container plants the right nutrients at the right time. If you don't, you know what can happen. You may be the first to hear from the SPCCP (Society for Prevention of Cruelty to Container Plants).

As you discover in this chapter, different plants need different feeding. Read about special demands in the chapters devoted to types of plants (annuals, cactus, shrubs, and so on). Most importantly, find out why plants need nutrients — and how you can fill those requirements.

Preparing a Good Diet — Plant-Wise

For healthy growth, plants need 16 different elements. Carbon, hydrogen, and oxygen — the foundation blocks for photosynthesis — are required in large quantities, whether provided by nature or by your watering hose.

Plants also need relatively large amounts of nitrogen, phosphorus, and potassium. These elements are called macronutrients. Secondary nutrients — calcium, magnesium, and sulfur — are required in smaller quantities. And the micronutrients — iron, manganese, copper, boron, molybdenum, chlorine, and zinc — you guessed it, are needed in even smaller amounts.

Macronutrients, secondary nutrients, and micronutrients are mostly absorbed from the soil by plant roots. (These nutrients can also be absorbed by the foliage, but we don't want to get ahead of ourselves.) If any of these nutrients is missing from the soil in sufficient quantities, or is present in a form that the plant can't absorb, fertilizer's in order — or correction of the conditions that make absorbtion difficult.

For plants grown in the ground, most soils already contain enough nutrients needed for healthy growth. Many gardeners find that nitrogen is the only nutrient that they need to apply through fertilizers.

For plants grown in containers, the story changes. If you choose soil mixes sold in bags, fertilizer's already added; if you mix your own soil, you have to incorporate fertilizer as described in Chapter 4. As these nutrients are washed out of the container's soil with frequent watering, you have to replace them.

Why do plants need more nitrogen? Look toward healthy growth. As a key part of plant proteins and chlorophyll, the plant pigment that plays a vital role in photosynthesis, nitrogen is responsible for the green color of plant leaves. Plants that are nitrogen deficient show a yellowing of older leaves first, along with a general slowdown in growth.

Phosphorus and potassium also play important roles in plant growth. Phosphorus is associated with good root growth, plus flower, fruit, and seed production. Potassium is also necessary for healthy roots, disease resistance, and fruiting. Deficiencies in either nutrient are hard to read through symptoms on a plant. Only a soil test can tell for sure; you can buy small soil test kits or have your soil tested through your local cooperative extension service.

Because phosphorus and potassium are less mobile than other nutrients, you can't apply them with watering like you do with nitrogen. Mixing phosphorus and potassium with your soil assures that your roots can absorb the important nutrients.

Translating the Chemistry Listed on Labels

At first glance, a nursery shelf lined with fertilizers is a bewildering sight. But confusion doesn't have to crowd your senses. Among all the colorful bags, bottles, and jars, consistency in labeling can guide you through the jungle of jargon and lead you to the fertilizer that's best for you.

When you buy a commercial fertilizer, the guaranteed analysis is listed on the label with three numbers. These three numbers tell you how much of each of the macronutrients is in the fertilizer. The first number indicates the percentage of nitrogen; the second, the percentage of phosphate; and the third, the percentage of potash, which is chemical mumbo jumbo for potassium. A 10-5-5 fertilizer is 10 percent nitrogen, 5 percent phosphate, and 5 percent potash.

Do the math and you find that a 100-pound bag of 10-5-5 fertilizer contains 10 pounds of nitrogen, 5 pounds of phosphorus, and 5 pounds of potash — a total of 20 pounds of usable nutrients. Although the remaining 80 pounds contain some useful nutrients (also listed on the label), most of the balance is either filler or carrier left over from manufacturing.

A fertilizer's guaranteed analysis is your best shopping guide. But before we dig deeper into the numbers and what they mean, check out some important fertilizer terminology.

First, most fertilizers are sold either in granular or liquid form.

Granular fertilizers

Granular fertilizers are most common. Available in bags or boxes, either partially or completely soluble, granular fertilizers can be scattered over the soil and watered in, or worked into the soil before planting. Completely soluble types are mixed with water and applied when you irrigate. Except for the completely soluble types, granular fertilizers are not ideally suited for feeding container plants. Spreading granules evenly over the top of soil in a pot is difficult — half the container may get more fertilizer than the other half. Because granules take time to dissolve, nutrients may not readily reach plant roots.

Liquid fertilizers

Liquid fertilizers are available in bottles or jugs. On a per nutrient basis, most liquid fertilizers are more expensive than granular ones. Most liquid fertilizers need to be diluted in water before you apply them, but some are ready to use. Liquid fertilizers are applied when you water and can be injected into irrigation systems, which is the reason many professional growers prefer them. Liquids are particularly well-suited for plants grown in containers. Some liquid fertilizers are sold in hose-end applicators, which eliminate the need for mixing.

Fertilizer lingo to know

Before you venture off to ring up your newfound fertilizer knowledge, consider a few more words of wisdom on the language of container plants:

- ✔ **Complete fertilizers** contain all three macronutrients — nitrogen (N), phosphorus (P), and potassium (K). The term "complete" is linked more to fertilizer industry laws and regulations than to satisfaction of the plant's actual requirements for nutrients.

- ✔ An **incomplete fertilizer** is missing one or more of the major nutrients, usually the P or the K. Fish emulsion, which usually has a guaranteed analysis of 5-0-0, is an incomplete fertilizer. Incomplete is not necessarily bad. In fact, less is sometimes good enough. Incomplete fertilizers are usually less expensive; if your soil has plenty of P and K, why apply more? Too much can harm your plants.

- ✔ **Chelated micronutrients** are in a form that allows them to be absorbed into a plant quicker than the more commonly available sulfated forms. If your plants just won't green up (they stay mottled yellow and green, or just plain yellow), no matter how much nitrogen you apply, you probably have a micronutrient deficiency of iron, zinc, or manganese. Chelated micronutrients are the quickest fix, although you may also have a soil pH problem that's preventing the nutrients from being absorbed by the plant (see Chapter 4 for more information on pH).

- ✔ **Foliar fertilizers** are applied to the leaves of plants rather than to the roots. Amazing — and logical — as it may seem, leaves can absorb nutrients too. Leaves aren't as effective as roots, but they do absorb quickly — so foliar feeding is a good fast feed. Most liquid fertilizers can be used as foliar fertilizers, but make sure that the label instructs you accordingly. Don't apply fertilizers in hot weather because they may burn the leaves.

✔ **Organic fertilizers** derive their nutrients from something that was once alive. Examples are blood meal, fish emulsion, and manure. Usually, organic fertilizers contain significant amounts of only one of the major nutrients; for example, bonemeal contains mostly phosphorus. (The nutrient contents of the most common organic fertilizers are listed in Table 19-1.) Nutrients in organic fertilizers are made available to plant roots after breakdown by soil microorganisms, which usually takes place faster in warm soil. Fish emulsion, a liquid organic fertilizer, is one of the more useful for container plants. Fish emulsion dissolves easily in water and gives good results, but is a bit smelly. Most dry organic fertilizers are best mixed with the soil before you plant. However, they must be used carefully to avoid burning the plants.

✔ **Slow-release fertilizers** provide nutrients to plants at specific rates under particular conditions. For example, Osmocote fertilizers release nutrients in response to soil moisture. The nutrients inside the tiny beads "osmose" through a resin membrane. Some slow-release, often called timed-release, fertilizers can deliver the benefits of their nutrients for as long as eight months. Slow-release fertilizers are very useful for container plants that otherwise need frequent fertilizing. Be warned: Slow-release fertilizers are very expensive. And when plants are growing quickly, they made need more nitrogen than the slow-release fertilizer can provide. Watch your container plants carefully. If plants grow slowly or are a bit yellowish even on a diet of slow-release fertilizer, give them a boost with an application of regular fertilizer.

✔ **Specialty fertilizers** are supposedly formulated for specific types of plants. For example, you may find that a fertilizer labeled Flower Food with an analysis of 0-10-10. The logic behind such a fertilizer is that a blooming plant needs more P and K than it does N. That's because the P and K are important in the formation of flowers, and the N promotes leaves. And we want flowers right? Well, not so fast. Remember that we told you how P and K don't move into the soil as well as N does. So you can apply all the P and K that you want and these major nutrients may not get to the roots. Besides, if you are using a good potting mix, there's probably plenty of P and K already.

The truth be told, we think specialty fertilizers are more marketing strategy than high-tech solution — and more expense than can be expected with other fertilizers. If your container plants need nitrogen, and they probably do, then that, and only that, is what you need to apply.

Shopping for Fertilizer Bargains

Now that you're pretty familiar with different types of fertilizers, especially those that offer the ever-important nitrogen, consider a closer look at product labels to find out how they can help make you a better shopper.

Fertilizer prices are all over the place. Premixed liquid fertilizers are among the products that don't cost-compare equally with the amount of nutrients they contain. Fertilizers may be filled with a lot of water, which makes them heavy and more expensive to ship, so they're even pricier. However, premixed varieties are also easy to use on container plants. A simple formula can help you compare the costs of nutrients in different fertilizers.

If a 10-pound bag of fertilizer contains 10 percent nitrogen, it includes 1 pound of what's called actual nitrogen (determined by multiplying the weight of the package by the percentage of nitrogen). By figuring out the actual nitrogen in different packages of fertilizer, you can compare the price of nutrients. For example, say the 10-pound bag of fertilizer with 10 percent nitrogen costs $5. The price of the one pound of actual nitrogen is $5 (the price divided by the pounds of actual nitrogen). Compare it to a 20-pound bag with 20 percent nitrogen, or 4 pounds of actual nitrogen, costing $10; the cost of the actual nitrogen is $2.50. The larger bag is a better deal. You can not only calculate your way to a bargain, but also treat your plants to a healthy meal — although they probably don't care how much you spend. You can make similar comparison for liquid fertilizer by multiplying the percentage of nitrogen by the ounces of fertilizer in the bottle.

The amount of actual nitrogen in a package of fertilizer also influences application rates. The more actual nitrogen, the less you use with each application. But don't try to figure that out; the manufacturer gives you recommended application rates on the package.

Preparing a Fertilizer Plan

Without doubt, we now really know our fertilizers — the nutrients they contain, the types, and how to shop for them. Next step: fertilizing some container plants.

Plants growing in containers need more water than those growing in the ground. The more you water, the more you flush nutrients from the soil, and the more often you have to fertilize.

You can offset some of this constant loss of nutrients by mixing slow-release fertilizers into the soil mix before planting. But we also recommend the less-food-more-often approach — the best-looking container plants we encounter are on a constant feed program. In other words, they're given a little liquid fertilizer every time, or every other time, that they're watered. Cut the recommended rates on the bottle of fertilizer in half or into quarters, using only about a teaspoon or so of fertilizer per watering. Wait until you see the results. Bloom city!

If frequent feeding poses too much hassle for you, use a liquid or water soluble fertilizer once every week or two. Follow the rates recommended on the label. Your container plants can still respond well.

You can use granular fertilizers on container plants, especially in raised beds. In fact, we often use a lazy person's approach to feeding and just sprinkle a little granular fertilizer in all the pots. Just beware, it's not a very precise technique, and you may burn plants if you put on too much — which we admit to doing more than once.

Discovering Organic Fertilizers

Many people prefer the natural "feel" of organic fertilizers. Truthfully, your plants don't care whether the nutrients they use come from an organic or synthetic form. But organic fertilizers have an advantage in that, besides providing nutrients, they also add bulk to the soil and improve its structure in ways synthetic fertilizers cannot. However, organic fertilizers are often difficult to handle, their nutrient contents are unpredictable, and the nutrients they do contain are not always immediately available to the plant.

You can supply all the nutrients that your container plants need by using only organic materials. Dry types are best worked into the soil before you plant. Liquids like fish emulsion are great to apply to growing plants.

Manures from horses, cows, and poultry are among the more commonly used organic sources of nitrogen. The salts in fresh manure can burn plants; be sure that manures age for a while or are completely composted before mixing them with the soil. Many gardeners work manures into raised bed soils in fall and then wait until spring to plant so that the manure has plenty of time to "mellow." Fish emulsion and blood meal are other organic sources of nitrogen.

Bonemeal is a good organic source of phosphorus, but once in the ground, it takes a long time to break down into a form that plants can use. Greensand is an excellent organic source of potassium and also includes many micronutrients. Mail-order suppliers of organic fertilizers are included in the Appendix.

Table 19-1 lists some common organic fertilizers, their average nutrient analysis, and moderate rates at which they can be applied. Remember that nutrient contents of organic fertilizers can vary greatly. Use less if you have doubts.

Table 19-1	Common Organic Fertilizers	
Organic Fertilizer	*Average Nutrient Analysis*	*Application Rate for 100 Square Feet of Raised Bed*
Blood meal	10-0-0	2 lbs
Bonemeal (steamed)	1-11-0	2 lbs
Cow manure	2-2-2	10 to 15 lbs
Fish emulsion	4-1-1	15 to 20 gallons (1T per gallon)
Greensand	0-0-7	5 lbs
Horse manure	2-1-2	10 to 15 lbs
Poultry manure	4-4-2	5 lbs

Recognizing Too Much of a Good Thing

Overfertilizing can be much worse than not applying enough nutrients. Excess nitrogen, for example, can burn the edges of leaves and even kill a plant. Besides that, if you apply too much, fertilizer can leach into ground water, and then you're a nasty polluter. Always follow label instructions and only apply nutrients that you know are needed — too much of any additive can cause problems with plants and the environment. If you have doubts, have your soil mix tested.

Also, don't apply fertilizer to dry plants or during extremely hot or windy weather, conditions that can cause burn to your container garden.

Chapter 20

All the Other Chores

In This Chapter

▶ Understanding repotting basics

▶ Keeping containers clean

▶ Preserving wood containers

▶ Painting and staining containers

▶ Moving heavy containers

*I*f we report that everything about container gardening is glamorous and exciting, we're missing the truth by just a hair: There are a few tasks that don't quite fall into that category. Think of these exceptions as necessary, but not noteworthy. In this chapter we take you through the basics of various odd jobs because, in the long run, they help you grow better plants.

We're being practical here: We help you repot plants, as well as clean, paint, and repair containers. We shore up everything from ceramic to wood to metal so that your containers are shiny and shipshape when you plant. You find out how to move heavy planters and store everything efficiently and easily. All this is designed to make your gardening activities easier and more successful. Thrilling and exhilarating may not describe this stuff, but important and useful certainly does.

When It's Time to Move On: Replanting

Eventually the time comes when your plants outgrow the containers they're in. Repotting them is no big deal. With a few basic tips, you can quickly become an expert at recognizing what needs to be repotted, when moving's in order, where to relocate, and how to give your planter royal treatment for a healthy new life.

With repotting, you have two goals. First, many of your plants need to go into larger containers to allow room for increasing growth as they head toward maturity. With others, repotting can reduce or slow growth so that plants stay happy and healthy in the same size container. The first order of business is answering key questions, followed by a few additional tips that can make the entire process go smoothly.

What to repot?

Any plant that has restricted roots obviously needs more space. If you see lots of roots coming through the drain hole, or find matted roots near the soil surface, it's time for a move. Repotting applies to long-term plants as well as annuals that you start from seed or small transplants that need space for more and more roots. How often does the need arise? Good question. A general rule is every few years with permanent plants, as often as every month or so with seasonal bedding plants and annuals.

When to repot?

Timing depends on what kind of plant you're dealing with. Permanent plants are best repotted when growth is slow or when they're dormant, well before or after flowering. With this schedule, plants have a chance to recover from these rather dramatic changes. Repot spring blooming permanent plants in fall, evergreens in spring or fall, and spring-flowering bulbs in fall. For summer-flowering bulbs, repot in winter or spring. With bedding plants and annuals, repot as needed through the growing season before the full flush of flowering hits.

Where to put the plant?

If you want to increase growth, you need to give plants more room for roots by transplanting into larger pots. How much larger? Well, moving up little by little to a new pot that's only a few inches larger in diameter is advisable. If you want to control growth and keep the plant from getting too big, you need to trim the roots and return the plant to a pot of the same size.

How do you repot?

Here you follow the same steps that you apply to regular planting, but first you have to get the plant out of its current home. This may be easy, or it may take some effort if the root ball is a tangled mess. Turn the container upside down, tap the rim, and slide the plant out. In some cases, you may have to trim off large roots poking through the drain hole. For plants going into larger containers, gently pull apart tangled roots, then set the plant in its new or newly filled existing pot. For some permanent plants, you need to go further than teasing apart roots — a little root-pruning's probably in order.

What is root pruning?

Just what it says — using shears to cut away root growth. You do this on plants that are pot-bound after they reach a desired size. Root pruning controls growth and forces plants to grow new roots, which leads to limited but healthy new growth. To root-prune properly, remove about a quarter of the soil and untangle as much of the root mass as you can. Using shears, cut between one-half and one-third of the roots. For tightly balled roots, slice off one-half inch all around the outside and make vertical cuts top to bottom in several places. And, please, do this without flinching. Snipping away at a living organism may seem harsh, but in the long run you're helping the plant and new roots to grow. Really, you are — the roots' response can be confirmation!

With those basic questions answered, your repotting can go off smoothly. Some cases may be tricky, though, so here are a few extra tips to help you avoid trouble and cover those unusual situations:

✔ Be aware of the obvious signs that repotting's required: poor flowering, quickly dried out soil, stunted leaves and stems, and even leaf drop and die-back (parts of the plant turn brown and die). Plants give these signals because they're not able to draw enough nutrients and moisture from their current root situation.

✔ With large containers, let the roots dry out first (this tends to shrink them) before removing the plant. Always let gravity help and pull by gripping the main stem or trunk. You may need to use a rubber mallet to tap the sides if the root mass is stubborn. And for some, sliding a knife down the sides and around the pot can help.

✔ When the plant goes back into the same pot, take the time to thoroughly wash the pot using hot water and even a 5 to 10 percent bleach solution to remove bacteria.

✔ If you can't get to a complete repotting job, a temporary solution is to replenish the top few inches of potting soil with fresh potting material and a little added fertilizer.

✔ Protect ceramic and clay pots from chipping or cracking by wrapping an old towel or piece of carpeting around the outside before you tilt and tap the sides.

Container Cleanup

Come on. They're outside, they get wet, they hold dirt, why should we bother to clean containers? That's an easy question. Things grow better in a clean and sterile environment, and you lower the chances of having pests and diseases hanging around to harm your new plants. While you're at it, be

sure to clean any stakes or plant supports that have seen duty in pre-
viously planted pots. Here are some quick and easy steps for keeping
containers clean:

- Get rid of potting soil and debris by brushing the inside and outside of
  the container thoroughly. Use a stiff plastic or wire brush for the job.

- Wash small containers in a basin filled with warm to hot soapy water.
  Use a bucket for larger containers. For added security or with especially dirty pots, add a few drops of liquid household bleach to the
  water; wear rubber gloves for this job. Be sure to scrub both inside
  and out.

- Rinse the container well and allow it to air dry overnight before replanting. Choose a sterilized potting soil for seeds and small transplants.

Humpty-Dumpty Duty — Repairing Broken Pots

It had to happen. That wayward pass ended up in the pansies and the
football found your favorite pot, which took a tumble and is now in pieces.
All is not lost. If the damage isn't too bad, you can repair the pot and return
the world to peace and harmony. If the pieces still fit tightly and you use the
right adhesive, these tricks can help you successfully mend your wounded
containers:

- Choose an epoxy glue. You mix the two components — one part glue,
  one part hardener — before you cement the pieces. Read the package
  directions for mixing, then apply the mending goo to both parts before
  joining them.

- Fit the pieces together and use some method to tie the pot so that it's
  securely held in place, as shown in Figure 20-1. Use cord or rope for
  large pots; try tape for small ones.

- Wipe off any glue that spills out of the cracks when you fit the pieces
  together. You can use sandpaper after the glue is dry to remove any
  residue.

The time may come, too, when you need to repair wooden containers. While
the damage may not be as earth-shattering as broken pottery, boxes, tubs,
and barrels still require care to stay in good working order. Constant moisture and the natural breakdown of materials may leave you with loose
boards and poorly fitted joints. Here are a few things to look out for and a
few ways to mend any wear and tear that you find:

Figure 20-1:
Using rope
or tape can
help you
repair a
broken pot.

✔ Prevent or at least reduce the chance of rot with wooden containers by raising them off the ground. Bricks, pavers, or even wooden blocks placed underneath the containers can give them just the lift they need. Raising the container allows the wood to dry between watering. Use enough supports so that the box or tub is stable and level.

✔ Watch for new or widening gaps where pieces join. Check planters, window boxes, wooden troughs, and barrels often — at least every couple of months.

✔ If containers suddenly show signs of excessive drainage and you see water pouring out, check to see if some part has come loose or started to rot away. Make these repairs without delay.

✔ Look for exposed nails, staples, or screws. Sometimes manufacturers assemble wooden containers with staples, and over time these can pull away. Small gaps only become larger under the weight and pressure of the soil and plants.

✔ Rejoin boards using galvanized wood screws long enough to penetrate each piece by an inch or more. You get the best hold over the long run.

✔ Reinforce wooden sections that may be starting to rot by adding new pieces on the inside of the container. Use redwood or cedar blocks on corner or end joints and insert screws through the original wood and well into the new piece.

> ✔ With barrels, you may need to reposition and reattach staves that are beginning to slip. Slide the stave up into its original spot and use small nails with large heads to secure it in several places around the container.

Well-Preserved Wood Containers

You can save work in the long run if you make sure that wooden containers are ready to hold up to the elements before you begin planting. Choosing rot-resistant materials in the first place is a wise decision; redwood and cedar are your best bets. These materials survive for years without any additional help.

Prolong the life of wooden containers — especially those made of soft woods — with a wood preservative safe for plants. Many nontoxic products can do the job. Check label directions and cautions before you buy to be sure that they're not harmful to plants. Treating the inside helps the container last; treating the outside preserves its looks. Use preservative on the outside of cedar and redwood to help containers retain their natural wood color. Otherwise they weather to gray, which actually can be attractive, too.

Another option is to paint or stain your containers — a good route to go with window boxes, since they then better match your house. These surface treatments give wood longer life, and allow you other decorating angles as well.

Some claims to growing success suggest lining the inside of wood containers with 4- to 6-mil black plastic. Lining does help keep moisture away from the actual wood surfaces, but only works for the sides because you need to poke holes in the bottom for drainage. Be sure to trim the plastic at the top of the soil level so that it doesn't show.

Large Containers Looking for New Locations

Consider carefully where you want large pots, planters, and barrels to go before you move them into place or even before you plant them (much easier to move). If you have to move large pots later on, there are a few tips to keep in mind.

For relocating large pots, tubs, and some barrels, you can buy wooden rolling plant dollies or plastic saucers with wheels. These are ideal for many planters, but you need to be sure they can hold up to the weight of the planted, watered container. And if you can plan ahead, hold off on watering to lighten the load.

To move other large and heavy containers like planter boxes and concrete or stone pots, try using an old piece of carpeting or a throw rug. With a helper, tip the container and slide the end of a long carpet strip underneath. Slide the container so that it rests completely on the carpet; then you can tug it along as your assistant steadies it. Cardboard, blankets, and large sacks can work this way, too.

Sometimes an old-fashioned hand truck or furniture dolly can be called in if the plants aren't generally upright. Take care to move long stems away from the sides as you balance the container on the foot of the dolly. A hand truck works for long rectangular containers that you can balance.

If you have to go up or down stairs, use a pair of long wooden planks to form a ramp and tie the container to a rope. With a helper, pull or gently lower the container slowly and securely.

Figure 20-2 illustrates the many ways to move large pots.

Where to Store All the Goods

We know that you're organized. You know exactly where to find the file with your 1984 tax return, if anyone asks (we won't), and you can quickly locate the ¹/₂-inch socket wrench in your garage. So why not extend this high level of efficiency to your containers and supplies? Important ingredients in your container gardening pursuit can be found easier, and you can expect many containers and other materials to hold up longer if they're stored properly. Here are some quick storage ideas for you to consider (someday at least!):

- ✔ Make a place for all your movable pots and materials, including soil, fertilizer, stakes, tools, and so on. Your reward arrives when you're ready to plant.

- ✔ A storage shed is ideal. But if you don't have one, designate a place in the garage for your gardening essentials. A generous cabinet may do the trick. Safe storage is especially important with chemical and toxic materials that need to be locked away from curious eyes, hands, and mouths.

- ✔ Make it a practice to wash containers before you store them. Brush them down inside and out and use a bit of soapy bleach water if you see or suspect mold and mildew. Let them air-dry completely before storing.

Figure 20-2:
Many ways
to move
large pots.

✔ Invert pots, planters, and barrels if you must store them outside, so that moisture, debris and rainwater doesn't collect inside. Cover everything with a waterproof tarp if you don't have any other shelter available.

✔ Look through chemicals — fertilizers, insecticides, and herbicides — at the end of the growing season to check effective dates. Dispose of outdated chemicals properly. Check with local authorities to discover proper methods and sites for disposal.

Maintenance Musts: Sanding, Painting, Staining

Awesome flowers in shabby containers or pretty pots in chipped and peeling plant stands don't provide the good looks that we bet you're going for. Naturally, containers exposed to the elements invariably fall into disrepair. Here's a quick and painless course on the how-to's of refurbishing various types of garden materials.

Metal or wire plant stands, brackets, hanging baskets

Here's how to keep your metal pieces in good condition:

1. **Inspect these items at the start of the season and look for any signs of rust or chipped or cracked paint.**

   If the metal surface is exposed, expect it to sustain damage under outdoor conditions.

2. **Wash off any dirt and debris and let items dry thoroughly.**

3. **Select new paint; choose a rust-free type that's designed for exterior applications.**

   Check out new "textured" paints that leave a stonelike finish. Read the instructions before you begin.

4. **On a dry warm day, find a covered or protected spot outdoors for painting.**

   If you must work indoors, choose a well-ventilated garage or toolshed.

5. **Protect surrounding surfaces with a drop-cloth or newspapers, especially if you're using spray paint or spraying on a sealer.**

6. **Sand all surfaces to remove rust or mineral deposits and to smooth the metal so that paint can adhere adequately.**

   Use steel wool or sandpaper in medium to fine grade.

7. **Spray or paint on a light coat and let it dry.**

   Sand lightly between coats with very fine grade steel wool. Repeat this process one to three times. Several thin layers give good protection.

8. **Finish with a coating of clear protectant designed for outdoor use.**

   Marine varnish offers excellent protection. Choose between glossy or matte finish and, again, go for a couple of applications.

Wood

For wood, you basically follow the same steps just described, although there are a few key points to keep in mind when you're painting or staining wooden containers.

- ✔ Make sure to use exterior grade paint or stain. This is critical, unless you particularly like the whole process of refinishing wood — over and over.

- ✔ Don't skimp on preparing the surface. Sand. Sand. Sand. Smooth surfaces are much easier to paint or stain evenly. Follow directions for what to do between coats, and use a tacky cloth to pick up any fine particles or sawdust.

- ✔ Consider penetrating oils. They're as easy to apply as stain, and they repel water very well. Some even come in different colors.

- ✔ Test your paint, stain, or oil on the underside of the container first. That's how you avoid surprises after application — brochure pictures and paint can labels are not always what they seem.

- ✔ For planters, boxes, and barrels that have quite a coat of grunge from mold, mildew and water stains, consider a chemical wash first. Usually designed to clean decks or siding, these products can be found in home centers and hardware stores. Generously spray or paint the wash liquid on, let it work for several minutes, and wash it off. For very bad surfaces, you may have to scrub with a wire brush or repeat the process. After treatment, your container is all set for painting, staining, or oiling.

There you have it — the practical and pragmatic part of container gardening. You can try to ignore these little responsibilities, but they somehow always seem to pop up. As with your other garden chores, the key is paying attention before the tasks become overwhelming.

Chapter 21

When Bad Things Happen: Pests and Diseases

In This Chapter

▶ Preventing pests from harming your container plants

▶ Using beneficial insects to control insect pests

▶ Taking insect control measures

▶ Identifying insects that prey on container plants

▶ Preventing plant diseases

▶ Identifying diseases that infect container plants

*T*he big, wide, wonderful world of container plants — everything from annuals to trees to cactus — also includes the big, wide, wonderful world of pests and diseases that afflict all this plant diversity.

But fear not, pests usually trouble our container plants less than they bug the same plants in other areas of the garden. The reason is in the way that you grow plants in containers — nearby, up close, right there. In other words, you're more intimate with container plants, and you can keep an eye on them much easier than you're able to do with outlying parts of the garden. Containers are where you are — on the patio, on the porch, on the deck. If a problem does develop, you usually see it right away and you can take care of it before it gets out of hand. And because container growing makes use of lightweight, sterile soils that start out free of insects and diseases, soil-borne problems are not common.

But when a pest problem develops on your container plants, you want to be able to handle it safely and effectively. And that's what this chapter is all about.

Preventing Pests and Diseases

Many gardeners, especially beginners, are truly surprised at how many pest and disease problems can actually be prevented or avoided. Now, we don't mean prevention through weekly sprays of pesticides that kill any insect or disease organism that approaches within 10 feet of your containers. An annihilator is not the kind of gardener we want you to be.

We want you to take a more well-rounded approach to pest control. And the key to this approach is knowledge. The more that you know about the plants you grow — the pests that prefer them, the types of pest control measures available, and how to protect the diversity of life that occupies your garden, the less likely you are to have to take drastic measures using strong chemicals.

Being a good observer is also important in our approach to pest control. Monitor your plants regularly; look under, over, between, and around the leaves and stems for any signs of infection and infestation. Don't throw a fit if you see nibblings of a few pests; these pests are food for beneficial predators like lady bugs and lacewings. But if you find masses of crawling insects or rapidly spreading diseases, you need to act fast and take measures to prevent problems from getting out of hand.

Identify any suspicious insect, leaf spot, or growth that you find so that you can determine whether it's a problem. For a start, consult our list of common pests and diseases coming up later in this chapter. If you need more help, contact a full-service garden center that has a variety of reference books to consult as well as personal experience with local problems. At your nursery or library, ask to see *The Ortho Problem Solver,* a 1,000-page encyclopedia of garden pest problems, each one with a color picture. Also check with a botanical garden or local extension service office; look for the telephone number of your extension office in the telephone book under county listings for cooperative extension or farm advisor.

Smart gardening to prevent pests

If you do the right things for your plants, they're better equipped to fend off insect attacks. Here's a list of common-sense pest prevention measures.

Plant in the right location

Many pests become more troublesome when plants are grown in conditions that are less than ideal. For example, when sun-loving plants are grown in shade, mildew problems often become more severe.

Grow healthy plants

How many times do we need to say it? Healthy plants are less likely to have problems. Start with a good soil mix as recommended in Chapter 4. Water and fertilize regularly so that plants grow strong and more pest-resistant.

Choose resistant plants

If you know a certain disease is common in you area, choose plants that are not susceptible or that resist infection. Some varieties of annuals are resistant to specific diseases. For example, some varieties of snapdragons resist rust, and several varieties of both delphiniums and zinnias resist mildew. Some varieties of roses are more disease-resistant than others, as are many varieties of vegetables.

Encourage and use beneficial insects

Beneficial insects are the good bugs that live in the garden — the insects that feed on the bugs that bother your plants. You probably have a bunch of different kinds in your garden already, but you can also purchase them and release them into your garden. You can also plant flowers that attract beneficial insects. We talk about those later in this chapter.

Keep your garden clean

Simply by cleaning up spent plants and other garden debris, you can eliminate hiding places for many pests.

Know the enemy

The more that you know about specific pests and diseases common to your area — when they occur and how they spread — the more easily you can avoid them. For example, some diseases, like rust, black spot, and botrytis, run rampant on wet foliage. By simply adjusting your watering so that you don't wet the leaves of the plant, or by watering early in the day so plants dry out quickly, you can reduce the occurrence of these diseases.

Encouraging good insects

Gardens typically are populated by huge numbers of different insects, most neither good nor bad. The critters are just hanging out at no expense to the plants. But some insects are definitely beneficial, waging a constant battle with the insects that are bugging our plants.

Good bugs are no fools. They hang out in gardens that offer the most diverse and reliable menu. That's why eliminating every last insect pest from your garden makes no sense — and can be detrimental to your plants.

Our approach to pest control is founded on maximum diversity in the garden. Variety means having some "bad" bugs around all the time. Aphids are like hors d'oeuvres for some many helpful insects, so you always hope to have a few potential meals in your garden. Otherwise, how do you think the good bugs survive? But accepting the bugs also calls for expecting a little damage once in awhile. So you're really just trying to manage the pests, not nuke them off the face of the earth. You want to keep them at acceptable levels, without letting them get out of control.

That's why being a good observer is so important. Spend time in your garden snooping around. Check your plants frequently, if not daily. If an insect or disease does get out of hand, you want to treat it effectively without disrupting all the other life in the garden, from good bugs all the way to birds. Control measures may be as simple as hand-picking and stepping on snails, or knocking off aphids with a strong jet of water from the hose. You find other physical control measures listed under the individual pests later in this chapter.

To get the good insects to stick around, follow these tips:

✔ Avoid indiscriminate use of broad-spectrum pesticides, which kill the bad bugs *and* the good bugs. If you do spray, use a product that specifically targets the pest that you want to eliminate with minimal effect on beneficial insects.

✔ Maintain a diverse garden with many kinds and sizes of plants. Doing so gives the beneficials places to hide and reproduce. Variety can also provide an alternative food source, because many beneficials like to eat pollen and flower nectar, too. Some plants that attract beneficials include Queen Anne's lace, parsley (especially if you let the flower develop), sweet alyssum, dill, fennel, and yarrow.

✔ If beneficials are not as numerous in your garden as you want, you can buy them from mail-order garden suppliers (we list several in the Appendix). If you know that a particular pest is likely to appear, order in advance. That way you can release the beneficials in time to prevent problems.

Following are some beneficial insects that you can buy to help control pests that trouble annuals:

✔ **Lady beetles:** These are your basic ladybugs. Both the adult and the lizard-like larvae are especially good at feeding on small insects like aphids and thrips. Releasing adults is sometimes not very effective because Mother Nature has preprogrammed them to migrate on down the road, so they leave your garden quickly. Try preconditioned lady beetles, which have been deprogrammed (you don't want to know how); they're more likely to stick around. And release them just before sundown. That way, they at least spend the night. Release a few thousand of them in spring as soon as you notice the first aphid.

✔ **Green lacewings:** Their voracious larvae feed on aphids, mites, thrips, and various insect eggs. These insects are among the more effective pest control forces. Release them in your garden in late spring, after the danger of frost has passed.

✔ **Parasitic nematodes:** These microscopic worms parasitize many types of soil-dwelling and burrowing insects, including cutworms and grubs of Japanese beetles. Because grubs usually inhabit lawns, you have to apply these worms there, too. Also apply parasitic nematodes to the soil around the base of your plants once in spring.

✔ **Predatory mites:** This type of mite feeds on spider mites and thrips. Add them to your garden in spring as soon as frost danger has passed.

✔ **Trichogramma wasps:** Harmless to humans, these tiny wasps attack moth eggs and butterfly larvae (that is, caterpillars). Release trichogramma when temperatures are above 72°F.

When trouble begins

If friendly bug-eaters don't do the trick, take further action with what we consider our first line of defense against pest outbreaks: pesticides that can be very effective against a certain pest, are pretty safe to use, and have a mild impact on the rest of the garden's life forms.

In general, these products are short-lived after you use them in the garden — that's what makes them so good. However, in order to gain effective control, you often have to use them more frequently than stronger chemicals.

Here are our favorite controls:

✔ **Biological controls:** This method involves pitting one living thing against another. Releasing beneficial insects is one example of biological control, but you can also use bacteria, that while harmless to humans, make insect pests very sick and eventually, very dead. The most common and useful are forms of *Bacillus thuringiensis,* or Bt, which kills the larvae of moths and butterflies — also known as caterpillars. One type of Bt (sold as milky spore) kills the larvae of Japanese beetles.

✔ **Botanical insecticides:** These insecticides are derived from plants. The following are most useful against the pests of annual flowers:

• **Neem** comes from the tropical tree *Azadirachta indica.* It kills young feeding insects and deters adult insects but is harmless to people and most beneficials. Neem works slowly and is most effective against aphids, thrips, and whitefly, but it also repels Japanese beetles.

We prefer neem *oil* over neem *extract* (check the product label) because oil is also effective against two common diseases, powdery mildew and rust. Neem oil gets thick when cool, so you need to warm it up before mixing it with water.

Use either kind of neem before you have a major pest problem. Neem is most effective when applied early in the morning or late in the evening when humidity is high. Reapply after rain.

Currently, you can buy neem oil only from Green Light Co., Box 17985, San Antonio, TX 78217; 210-494-3481. An 8-ounce container costs about $13, and you need to use 2 tablespoons per gallon of water.

- **Pyrethrins** are derived from the painted daisy, *Chrysanthemum cinerariifolium*. A broad-spectrum insecticide, pyrethrins kill a wide range of insects, both good (spray late in the evening to avoid killing bees) and bad. That's the downside. The upside is that this insecticide kills pests like thrips and beetles quickly, and has low toxicity to mammals, which means it's essentially harmless to humans and the environment.

  The terminology can be confusing, however. *Pyrethrum* is the ground-up flower of the daisy. *Pyrethrins* are the insecticide components of the flower. *Pyrethroids,* such as permethrin and resmethrin, are synthetic compounds that resemble pyrethrins but that are more toxic and persistent. Consequently, we prefer to avoid pyrethroids for home garden use.

- **Rotenone** is derived from the roots of tropical legumes. It breaks down quickly but is more toxic than some commonly used traditional insecticides. Rotenone is a broad-spectrum insecticide, killing beneficials, including bees, and pests alike. Use as a last resort to control various caterpillars, beetles, and thrips.

✔ **Summer oil:** When sprayed on a plant, this highly refined oil smothers pest insects and their eggs. The words "highly refined" mean that the sulfur and other components of the oil that damage the plant are removed. Summer oil is relatively nontoxic and short-lived. Use to control aphids, mites, thrips, and certain caterpillars.

Make sure that you do not confuse summer oil with dormant oil. Dormant oil is meant to be applied to leafless trees and shrubs during winter. It is very useful for smothering overwintering pests on roses and fruit trees and is often combined with a fungicide like lime sulfur or fixed copper.

Double-check the product label to make sure that it says it can be used on plants during the growing season. Then follow the mixing instructions carefully. Water the plants before and after applying and don't spray if temperatures are likely to rise above 85°F. When it's that hot, the oil can damage plant leaves.

✔ **Insecticidal soaps:** Derived from the salts of fatty acids, insecticidal soaps kill mostly soft-bodied pests like aphids, spider mites, and whiteflies. Soaps can also be effective against Japanese beetles. They work fast, break down quickly, and are nontoxic to humans. Insecticidal soaps are most effective when mixed with soft water. Soaps sometimes burn tender foliage.

Using synthetic insecticides

You can successfully control most insect problems using the techniques and products we just covered. If, however, a pest really gets out of hand on a prized planting, you may want to use something more serious. Try other control measures before you resort to synthetic pesticides because using them may disrupt the balance of your garden. When you use any pesticide, make sure that you have the pest identified correctly and follow labeled instructions precisely.

Pesticide safety

No matter which pesticides you decide to use, you must use them safely. Even pesticides that have relatively low impact on your garden environment, including several commonly used botanical insecticides, can be toxic to humans and pets.

Always follow instructions on the product label exactly. Doing otherwise is against the law. Both the pest you're trying to control and the plant you're spraying (sometimes plants are listed as groups, such as flowers) must be listed on the label.

Wear gloves when mixing and spraying pesticides. Spray when the winds are calm. Store chemicals in properly labeled containers well out of reach of children (a locked cabinet is best). Dispose of empty containers as described on the label, or contact your local waste disposal company for appropriate disposal sites.

Insects That Prey on Container Plants

Here are the most common insect pests that you're likely to find infesting your container plants and the best ways to control them:

Aphids

Aphids are tiny, pear-shaped pests (see Figure 21-1) that come in many colors including black, green, and red. They congregate on new growth and flower buds, sucking plant sap with their needlelike noses. Heavy infestations can cause distorted growth and weakened plants. Many plants can be infested including annuals, roses, and many vegetables. Aphids leave behind a sticky sap that may turn black with sooty mold.

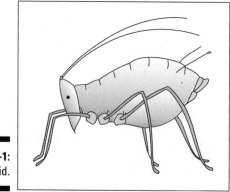

Figure 21-1:
An aphid.

Aphids are easy to control. You can knock them off sturdy plants with strong jets of water from a hose, or use insecticidal soap or pyrethrins. The soap also helps wash off the sooty mold (the harmless black gunk that comes with aphids). If you just wait a week or two, the aphid population boom is followed by a buildup of beneficials, especially lady beetles, and they usually take matters into their own hands before serious damage occurs.

Borers

Several kinds of beetle and caterpillar larvae (they look like small worms and are usually less than an inch long) tunnel into the wood or stems of fruit trees, white birches, dogwoods, shade trees, rhododendrons, and German iris. The boring weakens the plant and makes it more susceptible to disease. The damage can also cut off nutrient flow to the infested limb. Choose varieties that are less susceptible. For example, try Siberian irises instead of German irises. Keep susceptible plants growing vigorously and watch for signs of borer damage — dead bark, sawdust piles, poor performance. When you find borers, cut off and destroy severely infested limbs. Inject parasitic nematodes into remaining borers holes. You can also use preventive insecticide sprays to kill mating adults or hatching larvae.

Caterpillars and worms

Moth and butterfly larvae are avid eaters and can cause a lot of damage to a variety of plants. Some are hairy caterpillars, others are smooth-skinned and more wormlike. You can hand-pick them to reduce numbers or release trichogramma wasps. But the most effective way to get rid of caterpillars is to spray with Bt. Pyrethrins also work.

Geranium budworms

Geranium budworms are very frustrating pests of geraniums, nicotiana, ageratum, and petunias. The small caterpillars bore into flower buds and eat the flowers before they open, or they just feed on open blooms. The result is no flowers, just leaves. Great. To confirm the presence of these heartless monsters, look for small holes in geranium blossoms, or the tiny black droppings the caterpillars leave behind. You may also see the worms on the flowers. To control, pick off infested geranium buds and spray with Bt. Pyrethrins, carbaryl, and acephate also work.

Japanese beetles

Japanese beetles can really be troublesome east of the Mississippi River. The 1/2-inch-long beetles have coppery bodies and metallic green heads. They feed on both flowers and foliage, often skeletonizing leaves. They particularly love zinnias, marigolds, and roses.

Control can be tough. Treating your lawn and garden soil with parasitic nematodes or milky spore (a form of Bt) may reduce the white C-shaped larvae, but more adults may fly in from your neighbor's yard. Floral-scented traps that attract adult beetles are available, but the traps may attract more beetles than you had before. If you try the traps, keep them at least 100 feet from your flowers.

Neem, insecticidal soap, and pyrethrins are effective against adult beetles. Traditional chemicals that may help include carbaryl and acephate. You can also just pick the beetles off your flowers and stomp on them.

Mealybugs

These small sucking insects, most common on houseplants, cover their bodies with a white cottony substance that makes them easy to identify. They usually feed in groups, forming a cottony mass on branches and stems. Wash off small numbers with cotton dipped in rubbing alcohol; for larger infestations, spray with insecticidal soap or neem.

Cutworms

Cutworms are $\frac{1}{2}$-inch-long, grayish caterpillars. They emerge on spring and early summer nights to eat the stems of young seedlings, causing them to fall over like small timbers. They also move onto older plants and feed on leaves and flowers.

To protect seedlings, surround their stems with a barrier that prevents the cutworms from crawling close and feeding. These barriers can be as simple as an empty cardboard toilet paper roll, a Styrofoam cup with the bottom cut out, or a collar made from aluminum foil — just make sure that it encircles the stem completely and is set 1 inch deep in the soil. You can also trap cutworms by leaving boards around the garden. The worms hide there during the day when you can collect them. Parasitic nematodes are also effective against cutworms.

Scale

Like bumps on plant stems and leaves, these tiny sucking insects cling to plant branches, hiding under an outer shell cover that serves as a shield. These pests suck plant sap and can kill plants if present in large numbers. Look for sticky, honeylike sap droppings, one clue that scale may be present. Remove and destroy badly infested stems. Clean off light infestations with a cottony ball soaked in rubbing alcohol. Spray with dormant oil in winter or summer oil during the growing season.

Snails and slugs

Snails and slugs are soft-bodied mollusks that feed on tender leaves and flowers during the cool of the night or during rainy weather. Snails have shells, slugs don't. (A slug is shown in Figure 21-2). Both proliferate in damp areas, hiding under raised containers, boards, or garden debris. To control snails and slugs, you can roam the garden at night with a flashlight and play pick-and-stomp, or you can trap them with saucers of beer with the rim set at ground level. Refill regularly. Snails and slugs refuse to cross copper, so you can also surround raised beds or individual containers with a thin copper stripping sold in most nurseries or hardware stores. In southern California, you can release decollate snails, which prey on pest snails. Ask your cooperative extension office for information. If all else fails, you may want to put out poison snail bait.

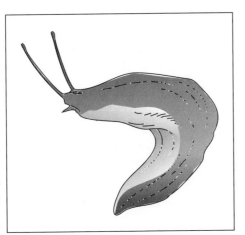

Figure 21-2:
A slug.

Spider mites

Spider mites are tiny, spiderlike arachnids that you can barely see without a magnifying glass. One is shown in Figure 21-3. If the population gets big enough, you can see telltale fine webbing beneath the leaves. And as the mites suck plant juices, the leaves become yellowish with silvery stippling or sheen. The plant may even start dropping leaves. Mites are most common in hot, dry summer climates, and on dusty plants. Houseplants, tomatoes, and roses are commonly infested.

A daily bath with a strong jet of water from a hose can help keep infestations down. You can control spider mites with insecticidal soap, which also helps to clean off plant leaves. Summer oil is also effective, as is releasing predatory mites.

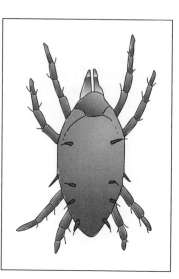

Figure 21-3:
A spider
mite.

Thrips

Thrips are another almost-invisible troublemaker. They feed on flower petals, causing them to be discolored and the buds to be deformed as they open. They also feed on leaves, causing them to be deformed and giving them a stippled look (which can be distinguished from similar spider mite damage by the small fecal pellets that thrips leave behind). Impatiens, roses, and gladiolus are commonly infested.

Many beneficials feed on thrips, especially lacewings. Insecticidal soaps are also effective against thrips, as are several stronger insecticides, including acephate.

Whiteflies

Whiteflies look like small white gnats (see Figure 21-4), but they suck plant juices and can proliferate in warm climates and greenhouses. They tend to congregate on the undersides of leaves. You can trap whiteflies with yellow sticky traps sold in nurseries. In greenhouses, release Encarsia wasps, which prey on greenhouse whiteflies. Insecticidal soaps, summer oil, and pyrethrins are effective sprays.

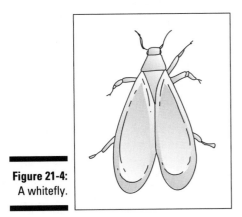

Figure 21-4:
A whitefly.

Preventing Diseases

Only a few diseases really do much damage to container-grown plants, and most of those maladies can be prevented or at least reduced in severity with good cultural practices or by planting resistant varieties. If you know a certain disease is a problem on a particular plant in your area, simply grow something else. There are surely many other choices and you may have a good time finding them.

Here are some cultural practices that can help avoid plant diseases. Some of these we mentioned earlier, but they're worth repeating here:

- ✔ **Remove infected plants.** As soon as you notice a plant with a problem, give it the yank. Even picking off infected leaves helps prevent a disease from spreading.

- ✔ **Avoid overhead watering.** Or at least water early in the morning so that plants have a chance to dry out before nightfall. Using drip irrigation or watering in furrows also helps keep foliage dry. Overhead watering can cause more problems than just encouraging foliage disease organisms — it can ruin many flowers, causing them to be washed out or look like they somehow melted. Bloom damage often happens with petunias and geraniums.

- ✔ **Space plants properly.** Planting too close reduces air circulation between plants — a condition that invites disease. Unfortunately, planting close together is often the way to achieve the best look with container plantings like annuals. Just be aware that diseases are more common under these conditions, and keep your eyes open for developing problems.

✔ **Keep your garden clean and tidy.** Many diseases spread on plant debris, so rake up fallen leaves and remove dead plants. Keep the spaces under containers clean. Removing diseased leaves can slow the spread of some organisms.

✔ **Provide drainage.** Make sure that your pots can drain properly. You know that your pots must have holes in the bottom so that water can drain out. But frequent checks also allow you to be sure that the openings aren't clogged with roots. And if you have a catch pan under your pots, make sure that it isn't constantly full of water, preventing water from draining out of the pot. Believe this — constantly soggy soil is a big contributor to root-rot diseases.

✔ **Use fresh soil mix.** Don't replant in the same soil mix, especially if you're growing plants that may be susceptible to diseases. Dump out the old, refill with the new.

Seven Dastardly Diseases

Here are some tips on the prevention, identification, and — if possible — treatment of some common plant diseases.

Black spot

Like its name suggests, this fungus causes black spots on leaves and stems. Black spot is most troublesome on roses, but it can also attack various fruiting plants. On roses, the edges of the spots are fringed and the tissue around the spots often turns yellow. In bad infections, the plant may drop all its leaves. The disease is most common in warm, humid climates with frequent summer rain.

Our outlook on fungicides

Chemical fungicides are one of the nastier bunch of pesticides. If we can get away with it, we prefer not to use them. If, however, you develop a really stubborn disease in a prized planting, you may have no choice. But before you spray, make sure that you have the disease properly identified. Enlist the help from a local nurserymen or cooperative extension specialist to confirm your suspicions. Then use a product specifically labeled for the disease you're trying to cure. Follow the label instructions exactly.

The best advice to prevent black spot (besides planting disease-resistant varieties) is to clean up your winter prunings — the most common source of reinfection — and use a dormant spray that includes lime sulfur. Also, avoid overhead watering or water early in the morning so that leaves can dry out quickly. The baking soda-summer oil combination mentioned under "Powdery mildew" later in this chapter also provides some control, as does neem oil.

Botrytis blight

Also called gray mold, this fungal disease overwinters on plant debris and is common on strawberries, petunias, and other flowers. The blight is most notable as gray fuzz forming on old flowers and fruit, turning them to moldy mush, but it can also discolor or spot foliage. It's most troublesome on older plant parts and in cool, humid weather. Make sure that plants are properly spaced and avoid overhead watering. Remove and destroy any infected plant parts.

Damping off

This fungus attacks the base of seedling stems, causing them to wilt and fall over. The best way to prevent the disease is to plant seeds in sterile potting soil and avoid over-watering. To prevent recurring problems after an infestation, clean containers well and fill your pots with fresh soil. If the disease gains a foothold, it's hard to stop.

Powdery mildew

This fungus coats leaves and flowers with a white powder. The mildew is most common when days are warm but nights are cool, and is particularly troublesome on zinnias, dahlias, begonias, roses, squash, melons, and peas. Control is difficult, but there are resistant varieties. The disease also becomes less of a problem as the weather changes, so if you keep young plants growing vigorously, they may grow out of suspectibility. Neem oil may also help. Near the end of the season, you may want to pull annual plants out early and start with something new. Rose growers have some success using a mixture of 1 tablespoon of summer oil and 1 or 2 teaspoons of baking soda in a gallon of water; you have to use the mix often to protect new foliage. Another rose grower's technique: spraying plants with antitranspirants. These materials, sold with names like Cloud Cover or Wiltpruf, coat leaves with a thin waxy film that seems to prevent the mildew from getting established — worth a try.

Root rots

A number of soilborne fungi cause plants to basically do the same thing —
suddenly wilt and die, whether or not the soil is moist. Vinca is notorious for
checking out like this. The best way to prevent root rot is to use sterile soil,
make sure that your pots drain properly, and avoid overwatering — let the
soil dry partially between irrigations. Otherwise, all you can do is remove
the dead plants. Few other control measures are effective.

Rust

This fungal disease is easy to identify: It forms rusty pustules on the undersides of plant leaves. Gradually the upper sides of the leaves turn yellow and
the whole plant begins to decline. Snapdragons, roses, and hollyhocks are
common hosts. To avoid rust, plant resistant varieties. Also, space plants for
good air circulation, keep the garden clean, and avoid overhead watering.
Destroy infected plants.

Salt burn

Salt burn isn't actually a disease caused by a living organism, but rather a
malady caused by excess salts building up in the soil. It's common in windy
areas, where irrigation water is high in salts, or when plants are over-
fertilized. Japanese maples are particularly sensitive to salt burn. The
symptoms are pretty easy to recognize — leaf edges become dry and
crispy — much like what happens when a plant becomes too dry. If the
condition worsens, the whole leaf may dry up and drop, and tips of
branches may die. Similar symptoms occur if you let a plant get too dry. The
solution is to water the container heavily and leach the salts out of the soil.
To get all the salts out, you may have to fill the pot with water more than six
or seven times. As long as the container has good drainage, you really can't
overdo it. You may also want to reduce your fertilizing or move the pot to an
area that's protected from wind.

Part VII
The Part of Tens

In this part . . .

How do you spell "hush" in language that plants can understand? Green, growing stuff has a habit of sharing secrets — like where they really want to show off, hide out, grow best, grant grace and elegance, and avoid contact altogether. Every chapter presents you with at least ten opportunities to know your plants' potential. And, after all, sound advice never injured any brave expedition, right? Go ahead, rest your oars. With all this preparation, the ride may be pretty gentle. Surely, the coast is clear for a few good yarns about the big one that didn't get away — it grew up right inside your own front door!

Chapter 22

More Than Ten Container Plants for Special Situations

In This Chapter

▶ Several container plants for special situations (duh)

*U*se the following lists to help you choose container plants for different spots in your indoor and outdoor landscapes or for different purposes throughout your own little corner of the world. For more on the plants, look them up in various chapters throughout this book (annuals, perennials, bulbs, and so on).

Annual and Perennial Flowers for Shady Spots

- ✔ Astilbe
- ✔ Begonia
- ✔ Browallia
- ✔ Campanula
- ✔ Coleus
- ✔ Foxglove
- ✔ Hosta
- ✔ Lenten rose
- ✔ Impatiens
- ✔ Primrose

Shrubs, Trees, and Vines for Shady Spots

- Aucuba
- Boxwood
- Camellia
- Fuchsia
- Heavenly bamboo (*nandina*)
- Hydrangea
- Ivy
- Japanese maple
- Lily-of-the-valley shrub
- Star jasmine

Fragrant Plants

- Daphne
- Gardenia
- Hyacinth
- Narcissus
- Rose
- Star jasmine
- Stock
- Scented geranium
- Sweet olive (*Osmanthus fragrans*)
- Sweet pea

Easy Plants

- Bedding begonia
- Fatsia
- Geranium
- Impatiens
- Ivy
- Jade plant
- Juniper
- Marguerite daisy
- Marigold
- Vinca rosea

Specimen Plants (Substantial Enough to Stand Alone)

- Bamboo
- Citrus
- Crape myrtle
- Dwarf Alberta spruce
- Flowering plum
- Japanese black pine
- Japanese maple
- Loquat
- New Zealand flax
- Rhododendron

Gift Plants (Nice Enough to Pot and Present)

- ✔ Azalea
- ✔ Bougainvillea
- ✔ Camellia
- ✔ English holly
- ✔ Gardenia
- ✔ Japanese maple
- ✔ Lavender
- ✔ Rhododendron
- ✔ Rose
- ✔ Tree fern

Chapter 23

Ten Container Plants for Spring, Summer, Fall, and Winter

In This Chapter

▶ For every season: plants year-round

Depending on your climate, you can enjoy the company of appealing container plants at almost any time of year. (Of course, your options are limited in winter in cold climates.) Here are just a few of many annuals, perennials, bulbs, and permanent plants that perform particularly well at various seasons:

Spring

✔ Azalea

✔ Calendula

✔ Columbine

✔ Daffodil

✔ Felicia

✔ Iceland poppy

✔ Primrose

✔ Rose

✔ Snapdragon

✔ Tulip

Summer

- ✔ Geranium
- ✔ Dahlia
- ✔ Daylily
- ✔ Fuchsia
- ✔ Hibiscus
- ✔ Impatien
- ✔ Lobelia
- ✔ Marigold
- ✔ Petunia
- ✔ Zinnia

Fall

- ✔ Aster
- ✔ Chrysanthemum
- ✔ Dwarf pomegranate
- ✔ Flowering cabbage
- ✔ Heavenly bamboo
- ✔ Japanese maple
- ✔ Pansy
- ✔ Rose
- ✔ Sasanqua camellia
- ✔ Sweet olive *(Osmanthus fragrans)*

Winter

- Camellia
- Cyclamen
- Holly
- Pyracantha
- Primrose

Living Christmas Trees

- Colorado spruce
- Dwarf Alberta spruce
- Noble fir
- Scotch pine
- White fir

Chapter 24

Ten Handy Tools
for Container Gardening

In This Chapter

▶ Some tools you may find useful

Along with ordinary gardening tools (shovel, hose, trowel, and the like), some special equipment can simplify your container operations. Most of the following items are available at garden centers or through mail-order suppliers.

✔ **Hose-end bubbler:** Screw this attachment to the end of the hose and use it to soften the flow of water — so that you don't wash out soil. A metal hose-end extension allows you to water overhead baskets and containers that are normally beyond arm's reach.

✔ **Scrub brush:** Use a brush to nudge soil, moss, and salt deposits off your containers.

✔ **Hand truck:** You need one of these if you want to move heavy containers indoors, or if you do a lot of outdoor redecorating.

✔ **Watering can:** You may find yourself filling your watering can every day during hot weather. You can also apply liquid fertilizer as you water. If you have a lot of containers, watering with a hose or even an automatic drip system is probably preferable.

✔ **Soil scoop:** This tool comes in handy when filling containers with potting soil or when mixing small quantities of potting soil (for larger quantities, use a shovel).

✔ **Mister:** Indoor plants often need extra humidity. Apply moisture with a small hand sprayer.

✔ **Plant labels:** Keep track of your container plants, especially permanent ones. Labels are available in wood, zinc, copper, and other materials.

- **Soil-testing kit:** Determine the nutritional value and acidity/alkalinity of your soil mix.

- **Maximum-minimum thermometer:** A good gauge of when to move container plants into protection.

- **Potting bench:** A place to spread out can be especially appreciated if you do a lot of potting. Look for models with a roomy work surface and plenty of shelves for storing pots, seeds, bulbs, and tools.

Chapter 25
Almost Ten Words about Bonsai

- -

In This Chapter

▶ A little bit of info on bonsai plants

- -

At the risk of sounding like we're bringing up Renoir in a class on finger painting, we think it appropriate to wrap up this book with some thoughts on the apotheosis of container gardening: Bonsai.

Simply put, bonsai is the horticultural art of growing dwarf trees in small containers. The idea is to evoke nature in miniature — an ancient twisted pine on a rocky precipice or a forest of lacy maples with a mossy carpet underneath. Fine art is involved in selecting the plants and containers, and training and displaying the plants. Refined horticulture is responsible for growing the darn things — watering, pruning, feeding, and much, much more. Don't ever plan to take a vacation.

Bonsai is an engrossing hobby with dedicated followers all over the world. The pastime also revolves around an entire realm of special equipment and tools: the low, flat clay pots; special shears; special wire; and so on. If you want to know more about the subject, here are a few suggestions:

✔ Browse through the hundreds of bonsai volumes available at libraries and bookstores. Beginners can search out *The Complete Book of Bonsai* by Harry Tomlinson and *Bonsai* by the editors of Sunset Books and *Sunset Magazine*.

✔ Check out the Internet, which supports thousands of bonsai sites. An excellent place to start is www.bonsaiweb.com.

✔ Contact a bonsai club, local or more far-flung. Clubs are all over, from Iowa to Sweden. For membership information, write to the American Bonsai Society, Box 11336, Puyallup, Washington 98371-1136.

✔ Visit a bonsai show staged by a local club.

You can buy bonsai plants already trained. Figures 25-1 through 25-3 show some bonsai plants you're likely to see. Before taking one home, make sure that you have full directions on watering, feeding, pruning, and other care. Friendly advice: Never give someone else a bonsai plant as a gift unless you know that he or she wants take on the responsibility.

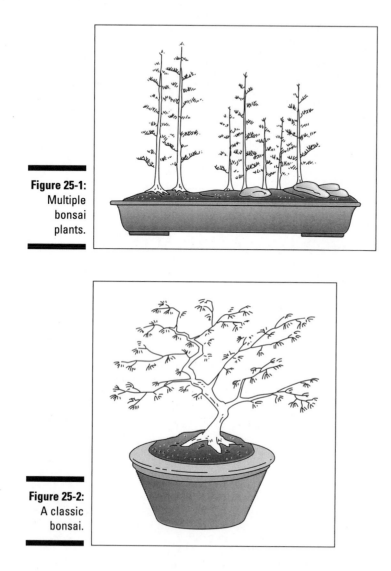

Figure 25-1:
Multiple
bonsai
plants.

Figure 25-2:
A classic
bonsai.

If you want to get a taste of what bonsai is about — to just put a toe in the water — you can experiment with small plants in containers. Some succulents look at home in bonsai pots and can thrive in their shallow soil; the common jade plant is one that actually starts to take on the aged look of a bonsai.

Or, browse nurseries looking for small pines, junipers, or false cypresses *(Chamaecyparis)* that have twisted branches or other signs of character at a young age. Prune the root ball of your selected plant by about as much as one-third, plant in a pot that's 4 or 5 inches wide, making sure that you add at least an inch of new soil around the root ball's sides. Prune the top a bit

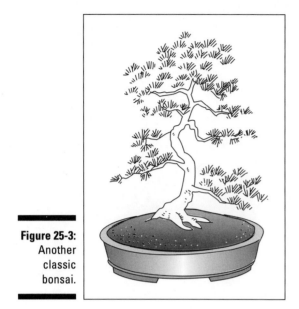

Figure 25-3:
Another
classic
bonsai.

to expose some of the trunk, trimming off a few side shoots up from the base. Sorry, that's about as specific as we can get — every plant is different, and particular in its requirements and responses. Keep the plant in part shade, and water often enough to ensure that soil stays moist. If you like doing this sort of thing and you enjoy how the plant looks, launch a full-fledged trip into the details of tending to these small-scale trees. Good luck.

Appendix
Additional Resources

● ●

*T*his chapter is filled with mail-order resources, organization contact info, Web site descriptions, book recommendations, and much more.

Mail-Order Suppliers of Seeds and Plants for Containers

Abundant Life, 930 Lawrence St., P.O. Box 772, Port Townsend, WA 98368; phone 360-385-5660, fax 360-385-7455 (Web site http://csf.Colorado.edu/perma/abundant). Catalog $2 optional donation. Nonprofit organization dedicated to preserving genetic diversity with specific emphasis on vegetable species not available commercially.

Berlin Seeds, 5371 County Rd. 77, Millersburg, OH 44654; phone 330-893-2030. Free catalog.

Bluestone Perennials, 7211 Middle Ridge Rd., Madison, OH 44057; phone 800-852-5243, fax 440-428-7198. More than 400 perennials.

Bountiful Gardens, 18001 Shafer Ranch Rd., Willits, CA 95490-9626; phone/fax 707-459-6410 (Website: http://countrylife.net/organic/). Free catalog in U.S. All seeds are untreated and open-pollinated.

Breck's, 6523 N. Galena Rd., Peoria, IL 61632; phone 309-691-4610, fax 309-589-2014. Bulbs direct from Holland.

Burrell's, P.O. Box 150, 405 N. Main St., Rocky Ford, CO 81067; phone 719-254-3318, fax 719-254-3319. Free catalog. Wide range of flower seeds.

W. Atlee Burpee Co., 300 Park Ave., Warminster, PA 18974; phone 800-888-1447, fax 800-487-5530 (Web site: www.burpee.com). Free catalog. Wide selection of heirloom flower and vegetables seeds, as well as the latest hybrids and transplants.

Busse Garden, 5873 Oliver Ave., S.W. Cokato, MN 55321-4229; phone 320-286-2654. Catalog $2. Cold-hardy and unusual perennials and native plants.

Carroll Gardens, 444 East Main St., Westminster, MD 21157; phone 800-638-6334, fax 410-857-4112. Catalog $3. Wide selection of rare and unusual perennials, herbs, vines, roses, and shrubs.

Comstock, Ferre & Co., 263 Main St., Wethersfield, CT 06109; phone 860-571-6590, fax 860-571-6595. Free catalog. Huge range of lesser-known varieties.

The Cook's Garden, P.O. Box 5010 Hodges, SC 29653-5010; phone 800-457-9703, fax 800-457-9705 (Web site http://www.cooksgarden.com). Extensive range of flower, herb and vegetable varieties, including European and hard-to-find salad greens.

The Daffodil Mart, 85 Broad St; Torrington CT 06790; phone 800-255-2852, fax 800-420-2852. More than 1,000 different flower bulbs.

DeGiorgi Seed Company, 6011 N St., Omaha, NE 68117-1634; phone 800-858-2580. Catalog free. Excellent selection of flowering annuals, perennials, grasses, herbs, vegetables and wildflowers.

Down on the Farm Seed, P.O. Box 184, Hiram, OH 44234; mail order only. Sells only untreated, open-pollinated, and heirloom seeds.

Dutch Gardens, P.O. Box 200, Adelphia, NJ 07710-0200; phone 800-818-3861, 908-780-7720. Great selection of bulbs.

Ed Hume Seeds, P.O. Box 1450, Kent, WA 98035; fax 206-859-06944, no phone orders (Web site http://members.aolcom/Humeseeds/). Catalog $1. Untreated Seeds for cool climates and short seasons.

Fedco Seeds, P.O. Box 520, Waterville, ME 04903; mail order only. Seed cooperative sells seeds of all kinds suited to cold Northeast climate.

Ferry-Morse Seeds, P.O. Box 488, Fulton, KY 42041-0488; phone 800-283-3400, fax 800-283-2700. Free catalog. Standards and new hybrids.

The Gourmet Gardener, 8650 College Blvd., Ste 202, Overland Park, KS 66210-1806; phone 913-345-0490 (Web site http://www.metrobbs.com/tgg/catalog.htm). Suppliers of containers, seed mixes, potting soil, and books for container gardening.

Gurney's Seed & Nursery Co., 110 Capital St., Yankton, SD 57079; phone 605-665-1930, fax 605-665-9718. Wide range of annuals, dwarf fruit trees, houseplants, and more.

Garden City Seeds, 778 Highway 93 North, Hamilton, MT; phone 406-961-4837, fax 406-961-4877. Organic, open-pollinated seeds selected for an early harvest.

Genesee Country Museum, P.O. Box 310, Mumford, NY 14511; phone 716-538-6822, fax 716-538-2887. Only 19th century heirlooms available.

Green Mountain Transplants, Inc., RR 1, Box 6C, East Montpelier, VT 05651; phone 800-514-4441, fax 802-454-1204, e-mail GMTranspl@aol.com. Greenhouse propagated transplants.

Harris Seeds, P.O. Box 22960, Rochester, NY 14692-2960; phone 800-544-4441, fax 716-442-9386. Vegetable and flower seeds, as well as seed-starting equipment and other gardening accessories.

Jackson & Perkins, #1 Rose Lane, Medford, OR 97501; phone 800-872-7673, fax 800-242-0329 (Web site http://www.jacksonandperkins.com). Free catalog. Excellent selection of roses, patio trees, miniatures, and containers.

Johnny's Selected Seeds, Foss Hill Rd., Albion, ME 04910-9731; phone 207-437-4301, fax 800-437-4290, e-mail homegarden@johnnyseeds.com (Web site http://www.johnnyseeds.com/). Source for seed-starting equipment; flower, herb, and vegetable seeds, as well as container gardening kits, seed collections, and soil mixes.

Jung Quality Seeds, 335 S. High St., Randolph, WI 53957; phone 800-247-5864, fax 800-692-5864. Wide selection of garden plants and products.

Kilgore's Florida Planting Guide, 1400 W. First St., Sanford, FL 32771; phone 407-323-6630. Free catalog. Specializes in annuals suited to Florida; catalog contains reference table for planting annuals and vegetables in Florida.

Liberty Seed Co., P.O. Box 806, New Philadelphia, OH 44663-0806; phone 800-541-6022, fax 330-364-6415. More than 1,000 varieties of annual and perennial flowers and vegetables.

Logee's Greenhouses, 141 North St., Danielson, CT 06239-1939; phone 860-774-8038, fax 888-774-9932, e-mail logee-info@logees.com (Web site http://www.logees.com). Offers over 1,500 rare and unusual flowering plants suitable for home, sunroom, patio, and conservatory display.

Nichols Garden Nursery, 1190 North Pacific Highway, Albany, OR 97321-4580; 541-928-9280, fax 541-967-8406, e-mail nichols@gardennursery.com (Web site http://www.pacificharbor.com/nichols/). Asian and unusual vegetables and herbs.

Nor'East Miniature Roses, Inc., 58 Hammond St., P.O. Box 307, Rowley, MA 01969; phone 978-948-7964. Great selection of miniature roses.

Nourse Farms, Inc., 41 River Rd., South Deerfield, MA 01373; phone 413-665-2658. A selection of small fruits.

Park Seed Co., 1 Parkton Ave., Greenwood, SC 29647-0001; phone 800-845-3369, fax 864-941-4206, e-mail info@park.com. (Web site http://www.parkseed.com). More than 1,800 kinds of bulbs and seeds.

Pinetree Garden Seeds, Box 300, New Gloucester, ME 04260; phone, 888-52-SEEDS, 207-926-3400, fax 207-926-3886, e-mail superseeds@worldnet.att.net (Web site http://www.superseeds.com). Wide assortment of standard, popular varieties in addition to lesser-known varieties.

R. H. Shumway's, P.O. Box 1, Graniteville, SC 29829; phone 803-663-7277, fax 803-663-9772. Wide selection of vegetable seeds.

Reliable Seeds, 3862 Carlsbad Blvd., Carlsbad, CA 92008; phone 760-729-3282. Catalog $2. Seeds for the Southern California garden.

Richters Herb Co., 357 Highway 47, Goodwood, ON L0C 1A0, Canada; phone 905-640-6677, e-mail orderdesk@richters.com (Web site http://www.richters.com). Extensive collection of herb seeds, plants, books, and products.

Roswell Seed Co., P.O. Bov bx 725, Roswell, NM 88202; phone 505-622-7701, fax 505-623-2885. Vegetables and flowers well-adapted to the Southwest and easily grown from seed.

Santa Barbara Heirloom Nursery, P.O. Box 4235, Santa Barbara, CA 93140; phone 805-968-5444, fax 805-562-1248 (Web site http://heirloom.com/heirloom/). Live heirloom seedlings, hanging garden basket kits, and windowsill herb kits.

Seeds Blum, HC 33, Idaho City Stage, Boise, ID 83706; phone 800-528-3658, fax 208-338-5658. Catalog $3. Seed kits suitable for container and porch gardens, seed collections, and books about growing vegetables in containers, salads in pots, and windowsill herbs.

Seeds of Change, P.O. Box 15700, Santa Fe, NM 87506-5700; phone 888-762-7333, fax 888-329-4762 (Web site `http://seedsofchange.com`). Organic, open-pollinated, old-time varieties, as well as new and interesting selections of seeds.

Seeds Trust, P.O. Box 1048, Hailey, ID 83333; phone 208-788-4363, fax 208-788-3452. Catalog $2. Open-pollinated wildflower annuals suited to high-altitude (short-season) gardening. Also drought-tolerant and native wildflowers.

Seymour's Selected Seeds, P.O Box 1346, Sussex, VA 23884-0346; phone 803-663-3084, fax 803-663-9772. Seeds of cottage garden plants from England.

Shady Oaks Nursery, 112 10th Ave. S.E., Waseca, MN 56093; phone 800-504-8006, fax 507-835-8772. Specialist in hostas and other shade perennials.

Shepherd's Garden Seeds, 30 Irene St., Torrington, CT 06790; phone 860-482-3638 (Web site `http://shepherdseeds.com`). Features European and Asian gourmet vegetables, herbs, and old-fashioned cottage garden flowers.

Springhill Nurseries, 6523 N. Galena Rd., Peoria, IL 61656; phone/fax 800-582-8527. Perennials, roses, shrubs, and vines.

Southern Exposure Seed Exchange, P.O. Box 170, Earlysville, VA 22936; 804-973-4703, fax 804-973-8717 (Web site `http://southernexposure.com`). Over 500 varieties of heirloom and traditional untreated, open-pollinated vegetables, flowers, and herbs, plus seed-saving supplies.

Stokes Seeds, Inc., P.O. Box 548, Buffalo, NY 14240-0548; phone 716-695-6980, fax 716-695-9649. Wide selection of flower seeds, including cultural information.

Territorial Seed Co., P.O. Box 157, Cottage Grove, OR 97424; phone 541-942-9547, fax 888-657-3131 (Web site `http://www.territorial-seed.com`). Hardy vegetable, herb, and flower seeds — especially varieties suited to the Pacific Northwest — as well as sprinklers, hoes, and wheelbarrows.

Thompson & Morgan Seed Co., P.O. Box 1308, Jackson, NJ 08527-0308; phone 800-274-7333 or 908-363-2225, fax 888-466-4769. Excellent selection of English flowers and vegetables.

Tomato Growers Supply Co., P.O. Box 2237, Fort Myers, FL 33902; phone 941-768-1119, fax 941-768-3476. Over 310 varieties of tomatoes, as well as peppers, supplies, and books.

Totally Tomatoes, P.O. Box 1626, Augusta, GA 30903; phone 803-663-0016, fax 888-477-7333. A tomato for every garden and the equipment to help you grow your own crop.

Twilley Seed Co., P.O. Box 65, Trevose, PA 19053-0065; phone 800-622-7333, fax 215-245-1949. Broad range of flowers and germination tips.

Van Bourgondien Brothers, 245 Farmingdale Rd., P.O. Box 1000, Babylon, NY 11702; phone 800-622-9997, fax 516-669-1228. Importers and distributors of bulbs and perennials.

Wetsel Seed Co., P.O. Box 956, Kittanning, PA 16201; phone 800-742-2510, fax 412-543-5338. Good selection of soil mixes, amendments, seed starter, peat moss, containers, window boxes, and seeds.

White Flower Farm, P.O. Box 50, Litchfield, CT 06759; phone 800-503-9624 or 860-496-9600, fax 860-496-1418. Lavishly illustrated catalog includes more than 700 varieties of annuals, perennials, bulbs, and shrubs. Good selection of elegant planters and containers.

Willhite Seed Inc., P.O. Box 23, Poolville, TX 76487; phone 817-599-8656, fax 817-599-5843. Good selection of warm weather vegetables.

Mail-Order Sources of Fruit Trees

Bay Laurel Nursery, 2500 El Camino Real, Atascadero, CA 93422; phone 805-466-3449. Free catalog. Tree fruits and ornamentals.

Classical Fruits, 8831 AL Hwy. 157, Moulton, AL 35650; phone 205-974-8813. Free catalog. Dwarf citrus trees for containers.

Four Winds Growers, P.O. Box 3538, Fremont, CA 94539; phone 510-656-2591 (Web site http://www.mother.com/fourwinds). Free catalog. Dwarf citrus trees; Web site includes an informative section on dwarf citrus.

Just Fruits, 30 Francis St., Crawfordville, FL 32327, 904-926-5644. Catalog $3. Temperate fruit trees suited for the southeast U.S. and many hard-to-find exotic trees.

Logee's Greenhouses, 141 North St., Danielson, CT 06239-1939; phone 860-774-8038, fax 888-774-9932, e-mail logee-info@logees.com (Web site http://www.logees.com). Catalog $3. Citrus trees and other exotics.

Miller Nurseries, 5060 West Lake Rd., Canandaigua, NY 14424; phone 800-836-9630, fax 716-396-2154. Free catalog. Hardy dwarf fruit trees suitable for containers.

Pacific Tree Farms, 4301 Lynwood Dr., Chula Vista, CA 91910; phone 619-422-2400. Catalog $2. Deciduous trees and other interesting sub-tropicals.

Raintree Nursery, 391 Butts Rd., Morton, WA 98356; phone 360-496-6400. Catalog $1. Deciduous, tropical, and citrus trees suitable for containers.

Stark Bro's., P.O. Box 10, Louisiana, MO 63353; phone 800-325-4180. Free catalog. Wide selection of deciduous fruit trees.

Mail-Order Sources for Water Gardening Plants and Supplies

Lilypons Water Gardens, 6800 Lilypons Rd., P.O. Box 10, Buckeystown, MD 21717; phone 800-723-7667, fax 800-879-5459. Free catalog. Specialists in all aspects of water gardening.

Maryland Aquatic Nurseries, 3427 North Furnace Rd., Jarrettsville, MD 21084; phone 410- 557-7615, fax 410-692-2837 (Web site `http://www.marylandaquatic.com`). Catalog $5. Full range of plants and supplies for water gardens, fountain gardens, and bonsai kits.

Paradise Water Gardens, 14 May St., Whitman, MA 02382; phone 781-447-4711, fax 781-447-4591. Catalog $3. All supplies for water gardening.

Slocum Water Gardens, 1101 Cypress Gardens Blvd., Winter Haven, FL 33884-1932; phone 941-293-7151, fax 800-322-1896 or 941-299-1896. Catalog $3. A nursery of aquatic plants.

Van Ness Water Gardens, 2460 N. Euclid Ave., Upland, CA 91784-1199; phone 800-205-2425 or 909-982-2425, fax 909-949-7217 (Web site`http://vnwg.com`). Catalog $4. Wide selection of water plants and supplies. Web site also provides detailed information on water gardening.

Mail-Order Sources for Container Gardening Tools, Supplies, and Structures

A. M. Leonard, Inc., 241 Fox Dr., Piqua, OH 45356; phone 800-543-8955, fax 800-433-0633. Catalog free. Professional nursery and gardening supplies.

Charley's Greenhouse Supply, 1599 Memorial Highway, Mount Vernon, WA 98273; phone 800-322-4707, fax 360-428-0310. Greenhouses and the accompanying tools and supplies.

E. C. Geiger, Inc., Rt. 63, P.O. Box 285, Harleysville, PA 19438; phone 800-443-4437, fax 215-256-6100. Wide selection of horticultural supplies.

Garden Trellises, Inc., P.O. Box 105, LaFayette, NY 13084; phone 315-498-9003. Galvanized steel trelliswork for vegetables and perennials.

Gardener's Eden, P.O. Box 7307, San Francisco, CA 94120-7307; phone 800-822-9600, fax 415-421-5153. Stylish garden supplies and accessories.

Gardener's Supply Company, 128 Intervale Rd., Burlington, VT 05401; phone 800-863-1700, fax 800-551-6712, e-mail info@gardeners.com (Web site http://www.gardeners.com/gardeners). Hundreds of innovative tools and products for gardeners, including containers and seed starting kits.

Gardens Alive!, 5100 Schenley Pl., Dept. 5672, Lawrenceburg, IN 47025; phone 812-537-8650, fax 812-537-5108. One of the larger organic pest control and organic fertilizer suppliers.

Garden Way, Troy, NY 12180; phone 800-828-5500. Wide range of equipment and accessories, from composters, carts, and tillers to apparel, books, and hand tools.

Home Harvest: Gardening Supply Online, 13624 Jeff Davis Hwy, Woodbridge, VA 22191; phone 800-348-4769, fax 703-494-2917, e-mail ugrow@homeharvest.com (Web site http://www.homeharvest.com). Full range of products, including materials for container gardening, special wood fiber nursery pots, HID grow lights, and hydroponic systems.

Hoop House Greenhouse Kits, Dept. N, 1358 Route 28, South Yarmouth, MA 02664; phone 800-760-5192.

HydroFarm Gardening Products, 1455 E. Francisco Blvd., San Rafael, CA 94901; phone 800-634-9999, fax 415-459-6096. Complete line of products for hydroponic gardening.

IPM Labs, P.O. Box 300, Locke, NY 13092-0300; phone 315-497-2063. Specialists in beneficial insects.

InterUrban WaterFarms, 5255 Canyon Crest Dr., Suite 71-347, Riverside, CA 92507; phone 909-342-7984, fax 909-342-7984. Full line of hydroponic gardening supplies. The Web site offers an overview of hydroponics, FAQs, visits to other gardens online, and online shopping.

Kinsman Company, River Rd., Pt. Pleasant, PA 18950; phone 800-733-4146, fax 215-297-0450. Gardening supplies and quality tools.

Langenbach, 638 Lindero Canyon Rd., MSC 290, Oak Park, CA 91301; phone 800-362-1991, fax 800-362-4490. Fine-quality tools and garden gifts.

Mellinger's, Inc., 2310 W. South Range Rd., N. Lima, OH 44452; phone 800-321-7444, fax 216-549-3716. Broad selection of gardening tools, supplies, fertilizers, and pest controls, as well as plants.

Natural Gardening, 217 San Anselmo Ave., San Anselmo, CA 94960; phone 707-766-9303, fax 707-766-9747. Organic gardening supplies; tomato seedlings.

Peaceful Valley Farm Supply, P.O. Box 2209, Grass Valley, CA 95945; phone 916-272-4769, fax 916-272-4794. Organic gardening supplies, containers, seed-starting kits, and quality tools.

Planet Nature, P.O. Box 3146, Bozeman, MT 59772; phone 800-289-6656 or 406-587-5891, fax 406-587-0223. Environmentally friendly products for lawn, garden, and home.

Plow & Hearth, P.O. Box 5000, Madison, VA 22727; phone 800-627-1712. A wide variety of products for home and garden.

Simple Gardens, Box 292 R.D.2, Richmond, VT 05477; phone 802-434-2624, fax 802-434-2624, e-mail smplgrdn@together.net. Features containers, window boxes, and baskets for container gardening and gardening in small spaces.

Simply Hydroponics, 1921 Starkey Rd., Largo, FL 33771; phone 813-531-5355 (Web site http://simplyhydro.com). Full line of hydroponic systems and accessories. Web site includes product information and FAQs.

Smith & Hawken, 2 Arbor Ln., P.O. Box 6900, Florence, KY 41022-6900; phone 800-776-3336, fax 606-727-1166. Wide selection of high-end tools, furniture, plants, and outdoor clothing.

The Urban Farmer Store, 2833 Vicente St., San Francisco, CA 94116; phone 800-753-3747 or 415-661-2204. Drip irrigation supplies. Catalog $1.

Walt Nicke Co., P.O. Box 433, Topsfield, MA 01983; phone 800-822-4114, fax 508-887-9853. Good selection of gardening tools.

How to Reach — or Become — a Master Gardener

The umbrella organization for all the regional programs is Master Gardeners International, 424 North River Drive, Woodstock, VA 22664; phone 540-459-5656. If you write to Master Gardeners for information, include a self-addressed, stamped envelope. The e-mail address is mgic@capaccess.org. The following list provides contact names and telephone numbers for each state and participating province:

Alabama: Mary Beth Musgrove, 334-844-5481

Alaska: Wayne Vandre, 907-279-6575

Arizona: Lucy Bradley, 602- 470-8086, ext. 323

Arkansas: Janet Carson, 501-671-2174

British Columbia: MG Coordinator, Van Dusen Botanical Gardens 604-257-8672

California: Pam Elam, 209-456-7554; or Nancy Garrison, 408-299-2635

Colorado: Marlo Meakins, 970-491-7887

Connecticut: Norman Gauthier, 860-241-4940

Delaware: Susan Barton, 302-831-2532

District of Columbia: M. Khan, 202-274-6907

Florida: Kathleen C. Ruppert, 352-392-8836

Georgia: Bob Westerfield, 912-825-6413

Hawaii: Dale Sato, 808-453-6059

Idaho: Dr. Michael Colt, 208-722-6701

Illinois: Floyd Giles, 217-333-2125

Indiana: Rosie Lerner, 317-494-1311

Iowa: Linda Naeve, 515-294-0028

Kansas: Charles Marr, 913-532-6173

Kentucky: Sharon Bale, 606-257-8605

Louisiana: Dr. Tom Koske, 504-388-4141

Maine: Lois Berg Stack, 207-581-2949

Maryland: Jon Traunfeld, 410-531-5572

Massachusetts: Bruce Roberts or Suzanne A. Siegel, 617-536-9280

Michigan: Mary McLellan, 517-353-3774

Minnesota: Dr. Mary H. Meyer, 612-443-2460

Mississippi: MG Coordinator, Mississippi State University, 601-325-2311

Missouri: Denny Shrock, 573-882-9633

Montana: Bob Gough, 406-994-6523

Nebraska: Susan Schoneweis, 402-472-1128

Nevada: Richard Post, 702-784-4848

New Hampshire: Virginia Hast, 603-796-2151

New Jersey: Rutgers Cooperative Extension, 908-704-9828

New Mexico: Dr. Curtis Smith, 505-275-2576

New York: Charles Mazza, 607-255-1791

North Carolina: Larry Bass, 919-515-1200

North Dakota: Dr. Ronald Smith, 701-231-8161

Ohio: Mary Riofrio, 614-292-8326

Oklahoma: Dale Hillock, 405-744-5158

Ontario: Laurie Scott, 519-767-3186

Oregon: Ann Marie VanDerZanden, 541-737-2503

Pennsylvania: Toni Bilik, 814-863-7716

Rhode Island: Roseanne Sherry, 401-792-2900

Saskatchewan: Sara Williams, 306-966-5593

South Carolina: Robert F. Polomski, 864-656-2604

South Dakota: David F. Graper, 605-688-6253

Tennessee: Dr. David Sams, 901-425-4721

Texas: Dr. Douglas Welsh, 409-845-7341

Utah: Dr. Dan Drost, 801-797-2258

Vermont: Margaret Andrews, 802-773-3349

Virginia: Sheri Dorn, 540-231-6524

Washington: Van Bobbitt, 206-840-4547

West Virginia: John Jett, 304-293-4801

Wisconsin: Helen Harrison, 608-262-1749

Wyoming: Rodney Davis, 307-235-9400

Web Sites about Container Gardening

California Garden Calendar (http://www.geocities.com/RainForest/1079/calendar.html) offers a detailed monthly calendar of seasonal gardening chores for California gardeners.

Contained Garden: A Web Site for Container Gardeners (http://www.anet-chi.com/~kmguise/) by Karen Guise. Provides design ideas and links (still to come) to other helpful sites.

Container Gardening (http://www.ext.vt.edu/pubs/envirohort/general/container.html) Sponsored by Virginia Cooperative Extension, written by Diane Relf, Extension Specialist, Environmental Horticulture. Covers all the basics (soil, light, water) and includes suggestions for varieties best suited for containers.

Container Gardening (http://www.umsl.edu/~silvest/garden/contain.html) by Doreen G. Howard. Special section on choosing varieties and planting tips for a broad range of container vegetables (including watermelon).

Container Gardening (http://www1.geocities.com/RainForest/1329/containers.htm) by Terry L. Yockey. Read about a small-space gardener's personal experiences.

Container Gardening of Culinary Herbs (http://httpsrv.ocs.drexel.edu/grad/sg95d362/) Information and links to other sites.

Dig the Net — The World of Gardening Online (http://www.digthenet.com/) A gardening database subsection of Time Warner's Virtual Garden.

The Virtual Garden (http://www.pathfinder.com/vg/) This site features an electronic encyclopedia, a database with information on about 3,000 plants grown in North America. Other resources include excerpts from Time-Life's gardening books, articles from *Sunset* and *Southern Living* magazines, and a tour of the New York Botanical Gardens.

USDA Home Gardening Page (http://www.usda.gov/news/garden.htm). This site is comprised of multiple sections, including a horticultural solutions, lawn and garden care, ecoregions map, and lots more.

USDA Partners of the Cooperative State Research, Education and Extension Service (http://www.reeusda.gov/new/statepartners/usa.htm) This site presents a directory of land-grant universities that are state partners of the Cooperative State Research Education and Extension Service, with links to all the partners.

USDA Plants Project (http://plants.usda.gov) This site offers a database and photo gallery of standardized information about plants found in the United States and its territories, with an emphasis on economically important plants.

WebGarden Factsheet Database (http://www.hcs.ohio-state.edu/hcs/webgarden/FactsheetFind.html) Complied by Ohio State University, this site offers online tutorials, a plant dictionary, and a searchable database of over 9,000 factsheets. Also provides weekly Ohio gardening news.

Books about Container Gardening

50 Recipes for Colorful Hanging Baskets. Richard Bird. Sterling Publications, 1997 ($22.95 hardcover).

A Growing Gardener. Abbie Zabar. Universe Publishing, 1996 ($22.50 hardcover).

Balcony and Roof Gardens: Creative Ideas for Small-Scale Gardening. Jenny Hendy. Time-Life, 1997 ($19.95 hardcover).

Colorful Containers. Friedrich Straus, Dagmar Straus. Crescent Books, 1996 ($19.99 hardcover).

Colorful Hanging Baskets & Other Containers. Debbie Patterson, et al. Sterling Publications, 1997 ($19.95 hardcover).

Contained Gardens: Creative Designs and Projects. Susan Berry, Steve Bradley. Garden Way Publishing, 1995 ($25.00 hardcover).

Container Gardening for Kids. Ellen Talmage, Bruce Curtis (Photographer). Sterling Publications, 1997 ($9.95 paperback).

Container Gardening Through the Year. Malcolm Hillier. Dorling-Kindersley, 1995 ($24.95 hardcover).

Container Plants: For Patios, Balconies, and Window Boxes. Halina Heitz. Barrons, 1992 ($22.95 hardcover).

Containers. George Carter, Marianne Marjerus. Stewart, Tabori & Chang, 1997 ($22.50 hardcover).

Gardening Without a Garden. Gay Search. Dorling-Kindersley, 1997 ($24.95 hardcover).

Hanging Baskets, Window Boxes, and Other Container Gardens : A Guide to Creative Small-Scale Gardening. David Joyce. Summit Books, 1992 ($20.50 hardcover).

Miniature Gardens (Gardener's Handbook, Vol 4). Joachim Carl, Martin Kral (Translator). Timber Press, 1990 ($26.95 hardcover).

Movable Harvests: The Simplicity & Bounty of Container Gardens. Chuck Crandall, Barbara Crandall. Chapters Publishing Ltd., 1996 ($19.95 paper).

Potted Gardens: A Fresh Approach to Container Gardening. Rebecca Cole, Richard Felber (Photographer). Clarkson Potter, 1997 ($27.50 hardcover).

Spectacular Hanging Baskets: Choice Plants and Plantings for Great Displays. John Feltwell. Sterling Publications, 1997 ($24.95 hardcover).

The Art of Gardening in Pots. Elisabeth De Lestrieax. Antique Collectors Club, 1996 ($59.50 hardcover).

The Book of Container Gardening. Malcolm Hillier. Simon & Schuster, 1991 ($27.50 hardcover).

The Container Gardener. Rupert Golby, et al. Stemmer House Publications, 1995 ($25.00 hardcover).

The Ultimate Container Gardener: Over 150 Glorious Designs for Planters, Pots, Boxes, Baskets and Tubs. Stephanie Donaldson. Lorenz Books, 1997 ($19.98 hardcover).

The Window Box Book. Karen Fausch. Little Bookroom, 1997 ($19.95 hardcover).

Window Boxes. Stephanie Donaldson, Marie O'Hara (Photographer). Lorenz Books, 1997 ($16.96 hardcover).

Windowbox Gardening. David Joyce. Globe Pequot Press, 1993 ($22.95 hardcover).

Magazines That Include Some Information about Container Gardening

The American Gardener. Published bimonthly. American Horticultural Society, 7931 East Boulevard Dr., Alexandria, VA 22308-1300; 703-768-5700. $45.

Country Home Country Gardens. Published quarterly. Meredith Corp., 1716 Locust St., Des Moines, IA 50309-3023. $16. Subscriptions: 1901 Bell Ave., Des Moines, IA 50315; 800-677-0484.

Country Living Gardener. Published bimonthly. The Hearst Corp., 224 W. 57th St., New York, NY 10019; 212-649-3824. $19.97. Subscriptions: Customer Service Dept., Country Living Gardener, P.O. Box 7335, Red Oak, IA 51591-0335; 800-777-0102.

Fine Gardening. Published bimonthly. The Taunton Press, 63 S. Main St., Newtown, CT 06470-5506; 800-477-8727. $32.

Garden Design. Published 8 times a year. Meigher Communications, 100 Avenue of the Americas, New York, NY 10013; 212-334-1212, e-mail gardendesign@meiger.com. $27.95. Subscriptions: P.O. Box 5428, Harlan, IA 51593.

Garden Gate. Published bimonthly. August Home Publishing Co., 2200 Grand Ave., Des Moines, IA 50312. $24.95. Subscriptions: P.O. Box 37115. Boone, IA 50037-2115; 800-341-4769.

Herb Companion. Published bimonthly. Interweave Press, 201 East Fourth St., Loveland, CO 80537-5655; 970-669-7672 (Web site http://www.interweave.com). $24.

Horticulture. Published 10 times a year. KIII Communications, 98 North Washington St., Boston, MA 02114-1913; 617-742-5600. $26. Subscriptions: P.O. Box 53880, Boulder, CO 80322-3880; 800-234-2415.

National Gardening. Published bimonthly. National Gardening Association, 180 Flynn Ave., Burlington, VT 05401; 802-863-1308, e-mail nga@garden.org; (Web site http://www.garden.org). $18.95. Subscriptions: P.O. Box 52874, Boulder, CO 80323; 800-727-9097.

Index

• A •

acanthocalycium glaucum, 159
acer palmatum, 117–118
achillea (yarrow), 90
acidity (pH) of soil mixes, 40–41, 250
acid-loving plants, 41
African violets (*saintpaulia*), 46, 168–169
agapanthus (Lily of the Nile), 85, 94
agave victoria-reginae (Queen Victoria century plant), 161
ageratum, 75, 78
aglaonema (Chinese evergreen), 168
air quality improvement through indoor plants, 163
air space, considerations for soil mixes, 40, 42–43
alkalinity (pH) of soil mixes, 40–41, 250
aloe vera (*aloe barbanensis*), 170
alstroemerias, 86
alyssum, 76, 78, 185, 187, 207, 222
amaryllis (*hippeastrum*), 100
amending soil mixes, 40
American Bonsai Society, 293
annuals
  advantages of growing in containers, 68–69
  caring for, 68, 73–74
  climate considerations, 19–20, 70
  crowding for effect, 72
  defined, 67–68
  hardy versus tender, 69
  mixing in containers, 77–78
  mixing with perennials, 13
  "new outlook" mixed planting, 186–187
  pinching and deadheading, 74
  planting, 72–73
  purchasing, 56, 70–71
  removing, 180
  seasons, considerations for, 69–70
  seed and seedlings, 56, 70
  selecting, 74–77
  selecting containers, 71–72
  for shady spots, 77, 283
  for sunny spots, 75–77
  "suspended animation" mixed planting, 185–186
  when to plant, 54
aphids, 268, 272
  See also pest control
apple trees, 143, 146–147
apricot trees, 147
aquatic plants. *See* water gardens
aralia, Japanese, 113
araucaria heterophylla (Norfolk Island pines), 119, 164, 170
arborvitae (thuja), 111
arbutus unedo, 124
areoles on cactus, 154
artemisia Powis Castle, 91
asparagus ferns, 86
aspidistra elatior (cast-iron plant), 168
asplenium nidus (bird's nest ferns), 164, 169
asters, 91
astilbe, 91
aucuba, 106
Australian tree ferns (*Cyathea cooperi*), 114
"autumn romance" mixed planting, 184–185
azaleas, 43, 106–107

• B •

bacillus thuringiensi (Bt), 269
balled and burlapped shrubs and trees, 55, 57, 63
bamboo, 15, 34, 107–108
  heavenly, 115
banana trees, 152
barberry, Japanese, 117

bare-root plants
  amount of soil mix to add when planting, 62
  fruits and berries, 145
  keeping moist, 60
  perennials, 82
  purchasing, 55
  selecting, 57
  when to plant, 54
bark chips for mulch, 63, 244
bark in soil mixes, 43, 45
barrels as containers, 27
basil, 138, 193, 215
baskets, hanging. *See* hanging baskets
beans, 133
beard tongue, 89
bedding plants, 55
  See also annuals; perennials
beehive cactus (*coryphantha
    missouriensis*), 159
bees for pollination, 142
beetles, 269, 272–274
  See also pest control
beets, 133
begonias, 15, 43, 77, 78, 102, 169, 207
bellflowers, 91, 228
benches for potting chores, 292
berberis thunbergii, 117
berries. *See* fruits and berries
bird's nest ferns (*asplenium nidus*), 164, 169
bishop's cap or miter (*astrophytum
    myriostigma*), 159
black spot, 278–279
blackberries, 147–148
blanketflower (*gaillardias*), 86
bleach, 258
blood meal, 84, 251, 254
blooms
  deadheading to encourage, 74, 83
  precocious, 56, 71
blue marguerites (*felicias*), 86
blueberries, 142, 145, 148
bolting, 131
bonemeal, 84, 251, 253, 254
bonsai, 7, 230, 293–295
Bonsai (Sunset Books), 293

books for container gardening enthusiasts,
    311–312
borers, 272–273
boron, 248
borzicactus celsianus
    (old-man-of-the-mountains), 160
Boston ferns (*nephrolepis bostoniensis*),
    114, 169
botrytis blight, 279
bougainvillea, 15, 125
boxwood, 12, 108
British Columbia chapter of Master
    Gardeners International, 306–308
broccoli, 133
browallias, 77
Brown, Deb, 20
brushes for scrubbing, 291
bubblers, hose-end, 291
bud unions, 143
budgetary considerations
  bargains in fertilizers, 251–252
  seeds, 54
budworms on geraniums, etc., 273
bugs. *See* pest control
bulb food, 97
bulb pans, 97
bulb pots, 32
bulblets, 93
bulbs
  beauties of, in containers, 93, 94–95
  chilling, 96–97
  described, 93–94
  in "early spring bouquet" mixed planting,
    182–183
  fertilizing, 97
  forcing blooms, 99–100
  growth pattern, 94, 97
  importance of timing, 54, 95, 96
  mail ordering, 95, 96, 297–302
  with "noses," 96
  planting, 54, 97–99
  purchasing, 95, 96, 297–302
  in saucers, 230
  selecting, 95–96
  selecting containers, 97

soil mixes for, 46, 97
for spring, 94, 100–101
storing, 96–97
for summer, 94, 102
in urns, 229
watering, 99
in window boxes, 223
burlapped shrubs and trees, 55, 57, 63
butterfly flowers, 207

• **C** •

cabbage, 133
cabbage palm, 229
cactus and succulents
    advantages, 153, 245
    areoles, 154
    caution on reflected heat, 24
    climate considerations, 154–155
    described, 154
    fertilizing, 158
    ideas for using, 12, 13, 15, 22, 34
    planting, 155–157
    repotting, 158
    in saucers, 230
    selecting, 159
    selecting containers, 155
    soil mixes, 155
    soil mixes for, 46
    watering, 157–158
caladium, 102
calceolarias, 207
calcium, 248
calendulas, 69, 75, 184, 207
callas (*zantedeschia*), 102
camellias, 43, 108
campanulas, 91
cannas, 102
carbon, 248
cardinal flowers, 194, 223
carnations, 43, 89
carrots, 133
cast concrete containers, 29, 227–230, 236
cast-iron plant (*aspidistra elatior*), 168
casual versus formal settings, 12
caterpillars, 269, 272–273
    See also pest control

catmint, 91, 213
cauliflower, 133
celosia, 70
cement. *See* concrete containers
charcoal in soil mixes, 45
chard, 126
chelated fertilizers, 250
cherry tomatoes, 136
cherry trees, 114, 149
Chinese evergreen (*aglaonema*), 168
chives, 138, 193
chlorine, 248
chlorophyll, 248
chlorophytum comosum (spider plant), 167
cholla, 160
Christmas cactus (*schlumbergera*), 169
Christmas trees, living, 109, 289
chrysanthemum frutescens (marguerites), 15, 89
chrysanthemums, 43, 87, 184
cilantro, 193
cineraria, 75
citrus trees, 34, 148–149
    lemon, 144, 164, 170
clay component of soil mixes, 39
clay loam, 43
clematis, 125
climate considerations, 103
    advantages of portability, 17, 24, 69, 84
    annuals and perennials, 19–20, 70
    cactus and succulents, 154–155
    caution on additional exposure of container plants, 19, 20
    first- and last-frost dates, 19–20
    fruits and berries, 144
    hardiness (cold tolerance), 18
    heat tolerance, 19
    permanent plants, 20–22
    shrubs and trees, 103
    sun or shade, 22–23
    tropical (Hawaii or Florida), 70
    watering, 236
    wintertime relocation of plants to indoors, 16
    See also seasons
Clivia, 94

cloudiness, and watering, 236
clubs
  bonsai enthusiasts, 293
  Master Gardeners International, 306–308
  See also Web sites
coco-fiber liners for hanging baskets, 203
coconut coir pith, 45
codiaeum variegatum (crotons), 164, 169
coleus, 77, 78, 170, 207
color
  complementary, 174
  design considerations, 12, 174–175
  of glazed pots with flowering annuals, 71
  of leaves, 55, 175
  of pots, and water retention, 237
"color connection" hanging basket design,
  212–213
combining plants in containers. *See* mixed
  plantings
complementary colors, 174
"complete" and incomplete fertilizers, 250
The Complete Book of Bonsai, 293
compost in soil mixes, 40, 45
composted bark in soil mixes, 45
computer research on container gardening.
  See Web sites
concrete containers, 29, 227–230, 236
conifers, 109–111
  See also pines; spruce
conservatories, 21
conserving water, 244–245
container gardening
  climate. *See* climate considerations
  designing with. *See* design considerations
  ease of, 7
  Master Gardeners International, 306–308
  origins and advantages, 1, 7–10, 11
  portability of containers, 8, 69, 84, 95
  problem of poor appearance in off-
    season, 16
  skill levels assumed, 2
  yard/plot size considerations, 7
  See also mixed plantings; plants
container plants. *See* plants
containers
  burying for over-wintering, 21
  burying for water conservation, 244

caution on freezability, 22, 26
caution on weight, 16
cleaning, 257–258, 261
combining in arrangements, 14
combining plants in. *See* mixed plantings
elevating above ground level, 33–34
gravel in bottom, caution on, 42
moving large, heavy, 260–261, 262
placement, 14, 177, 237
planting. *See* planting
preparing to receive plants, 58
removing plants from, 60–61, 256
repairing, 258–260
storing unused, 261, 263
unusual, 10, 29, 30, 219, 231
using doubled for water conservation, 244
containers: selecting for
  annuals, 71–72
  cactus and succulents, 155
  drainage, 26, 246
  fruits and berries, 145–146
  indoor plants, 164–165
  perennials, 81
  porosity, 25–26, 236
  shrubs and trees, 105
  size, shape, beauty, and function, 25, 29–32,
    71, 72, 81, 177–178
  vegetables and herbs, 130
  watering needs, 236
containers: types
  bulb pans, 97
  bulb pots, 32
  concrete, 29, 227–230, 236
  glazed clay, 26, 71
  hypertufa, 155, 228–229
  metal, 29, 236, 263–264
  paper pulp, 29
  plastic, 28, 178, 236
  raised beds, 29
  saucers, 33, 230
  strawberry jars, 226–227
  terra-cotta or unglazed clay, 26, 27, 58, 71,
    155, 177, 178, 187, 236
  troughs and stone sinks, 227–229
  unusual, improvised, homemade, "found,"
    10, 29, 30, 219, 231

urns, 229–230
water-filled, for aquatic plants, 34, 194–195, 223–225
window boxes, 220–223
wood, 27–28, 58, 178, 236, 264
See also hanging baskets
contamination of soils. *See* pest control; soil mixes
copper, 248
snails' refusal to touch, 275
coral bells (*heuchera*), 87
coreopsis, 87, 187, 207
corn, 133
Cornell soil-less mix recipe, 51
corylus avellana contorta, 115
coryphantha missouriensis (beehive cactus), 159
cosmos, 70, 75, 78, 190
cotoneaster, 112
crabapple trees, 114
crape myrtle, 112, 195
crassula (jade plant), 160
crassula pubescens, 160
crocuses, 99, 100
crotons (*codiaeum variegatum*), 164, 169
cub's paws (*cotyledon tomentosa*), 160
cucumbers, 133
currants, 152
cutting back. *See* pruning
cutworms, 269, 274
See also pest control
cycas revoluta, 123
cypress, false, 110, 229

● *D* ●

daffodils, 99, 100, 182
dahlias, 75, 102
daisies, 195
kingfisher, 206
paludosum, 184
Transvaal (gerberas), 77, 207
damping off, 279
daphne, 112–113
daylilies (*hemerocallis*), 87
deadheading, removing dead flowers to promote blooming, 74, 83, 179, 212

debris removal, 267, 278, 279
deciduous perennials, 80
delphiniums, 88
design considerations
color, 174–175
for containers. *See* containers: selecting
elevating containers above ground level, 33–34
ideas for, 15
styles, 12
water gardens, 225
See also hanging baskets; mixed plantings
dianthus, 34, 89, 190, 207, 214, 222
diascia, 91
dieffenbachia (dumb cane), 167, 169
digitalis (foxglove), 88
dill, 268
dirt. *See* soil mixes
diseases in soils, 44, 48
disposal of pesticides, 263, 271
dividing and repotting perennials, 84–85
dollies for large containers, 177
dolomite in soil mixes, 45
donkey tails, 217
dormant oil, 270–271
dracaena, 168
drain hole covers, 42, 57, 59–60
drainage
aiding in prevention of root rot, 278, 280
considerations for container selection, 26, 246
excessive, as sign of container breakage, 259
hanging baskets, 200
unusual containers, 231
See also water considerations
drill for making drainage holes, 60
drip irrigation, 239–241, 243, 244
dumb cane (*dieffenbachia*), 167, 169
dusty miller, 75, 78
dwarf fruit trees, 142–143
dwarfing rootstocks, 143

● *E* ●

"early spring bouquet" mixed plantings, 182–183

eastern exposures, 22
echeveria, 160
echinocactus grusonii (golden barrel cactus), 159
echinocereus viridiflorus (hedgehog cactus), 159
echinopsis (sea urchin), 160
"edible aerials" hanging basket design, 214–215
eggplant, 133
English ivy, 223
English laurel, 113
English primroses, 89–90, 207
"entryway elegance" mixed planting, 195–196
epiphyllum (orchid cactus), 160
epipremnum (pothos), 164, 170
erigeron, 91
euryops, 88
evergreens
  conifers, 109–111, 229
  perennials, 80
  See also shrubs and trees
exposure, of container plants to climate. *See* climate considerations

• *F* •

Fafard Mixes, 44
fall
  and "autumn romance" mixed planting, 184–185
  plants for, 288
false cypresses, 110, 229
  as bonsai, 294
fatsia, 113
feeding of container plants. *See* fertilizing
feijoa, 121
felicias (blue marguerites), 86
fennel, 268
ferns
  air space needs, 43
  bird's nest, 164, 169
  Boston, 114, 169
  ideas for, 15, 113–114
  maidenhair, 114, 192

as shade lovers, 22
  types, 113–114
fertilizers
  blood meal, 84, 251, 254
  bonemeal, 84, 251, 253, 254
  caution on salt burn, 178, 242, 253
  checking expiration dates and discarding, 263
  chelated, 250
  "complete" and incomplete, 250
  criticality of, 247
  essential elements in, 248
  fish emulsion, 84, 251, 253, 254
  foliar, 250
  granular, 249
  greensand, 253, 254
  liquid, 178, 250, 252, 253
  manure, 45, 251, 253, 254
  organic, 251, 253–254
  reading labels, 249
  shopping for bargains, 251–252
  slow- or timed-release, 84, 178, 203, 251, 252
  in soil mixes, 45, 48, 61
  "specialty," 251
fertilizing
  advantages for pest control, 267
  advantages of frequent, 252–253
  annuals, 73
  bulbs, 97
  cactus and succulents, 158
  caution, during hot or windy weather, 254
  caution on overfertilizing, 254
  hanging baskets, 212
  indoor plants, 167
  perennials, 83–84
  seedlings, 64
  shrubs and trees, 105
  vegetables and herbs, 131
  when planting, 61
fig trees, 149
filler plants, 207
firs, 110
fish, in water gardens, 225
fish emulsion, 84, 251, 253, 254
flax, 12, 229

flies
  for pollination, 142
  whiteflies, 276–277
Florida, southern/tropical, 70
flowering fruit trees. *See* fruits and berries
flowering plants
  in "autumn romance" mixed planting,
      184–185
  deadheading (removing dead flowers) to
      promote blooming, 74, 83, 179
  "entryway elegance" mixed planting,
      195–196
  "new outlook" mixed planting, 186–187
  "scented sensations" mixed planting,
      190–191
  "shade-lover's delight" mixed planting,
      192–193
  sun exposure, 24
  "terra-cotta collection" mixed planting,
      187–189
  See also annuals; fruits and berries;
      perennials
foliage
  color considerations, 175
  inspecting regularly for pests, 265, 266
  overhead watering to wash off dust, 178
foliage plants, 24
foliar fertilizers, 250
forcing blooms on bulbs, 99–100
form (shape) of plants, design consider-
      ations, 175–176
formality versus casual settings, 12
foxglove (*digitalis*), 88
fragrant plants, 284
freesias, 100
frost dates, first- and last-, 19–20
fruits and berries
  challenges, 141
  climate considerations, 144
  dwarfing rootstocks, 143
  dwarfs, 142–143
  flowering, 114
  graft or bud unions, 143
  mail order sources, 302–303
  maintenance considerations, 144

  in "nature's bounty" mixed planting,
      183–184
  pest control, 144
  pollination, 142
  pruning, 146
  rootstocks, 142–143
  scions, 142–143
  selecting containers, 145–146
  size considerations, 144
  thinning, 143
fuchsias, 114, 192, 206, 216
full sun, defined (seven hours in summer),
      22, 23
fungicides, 278
  See also pest control
funguses
  causing root rot, 278, 280
  damping off, 279
  powdery mildew, 279
  rust, 280
  See also pest control

• *G* •

gaillardias (blanketflower), 86
gardenias, 115
Gardening For Dummies, 19
gardens
  plot size considerations for container
      gardening, 7
  See also container gardening
garlic chives, 193
gazanias, 91, 183
general-purpose soil mixes, 46
genetic dwarf fruit trees, 143
gentian, 228
geranium budworms, 273
geraniums
  ideas for using, 43, 75, 78, 80, 185, 190, 207,
      213, 223
  ivy, 206, 212, 222
gerberas (Transvaal daisies), 77
germinating mix, 46
  See also soil mixes
gifts, plants nice enough to pot and present
      as, 286

glazed clay containers, 26, 71
glory lilies (*gloriosa rothschildsiana*), 102
gloves, 57, 156
    caution: use when mixing or spraying
        pesticides, 271
golden barrel cactus (*echinocactus
        grusonii*), 159
goldfish, in water gardens, 225
gooseberries, 152
graft unions, 143
granular fertilizers, 249
grape hyacinths (*muscari*), 101
gravel in bottom of containers, caution
        on, 42
gray mold (botrytis blight), 279
green lacewings, 269
greenhouses, 21
greensand, 253, 254
growing mix. *See* soil mixes
guavas, 152

• H •

hand truck, 291
hand watering, 238–239
hanging baskets
    advantages and disadvantages, 199
    described, 32
    design considerations, 204–207
    fertilizing, 212
    fiber or peat, pre-formed, 203
    hanging and support considerations, 204
    ideas for, 15, 173
        "color connection," 212–213
        "edible aerials," 214–215
        "scented sensations," 213–214
        "shady delight," 215–216
        "textured treasures," 216–217
        "wall basket collection," 217–218
    liners, 203
    location selection, 199–200
    planting, 208–211
    plastic, 202
    replanting, 212
    rotating, 212
    self-watering, 203

soil mixes, 46, 203
in "suspended animation" mixed planting,
        185–186
watering, 200, 211
wire, 201
wooden boxes, 202, 264
See also mixed plantings
hardiness zones, 18
hardy annuals, 69
Harry Lauder's walking stick, 115
Hawaii, 70
heat, reflective, as microclimate factor, 24
heat tolerance, 19, 237
    fish in water gardens, 225
    thermometers, 292
heath, 189
heavenly bamboo, 115
hedera helix, 126
hedgehog cactus (*echinocereus
        viridiflorus*), 159
heights
    plants compared to containers, 13
    varying, for collections of containers, 14
helichrysum, 206
hemerocallis (daylilies), 87
Henry, Peggy, 181
hens and chicks or houseleeks (*sempervivum*),
        160, 217
herbicides
    caution on, 44
    checking expiration dates and
        discarding, 263
herbs and spices. *See* vegetables and herbs
heuchera (coral bells), 87
Hibbard, Mike, 20
hibiscus, 116
hills (slopes) as microclimate factor, 23
hollies, 116
homemade and improvised containers, 29
horsetails, 223
hose-end bubblers, 291
hoses for hand watering, 238–239
hostas (plantain lilies), 88
hot peppers, 135
houseleeks or hens and chicks (*sempervivum*),
        160, 217

houttuynia, 223
humidity
  for indoor plants, 166
  and watering, 236
humus, 39
hyacinths, 93, 99, 100
hydrangeas, 9, 116–117
hydrogen, 248
hydroponic gardening. *See* water gardens
hypertufa containers, 155, 228–229
hypoestes phyllostachya (polka-dot plant), 170

• *I* •

Iceland poppies, 70, 75
icons used in this book, 4
impatiens, 12, 15, 77, 78, 192, 207, 216, 222
improvised and homemade containers, 29
India hawthorne, 117
indoor container gardening
  advantages, 163
  caution on window locations, 164
  container selection, 164–165
  direct light conditions, 170
  fertilizing, 167
  humidity, 166
  light considerations, 166–167
  low light conditions, 168
  medium light conditions, 168–170
  misting, 166, 291
  pest control, 164, 167
  plant selection, 164
  pruning, 167
  soil mixes, 165
  spending summers outdoors, 164
  temperature ranges, 166
  terrariums, 164, 165
  watering, 166
"infirmary" for off-season plants, 16
insecticidal soaps, 271
insects
  beneficial for pest control, 267–269
  in garden soil, 44
  for pollination, 142
  See also pest control
insulation, for container plants in winter-
    time, 21

Internet. *See* Web sites
iris, 101, 194
  Japanese, 223
iron, 248
ivy
  English, 223
  ideas for using, 12, 15, 34, 43, 126, 185, 187,
    195, 223
ivy geraniums, 206, 212, 222
ixia, 101

• *J* •

jade plant (*crassula*), 160, 217
Japanese aralia, 113
Japanese barberry, 117
Japanese beetles, 269, 273–274
  See also pest control
Japanese iris, 223
Japanese maples, 15, 20, 117–118, 229
Jiffy-Mix, 44
jovibarba heuffelii, 160
junipers
  as bonsai, 294
  ideas for using, 8, 110, 189

• *K* •

kale, 133
  ornamental, 76
kentia palms, 120
kingfisher daisies, 206
knives, 57
kumquats, 148

• *L* •

labels for plants, 291
lacewings, 269
ladybugs and ladybeetles, 268
lantana, 118, 206, 212
Lauder's walking stick, 115
laurel
  English, 113
  ideas for using, 15
  sweet bay, 124

laurus nobilis, 124
lavender (*lavandula*), 12, 34, 88–89
lemon trees, 144, 164, 170
Lenten roses, 91
lettuce, 129, 133
lewisia redidiva, 161
ligustrum, 122
lilies
  as bulbs, 101
  daylilies (*hemerocallis*), 87
  plantain (hostas), 88
  water, 223
Lily of the Nile (agapanthus), 85
Lily of the valley shrub, 118
lime in soil mixes, 41, 45
limestone, ground (dolomite), 45
liquid fertilizers, 178, 250, 252, 253
"living" Christmas trees, 109, 289
loam, 40
lobelia, 12, 75, 78, 185, 195, 206, 213, 216, 222
loquats, 152

• *M* •

macroclimates, 17
macronutrients, 248
macropores in soil mixes, 42
Madagascar dragon tree, 168
magazines for container gardening
    enthusiasts, 313
magnesium, 248
maidenhair ferns (*adiantum*), 114, 192
mail order purchases
  beneficial insects, 268
  bulbs, 95, 96
  fruit trees, 302–303
  neem, 270
  perennials, 82, 297–302
  plants and seeds, 297–302
  tools, supplies, and structures, 304–306
  water garden plants and supplies, 303
Malacoides primroses, 207, 218
mammillaria bombycina (pincushion
    cactus), 160
mandarin oranges, 148
mandevilla, 126
manganese, 248

manure in soil mixes, 45, 251, 253, 254
maples, Japanese, 15, 20, 117–118, 229
marguerites
  blue (*felicias*), 86
  chrysanthemum frutescens, 89
  ideas for using, 15, 187
marigolds, 13, 70, 76, 78, 183, 187, 207,
    212, 223
marsh marigolds, 223
Master Gardeners International, 306–308
mealybugs, 274
  See also pest control
Mediterranean fan palm, 120
metal containers, 29, 236, 263–264
Metro-Mix, 44
Meyer's lemon trees, 144, 164, 170
microclimates, 17, 22–24
micronutrients, 248
micropores in soil mixes, 42
mimulus, 207
misting of indoor plants, 166, 291
mites, 269
  spider, 275–276
  See also pest control
mixed plantings
  advantages, 173–174
  care of plants for continuing beauty,
    178–180
  color as design element, 174–175
  container selection, 177–178
  form, texture, and proportion in design,
    175–176
  ideas for, 13, 14, 15, 181
    "autumn romance," 184–185
    "early spring bouquet," 182–183
    "entryway elegance," 195–196
    "nature's bounty," 183–184
    "new outlook," 186–187
    "next on the menu," 193–194
    "reflective beauty," 194–195
    "scented sensations," 190–191
    "shade-lover's delight," 192–193
    "suspended animation," 185–186
    "terra-cotta collection," 187–189
    "timeless beauty, Old World charm,"
      189–190
  See also hanging baskets

moisture. *See* water considerations; watering
moisture sensors, 242
molybdenum, 248
Moon Valley pilea, 169
moth orchid (*phaleanopsis*), 169
mother-in-law's tongue (*sansevieria trifasciata*), 168
moving large, heavy containers, 260–261, 262
mulching, 63, 244
myrtle, 118
  crape, 112

• *N* •

nandina domestica, 115
narcissus, 100, 182
nasturtiums, 206, 215
Natural Organic Farmers Association (NOFA) soil mix recipe, 51
naturalized bulbs, 100
"nature's bounty" mixed plantings, 183–184
nectarine trees, 143, 150
neem, 269–270
nematodes
  parasitic, 269, 273
  See also pest control
nemesia, 76, 78
nepeta, 91
nephrolepis bostoniensis (Boston ferns), 114, 169
"new outlook" mixed planting, 186–187
New Zealand flax, 119, 229
"next on the menu" mixed planting, 193–194
nicotianas, 191
nitrogen, 248, 249
Norfolk Island pines (*araucaria heterophylla*), 119, 164, 170
northern exposures, 22
nursery mixes, 46

• *O* •

"Old World charm" mixed plantings, 189–190
old-man-of-the-mountains (*borzicactus celsianus*), 160

oleanders, 119
onions, 133
opuntia, 160
orchid cactus (*epiphyllum*), 160
orchids, soil mixes for, 46
oregano, 138
organic fertilizers, 251, 253–254
ornamental kale, 76
The Ortho Problem Solver, 266
outdoor plants. *See* annuals; bare-root plants; bulbs; cactus and succulents; evergreens; fruits and berries; perennials; shrubs and trees
outdoor plants. *See* vegetables and herbs
overhangs, for protecting frost-threatened plants, 21
oxygen
  considerations for soil mixes, 40, 42–43
  in fertilizers, 248

• *P* •

packing peanuts, caution on use in soil mixes, 51
palms, 120
  cabbage, 229
paludosum daisies, 184
pansies, 13, 15, 69, 70, 76, 185, 207, 218, 222
paper pulp containers, 29
parasitic nematodes, 269, 273
  See also pest control
parlor palms, 120
parodia, 160
parrot's feather, 194, 223
parsley, 138, 268
Part of Tens
  bonsai, 293–295
  handy tools, 291–292
  plants for seasons, 287–289
  plants for special situations and occasions, 283–286
part shade, defined, 22
peace lily (*spathiphyllum*), 168
peach trees, 143, 150, 183
pear trees, 150
peas, 133–134

peat-based "growing media," 44–46
  peat moss, 43, 46
pennisetum setaseum Rubrum (purple
    fountain grass), 90
penstemon, 89
peperomia, 170
peppers, 135, 193
perennials
  advantages and disadvantages in
      containers, 80–81
  advantages of, 79
  climate considerations, 19–20
  cutting back, 83, 84
  deadheading for more bloom, 83
  defined, 79–80
  downside of down time, 81
  fertilizing, 83–84
  mixing with annuals, 13
  planting in containers, 82–83
  purchasing by mail order, 82
  repotting, 84–85
  selecting candidates for containers, 85–91
  selecting containers for, 81
  "suspended animation" mixed planting,
      185–186
  "timeless beauty, Old World charm" mixed
      planting, 189–190
  watering, 83
  when to plant, 54
  winter care, 84
perlite in soil mixes, 42, 43, 45, 203
pest control
  by beneficial insects, 267–269
  caution on expired pesticides and discard-
      ing, 263, 271
  caution on overhead watering, 267,
      277, 279
  caution on use of pesticides, 271
  common diseases of plants,
    black spot, 278–279
    botrytis blight, 279
    damping off, 279
    powdery mildew, 279
    root rots, 280
    rust, 280
    salt burn, 280

common pests,
    aphids, 272
    borers, 272–273
    budworms, 273
    caterpillars and worms, 273
    cutworms, 274
    Japanese beetles, 273–274
    mealybugs, 274
    scale, 274
    snails and slugs, 268, 275
    spider mites, 275–276
    thrips, 276
    whiteflies, 276–277
  debris removal, 267, 278, 279
  and disease prevention, 277–278
  health of plants and disease resistance, 267
  importance of regular plant inspection,
      265, 266, 268
  indoor plants, 164, 167
    inspecting after stays outdoors, 164
  isolating containers/plants for spraying, 11
  location and relationship to problems, 266
  mail order purchase of beneficial
      insects, 268
  for old pots before reuse, 58, 257
  pesticides,
    bacillus thuringiensi (Bt), 269
    caution on use of, 271
    dormant oil, 270–271
    expired, discarding properly, 263, 271
    insecticidal soaps, 271
    isolating containers/plants for spraying, 11
    neem, 269–270
    pyrethrins, 270
    rotenone, 270
    snail bait, 57, 275
    summer oil, 270–271
  removing infected plants, 277
  for soil mixes, 44, 48
  spacing of plants for air circulation, 277
pets, caution on dangers of pesticides to, 271
petunias, 19–20, 70, 76, 78, 183, 195, 206,
      213, 222
pH of soil mixes, 40–41, 250
  soil-testing kits, 292
phaleanopsis (moth orchid), 169
philodendrons, 170

phlox, 189, 207, 228
phormium tenax, 119
phosphate, 249
phosphorus, 248
pieris japonica, 118
pinching off tip growth on annuals, 74
pincushion cactus (*mammillaria bombycina*), 160
pineapple guavas, 121, 152
pines
  basics, 110–111
  as bonsai, 294
  ideas for using, 15, 103
  Norfolk Island, 119, 164, 170
  shade and loss of needles, 24
pinks, 89, 228
pittosporum, 120
plant labels, 291
plantain lilies (hostas), 88
planting
  annuals, 72–73
  basics, 61–63
  bulbs, 97–99
  cactus and succulents, 155–157
  hanging baskets, 208–211
  loosening plant from original container, 60–61
  necessities for, 57
  perennials, 82–83
  readying containers and drain holes, 58–60
  seasons for, for various plants, 54
  seeds, 63–64
  shrubs and trees, 104
  and watering just-planted plants, 63
  See also fertilizing; soil mixes; watering
plants
  for acidic soil, 41
  attractiveness, in unusual settings, 8–9, 219
  combining in containers. *See* mixed plantings
  easy to grow, 285
  experimenting with locations, 10
  fillers, 207
  flowering, 24
  form, texture, and proportion in design, 175–176
  for fragrance, 284
  for gifts, 286
  in hanging baskets. *See* hanging baskets
  how sold, 54–55
  in impossible places, 8
  for indoors. *See* indoor container gardening
  loosening from original container, 60–61
  mail order sources, 297–302
  mature size considerations, 11, 81, 142–143, 144
  mulching, 63, 244
  selecting, 55–56
  space considerations in containers, 31
  specimen shrubs and trees, 104, 285
  stakes or ties for tall plants, 63, 179
  trailing, 206
  transplanting, 31
  trellises for vines, 57, 63, 179
  upright, 207
  watering just-planted, 63
  See also annuals; bare-root plants; bulbs; cactus and succulents; fruits and berries; perennials; shrubs and trees; vegetables and herbs
plastic containers, 28, 178
  hanging baskets and liners, 202, 203
plastic liners for wood containers, 260
plum trees, 114, 143, 150–151
podocarpus, 121
poinsettias, 43
polka-dot plant (*hypoestes phyllostachya*), 170
pollination of fruit blooms, 142
polystyrene packing peanuts, caution on use in soil mixes, 51
pomegranate, 121
poppies, Iceland, 70, 75
pores in soil mixes, 42
porosity
  considerations for container selection, 25–26, 236
  of soil mixes, 42
portability
  advantages for surviving climate change, 17, 84
  of container plants, 8, 69, 95

"pot feet," 34
potassium, 248
potatoes, 135
pothos (*epipremnum*), 164, 170
pots. *See* containers
potting benches, 292
potting soil. *See* soil mixes
powdery mildew, 279
precocious blooming, 56, 71
pricking out seedlings, 64
prickly pear, 160
primary colors, 174
primroses
  English, 89–90, 207
  ideas for using, 89–90, 182, 189, 228
  Malacoides, 207, 218
primula polyantha, 89–90
privet, 122
Pro-Gro, 44
Pro-Mix, 44
proportion and scale of plants, design
    considerations, 175–176
pruning
  cutting back perennials, 83, 84
  fruits and berries, 146
  indoor plants, 167
  need for, 179, 180
  roots, 257
  shrubs and trees, 105
publications for container gardening
    enthusiasts, 311–313
  See also Web sites
purchasing plants and supplies. *See* mail
    order purchases
purple fountain grass, 90
pygmy date palms, 120
pyracantha, 122
pyrethrins, 270

• *Q* •

Queen Anne's Lace, 268
Queen Victoria century plant (*agave
    victoria-reginae*), 161

• *R* •

radishes, 135
rain, and watering, 236, 245
raised beds, as form of container, 29
raised containers
  elevated above ground level, 33–34
  preventing pot-bottom rot, 27, 259
ranunculus, 101
raphiolepis, 117
raspberries, 151
Redi-Earth, 44
redwoods, 111
reflected heat, as microclimate factor, 24
"reflective beauty" mixed planting, 194–195
REMEMBER icon, 4
repair and refurbishment of broken pots and
    plant stands, 258–260, 263–264
repetition, as element in design, 13
repotting
  cactus and succulents, 158
  need for, 255–256
  perennials, 84–85
  removing plant from original pot, 60–61, 256
  shrubs and trees, 105
  timing of, 256
resources for container gardening enthusiasts
  books, 311–312
  magazines, 313
  See also mail order purchases; Web sites
rhododendrons, 43, 106–107
rock cress, 228
rock rose, 228
rock wool, 45
root balls, checking for moisture, 72, 237, 243
root pruning, 257
root rots, 278, 280
root-bound plants
  avoiding, 55, 56, 57, 60, 71, 72
  pruning root mass, 257
  water needs, 237
roots, criticality of proper soil conditions, 38
rootstocks, 142–143
rosemary, 138, 215
roses
  Lenten, 91

miniature, 34, 223
overview of types, 122–123
Roses For Dummies, 123
rotenone, 270
rust, 280

• S •

safety considerations of pot placement, 14
sage, 90, 139, 215
sago palm, 123
saintpaulia (African violets), 46, 168–169
salt burn, 178, 242, 253, 280
salvia, 76, 78, 207
sand component of soil mixes, 39, 43, 46
sansevieria trifasciata (mother-in-law's tongue), 168
saucers
  as containers, 33, 230
  for protection of surfaces from water damage, 33
  for water reabsorption by plant, 243, 246
savory, 139
sawdust in soil mixes, 43
saxifrage, 189, 228
scale and proportion of plants, design considerations, 13, 175–176
scale (insects), 274
  See also pest control
scallions, 133
"scented sensations" hanging basket design, 213–214
"scented sensations" mixed planting, 190–191
schefflera actinophylla (umbrella plant), 170
schlumbergera (Christmas cactus), 169
scions, 142–143
scoops, 57
screen, as drain hole cover, 42, 57, 59
scrub brushes, 291
sea urchin (*echinopsis*), 160
seasons
  considerations for annuals, 69–70
  for planting various plants, 54
  See also climate considerations; fall; spring; summer; winter

secondary nutrients, 248
sedum, 161, 217
seed packets, USDA zone maps on, 19
seed starting mix, 46
  See also soil mixes
seedlings
  acclimating after purchase, 56
  fertilizing, 64
  thinning, 64
seeds
  advantages, 54
  mail order sources, 297–302
  purchasing, 54
self-watering pots, 203, 241–242
semidwarf fruit trees, 143
shade
  annuals for, 77
  described, 22–23
  for water conservation, 244
"shade-lover's delight" mixed planting, 192–193
shades of color, 175
"shady delight" hanging basket design, 215–216
shapes, design considerations, 12
shears, 57
shellflowers, 194, 223
shrubs and trees
  balled and burlapped, 55, 57, 63
  bonsai, 7, 230, 293–295
  care considerations, 103
  climate considerations, 103
  fertilizing, 105
  "living" Christmas trees, 109, 289
  mature plants' suitability for container gardening, 11, 81, 142–143, 144
  planting, 104
  pruning, 105
  purchasing, 55
  repotting, 105
  selecting, 57
  selecting containers, 105
  for shady spots, 284
  soil mixes for, 43, 46, 48, 105
  tall, stakes or ties for, 63, 179
  watering, 105
  when to plant, 54

silt component of soil mixes, 39
size considerations
  bulbs, 96
  containers, 29–32, 177
  mature plants' suitability for container
      gardening, 11, 81, 142–143, 144
  plants in their containers, 13
slope as microclimate factor, 23
slow-release fertilizers, 84, 178, 203, 251, 252
slugs, 275
snail bait, 57, 275
snails, 268, 275
snapdragons, 12, 13, 15, 43, 69, 76
soaps, insecticidal, 271
societies of gardeners: Master Gardeners
      International, 306–308
soil mixes
  air space, 42–43
  alkalinity and acidity (pH), 40–41
  amendments, 40
  amount to add when planting, 61–63
  caution on reusing, 99, 278, 279
  caution on salt burn, 178, 242, 253, 280
  clay component, 39
  compost, 40
  contamination-free, 44
  criticality of, 37–38
  customizing in containers, 11
  humus, 39
  loam, 40
  mixing from scratch, 47–51
  peat-based "growing media," 44–46
  plain dirt's unsuitability for containers,
      42–44
  purchased, pre-mixed, 37, 44–47
  reusing, caution on, 99, 278
  sand component, 39
  shopping for, 46–47
  silt component, 39
  storing, 47, 50
  structure, 40, 41
  texture, 39
  for types of plants,
    cactus and succulents, 155, 165
    hanging baskets, 46, 203
    indoor plants, 165

    orchids, 165
    shrubs and trees, 105
    vegetables and herbs, 130
  water: moistening upon use, 61
  water infiltration and drainage, 42
  water moisture retention, 43, 237
  See also fertilizers; fertilizing; water
      considerations; watering
soil polymers and water-storing crystals,
      203, 244, 245–246
soil scoops, 291
soil-testing kits, 292
sourness (acidity, or pH) of soil mixes, 40–41
southern exposures, 23
spathiphyllum (peace lily), 168
specimen shrubs and trees, 104, 285
sphagnum peat moss
  as hanging basket liner, 203
  in soil mixes, 44, 45, 46
spices. *See* vegetables and herbs
spider mites, 275–276
spider plants (*chlorophytum comosum*), 167
spinach, 135
spring
  annuals, 70, 287
  bulbs, 94, 100–101, 287
  "early spring bouquet" mixed planting,
      182–183
  perennials, 80, 287
sprinklers, 239
spruce
  ideas for using, 15
  shade and loss of needles, 24
  types, 111
squash, 126
squirrel's foot ferns (*davillia*), 114
stains, water, 16
stakes for tall plants, 57, 63, 179
star jasmine, 126
state chapters of Master Gardeners Interna-
      tional, 306–308
statice, 91
stocks, 186–187
stone sinks and troughs, 227–229
stonecrop, 228
stones, as mulch, 63, 244

storing
  pesticides, 271
    and checking expiration dates, 263
  unused containers, 261, 263
strawberries, 144, 145, 151–152, 183
strawberry jars, 226–227
strawberry trees, 124
structure of soil, 40, 41
styrofoam packing peanuts, caution on use
    in soil mixes, 51
succulents. *See* cactus and succulents
sulfur, 248
summer
  annuals, 288
  bulbs, 94, 102
  perennials, 80, 288
summer oil, 270–271
sun
  annuals for, 75–77
  exposure, 22–23
sunflowers, 74, 76
"sunny" locations, 23
supplies, tools, and structures, mail order
    purchases, 304–306
"suspended animation" mixed planting,
    185–186
sweet alyssum, 76, 78, 185, 187, 207, 214,
    222, 268
sweet bay, 124
sweet flags, 223
sweet olive, 124
sweet peas, 76, 187, 213
sweet peppers, 135
sweet Williams, 76, 187, 218
sweetness (alkalinity, or pH) of soil mixes,
    40–41
Swiss chard, 126
sword ferns (*nephrolepis*), 114

● *T* ●

tarragon, 139
Tasmanian tree ferns (*Dicksonia
    antarctica*), 114
temperatures
  and watering, 236
  See also climate considerations

tender annuals, 70
"terra-cotta collection" mixed planting,
    187–189
terra-cotta (unglazed clay) pots, 26, 27, 58,
    71, 155, 177, 178, 187, 236
texture of plants, design considerations,
    175–176
texture of soil, 39
"textured treasures" hanging basket design,
    216–217
thermometers, 292
thinning of fruit, 143
thrift, 228
thrips, 276
thuja, 111
thyme, 139
ties for tall plants, 57, 63, 179
tiger flowers (*tigridia*), 102
timed- or slow-release fertilizers, 84, 178,
    203, 251, 252
"timeless beauty, Old World charm" mixed
    planting, 189–190
"tip and bury" method of aiding wintertime
    plant survival, 20
TIP icon, 4
tomatoes, 34, 44, 129, 136, 193, 215
tools
  mail order sources, 304–306
  toolkit contents, 57, 291–292
topsoil in soil mixes, caution on use, 46, 48
total porosity, 42
trachelospermum jasminoides, 126
trailing fuchsias, 206
trailing plants, 206
transplanting
  annuals, 70–73
  nursery plants. *See* planting
  rootbound plants for water
    conservation, 244
  seedlings, 64
Transvaal daisies (gerberas), 77, 207
trays for large containers, 177
tree ferns
  Australian, 114
  Tasmanian, 114
trees. *See* citrus; conifers; fruits and berries;
    shrubs and trees

trellises for vines, 57, 63, 179, 304
trichogramma wasps, 269, 273
  See also pest control
troubleshooting
  needle loss on conifers, 24
  sickly appearance of plants, 22, 23
troughs and stone sinks, 227–229
trowels, 291
tuberous begonias, 102
tulips, 14, 93, 99, 101

• *U* •

umbrella plant (*schefflera actinophylla*), 170
upright plants, 207
urns, 229–230
USDA zones
  described, 18
  subtracting two for safety margin, 18, 19

• *V* •

vegetables and herbs
  attractors for beneficial insects, 268
  container selection, 130
  "edible aerials" hanging basket design,
    214–215
  fertilizing, 131
  ideas for herbs, 34, 136–139
  ideas for vegetables, 34, 132–136
  need for sun, 131
  "next on the menu" mixed planting,
    193–194
  size considerations, 132
  soil mixes, 43, 130
  watering, 131
  when to plant, 54
verbena, 206
vermiculite in soil mixes, 43, 44, 45, 46, 203
vinca, 207
  rosea, 70, 77
vines
  examples, 124–127
  for shady spots, 284
  "suspended animation" mixed planting,
    185–186

trellises for, 57, 63, 179
violas, 76, 78

• *W* •

Walheim, Lance, 123
walking stick, 115
"wall basket collection" hanging basket
    design, 217–218
wall rockcresses, 189
WARNING icon, 4
wasps, trichogramma, 269, 273
water clover, 223
water considerations
  amount, 243
  caution on overhead watering, 239, 267,
    277, 279
  caution on salt burn, 178, 242, 253, 280
  climate, 236
  conservation, 244–245
  containers' porosity, 25–26, 236
  drip irrigation, 239–241, 243, 244
  frequency, 242
  genetic dispositions of plants, 238
  hand watering, 238–239
  importance of, 10–11, 178, 235
  long, deep soakings, 178
  and pest control, 267
  pot type and color, 236–237
  root-bound plants, 237
  self-watering pots, 203, 241–242
  soil mixes: water infiltration, retention, and
    drainage, 42, 43
  sprinklers, 239
  terra-cotta pots: soaking before planting, 58
  watering cans, 291
  weather, 23, 236
  wetting agents for soil mixes, 45, 46
  wick watering, 245
  See also drainage
water damage to surfaces
  considerations for hanging baskets, 200
  saucers as protection from, 16, 33
water gardens
  mail order sources, 303
  plants for, 34, 194–195, 223–225

"reflective beauty" example of mixed planting, 194–195

water hyacinths, 194

water lilies, 223

watering
  annuals, 73
  bulbs, 99
  cactus and succulents, 157–158
  hanging baskets, 200, 211
  indoor plants, 166
  just-planted annuals, 73
  just-planted perennials, 83
  just-planted plants, 63
  shrubs and trees, 105
  vegetables and herbs, 131
  with water-storing crystals or soil polymers, 203, 244, 245–246

waterpoppies, 223

weather. *See* climate considerations

Web sites
  bonsai enthusiasts, 293
  container gardening enthusiasts, 308–311
  perennials, 80
  plant ordering opportunities, 80
  See also clubs

weeding for water conservation, 244

weight, considerations for containers, 16

western exposures, 23

wetting agents for soil mixes, 45, 46

whiteflies, 276–277

wick watering, 241, 245

wind
  caution on spraying of pesticides, 271
  as microclimate factor, 23, 236

window boxes, 220–223

winter
  annuals (after last frost), 69, 289
  caution of freezability of drip irrigation systems, 241, 243, 244
  caution on freezability of containers, 22, 26
  and hardiness, 18, 20
  "living" Christmas trees, 109, 289
  methods of aiding survival of permanent plants, 20–22
  perennials, 84, 289
  relocation of plants to indoors, 16
  shrubs and trees, 289

wire baskets and plant stands, 201, 263–264

wisteria, 127

wood containers
  advantages, 178
  described, 27
  hanging baskets, 202
  moisture retention, 236
  prolonging life with preservatives, 58, 260
  repairing, 258–260, 264
  window boxes, 220–221

World Wide Web, plant ordering opportunities, 80

worms, 273

● *Y* ●

yarrow, 90, 268

● *Z* ●

zantedeschia (callas), 102

zinc, 248

zinnias, 12, 22, 23, 70, 77, 207

zones. *See* USDA zones

BUSINESS, CAREERS & PERSONAL FINANCE

0-7645-5307-0   0-7645-5331-3 *†

Also available:

- ✔ Accounting For Dummies †
  0-7645-5314-3
- ✔ Business Plans Kit For Dummies †
  0-7645-5365-8
- ✔ Cover Letters For Dummies
  0-7645-5224-4
- ✔ Frugal Living For Dummies
  0-7645-5403-4
- ✔ Leadership For Dummies
  0-7645-5176-0
- ✔ Managing For Dummies
  0-7645-1771-6

- ✔ Marketing For Dummies
  0-7645-5600-2
- ✔ Personal Finance For Dummies *
  0-7645-2590-5
- ✔ Project Management For Dummies
  0-7645-5283-X
- ✔ Resumes For Dummies †
  0-7645-5471-9
- ✔ Selling For Dummies
  0-7645-5363-1
- ✔ Small Business Kit For Dummies *†
  0-7645-5093-4

HOME & BUSINESS COMPUTER BASICS

0-7645-4074-2   0-7645-3758-X

Also available:

- ✔ ACT! 6 For Dummies
  0-7645-2645-6
- ✔ iLife '04 All-in-One Desk Reference
  For Dummies
  0-7645-7347-0
- ✔ iPAQ For Dummies
  0-7645-6769-1
- ✔ Mac OS X Panther Timesaving
  Techniques For Dummies
  0-7645-5812-9
- ✔ Macs For Dummies
  0-7645-5656-8

- ✔ Microsoft Money 2004 For Dummies
  0-7645-4195-1
- ✔ Office 2003 All-in-One Desk Reference
  For Dummies
  0-7645-3883-7
- ✔ Outlook 2003 For Dummies
  0-7645-3759-8
- ✔ PCs For Dummies
  0-7645-4074-2
- ✔ TiVo For Dummies
  0-7645-6923-6
- ✔ Upgrading and Fixing PCs For Dummies
  0-7645-1665-5
- ✔ Windows XP Timesaving Techniques
  For Dummies
  0-7645-3748-2

FOOD, HOME, GARDEN, HOBBIES, MUSIC & PETS

0-7645-5295-3   0-7645-5232-5

Also available:

- ✔ Bass Guitar For Dummies
  0-7645-2487-9
- ✔ Diabetes Cookbook For Dummies
  0-7645-5230-9
- ✔ Gardening For Dummies *
  0-7645-5130-2
- ✔ Guitar For Dummies
  0-7645-5106-X
- ✔ Holiday Decorating For Dummies
  0-7645-2570-0
- ✔ Home Improvement All-in-One
  For Dummies
  0-7645-5680-0

- ✔ Knitting For Dummies
  0-7645-5395-X
- ✔ Piano For Dummies
  0-7645-5105-1
- ✔ Puppies For Dummies
  0-7645-5255-4
- ✔ Scrapbooking For Dummies
  0-7645-7208-3
- ✔ Senior Dogs For Dummies
  0-7645-5818-8
- ✔ Singing For Dummies
  0-7645-2475-5
- ✔ 30-Minute Meals For Dummies
  0-7645-2589-1

INTERNET & DIGITAL MEDIA

0-7645-1664-7   0-7645-6924-4

Also available:

- ✔ 2005 Online Shopping Directory
  For Dummies
  0-7645-7495-7
- ✔ CD & DVD Recording For Dummies
  0-7645-5956-7
- ✔ eBay For Dummies
  0-7645-5654-1
- ✔ Fighting Spam For Dummies
  0-7645-5965-6
- ✔ Genealogy Online For Dummies
  0-7645-5964-8
- ✔ Google For Dummies
  0-7645-4420-9

- ✔ Home Recording For Musicians
  For Dummies
  0-7645-1634-5
- ✔ The Internet For Dummies
  0-7645-4173-0
- ✔ iPod & iTunes For Dummies
  0-7645-7772-7
- ✔ Preventing Identity Theft For Dummies
  0-7645-7336-5
- ✔ Pro Tools All-in-One Desk Reference
  For Dummies
  0-7645-5714-9
- ✔ Roxio Easy Media Creator For Dummies
  0-7645-7131-1

* Separate Canadian edition also available
† Separate U.K. edition also available

Available wherever books are sold. For more information or to order direct: U.S. customers visit www.dummies.com or call 1-877-762-2974.
U.K. customers visit www.wileyeurope.com or call 0800 243407. Canadian customers visit www.wiley.ca or call 1-800-567-4797.

SPORTS, FITNESS, PARENTING, RELIGION & SPIRITUALITY

0-7645-5146-9

0-7645-5418-2

Also available:

- Adoption For Dummies
  0-7645-5488-3
- Basketball For Dummies
  0-7645-5248-1
- The Bible For Dummies
  0-7645-5296-1
- Buddhism For Dummies
  0-7645-5359-3
- Catholicism For Dummies
  0-7645-5391-7
- Hockey For Dummies
  0-7645-5228-7

- Judaism For Dummies
  0-7645-5299-6
- Martial Arts For Dummies
  0-7645-5358-5
- Pilates For Dummies
  0-7645-5397-6
- Religion For Dummies
  0-7645-5264-3
- Teaching Kids to Read For Dummies
  0-7645-4043-2
- Weight Training For Dummies
  0-7645-5168-X
- Yoga For Dummies
  0-7645-5117-5

TRAVEL

0-7645-5438-7

0-7645-5453-0

Also available:

- Alaska For Dummies
  0-7645-1761-9
- Arizona For Dummies
  0-7645-6938-4
- Cancún and the Yucatán For Dummies
  0-7645-2437-2
- Cruise Vacations For Dummies
  0-7645-6941-4
- Europe For Dummies
  0-7645-5456-5
- Ireland For Dummies
  0-7645-5455-7

- Las Vegas For Dummies
  0-7645-5448-4
- London For Dummies
  0-7645-4277-X
- New York City For Dummies
  0-7645-6945-7
- Paris For Dummies
  0-7645-5494-8
- RV Vacations For Dummies
  0-7645-5443-3
- Walt Disney World & Orlando For Dummies
  0-7645-6943-0

GRAPHICS, DESIGN & WEB DEVELOPMENT

0-7645-4345-8

0-7645-5589-8

Also available:

- Adobe Acrobat 6 PDF For Dummies
  0-7645-3760-1
- Building a Web Site For Dummies
  0-7645-7144-3
- Dreamweaver MX 2004 For Dummies
  0-7645-4342-3
- FrontPage 2003 For Dummies
  0-7645-3882-9
- HTML 4 For Dummies
  0-7645-1995-6
- Illustrator CS For Dummies
  0-7645-4084-X

- Macromedia Flash MX 2004 For Dummies
  0-7645-4358-X
- Photoshop 7 All-in-One Desk
  Reference For Dummies
  0-7645-1667-1
- Photoshop CS Timesaving Techniques
  For Dummies
  0-7645-6782-9
- PHP 5 For Dummies
  0-7645-4166-8
- PowerPoint 2003 For Dummies
  0-7645-3908-6
- QuarkXPress 6 For Dummies
  0-7645-2593-X

NETWORKING, SECURITY, PROGRAMMING & DATABASES

0-7645-6852-3

0-7645-5784-X

Also available:

- A+ Certification For Dummies
  0-7645-4187-0
- Access 2003 All-in-One Desk
  Reference For Dummies
  0-7645-3988-4
- Beginning Programming For Dummies
  0-7645-4997-9
- C For Dummies
  0-7645-7068-4
- Firewalls For Dummies
  0-7645-4048-3
- Home Networking For Dummies
  0-7645-42796

- Network Security For Dummies
  0-7645-1679-5
- Networking For Dummies
  0-7645-1677-9
- TCP/IP For Dummies
  0-7645-1760-0
- VBA For Dummies
  0-7645-3989-2
- Wireless All In-One Desk Reference
  For Dummies
  0-7645-7496-5
- Wireless Home Networking For Dummies
  0-7645-3910-8

Notes

Notes

Notes

Notes

Notes

Notes

Notes

Notes

Notes

Notes

Notes

Notes

Notes

Notes